university for the **creative arts**

Telling Stories:
Countering Narrative in Art, Theory and Film

Telling Stories:
Countering Narrative in Art, Theory and Film

Edited by

Jane Tormey and Gillian Whiteley

Telling Stories: Countering Narrative in Art, Theory and Film,
Edited by Jane Tormey and Gillian Whiteley

This book first published 2009

Cambridge Scholars Publishing

12 Back Chapman Street, Newcastle upon Tyne, NE6 2XX, UK

British Library Cataloguing in Publication Data
A catalogue record for this book is available from the British Library

ISBN (10): 1-4438-0532-7, ISBN (13): 978-1-4438-0532-2

CONTENTS

Contents

Part Three: The Cinematic Essay

PREFACE

JANE TORMEY AND GILLIAN WHITELEY

In recent years, there has been an increasing interest in the development of alternative forms of writing criticism and theory and in the reconfiguring of the relationship between writing and artistic practice. Such preoccupations derive perhaps from the performance of Jacques Derrida's writing and its encounters with creative themes, its challenge to the boundaries of disciplines and of the distinction between the rational and the subjective. Peggy Phelan speaks of the centrality of performance in contemporary thought[1] and uses "performative writing" to force a "different way of reading critical commentary," suggesting a different relation between the writer (performer) and the reader. She describes "performative writing" as an attempt to find a form for "what philosophy wishes all the same to say," and configures the form and manner in which something is *told* as integral to what it has to say *or* what it has to say as integral to the form which it takes.[2] This performative move could also be said to apply to forms of contemporary art practice: to what photography, film, objects wish to say.

Telling Stories: Countering Narrative in Art, Theory and Film explores these preoccupations through a series of writings and photo-essays which understand *contemporary making* and *writing practices* as multi-faceted, interdisciplinary and trans-medial. It aims to explore the performative exchange across and between verbal and experiential disciplines and to interrogate the manner, structure, assumptions and alternative conceptions of narration through theorising and practice. It sets out to consider how visual and performative encounters contribute to thinking. How might they *tell* theories?

It results directly from a series of symposia, *Telling Stories,* organised by Nelson Diplexcito, Mary O'Neill, Jane Tormey and Gillian Whiteley and held at Loughborough University School of Art and Design in February, April and September 2007. The programme, which included papers, screenings and performances, was based around the convenors' shared interests in the notion of *performative writing* and in the examination of interdisciplinary forms of narrative and counter-narrative. The call for papers invited writers, theorists, critics and practitioners to address and challenge the conventional expectations of meaning and objectivity emerging in current modes of both critical writing and the visual arts. This book, a collection of selected papers and presentations and commissioned essays, addresses this trend, investigating the manner of narrative/counter-narrative, authorial presence, style, language, rhetoric and the assertion of performance across a range of contemporary practice and theory. It specifically focuses on three aspects—experimental forms of *Theories and Criticism, Objects and Narrative* and the particular format of *The Cinematic Essay*. This edited collection is indicative of the nature of contemporary art practice and theories that set out to encounter the world, its social conditions, its global perspectives and the nature of aesthetic discussion that is no longer confined by formalism.

Trespassing disciplines and binding together practice and theory, *Telling Stories* crosses strange territories and occupies liminal spaces. It addresses a contemporary preoccupation with narrative and narration which is being played out across the arts, humanities and beyond.[3] In the context of such a vigorous debate, we hope that *Telling Stories: Countering Narrative in Art, Theory and Film* makes a useful contribution to a re-thinking, re-writing and re-telling of theories and practice.

Notes

With thanks to Sandra Leeland for all her help and support with the organisation of the symposia and final preparation of the text and index.

[1] Peggy Phelan,"Performance, Live Culture and Things of the Heart," *Journal Of Visual Culture*, Vol. 2(3) (2003): 291-302.
[2] Peggy Phelan. *Mourning Sex, Performing Public Memories* (London & New York: Routledge, 1997), 11.
[3] Our own symposia at Loughborough University followed the conference *Show/Tell: Relationships between Text, Narrative and Image*, University of Hertfordshire in 2005. Indeed, since *Telling Stories*, a series of subsequent conferences have explored similar territory, including *Disrupting Narratives, A Symposium for the Electronic Media Arts*, Tate Modern, July 2007; *Telling Places: Narrative & Identity in Art & Architecture* at Bartlett School of Architecture, UCL, December 2007 and *Engaging Objects*, ASCA International Workshop Amsterdam, March 2008, which forms part of a series entitled "Ways of Writing: The Object Speaks Back."

PART I

THEORIES AND CRITICISM

INTRODUCTION: THEORIES AND CRITICISM

MARY O'NEILL

The narrative achieves an amplitude that information lacks. [1]

The phrase *telling stories* is deceptively simple; it conjures up thoughts of childhood tales, fabulous beasts, magical lands and dream-like existences. It is associated with *in the beginning* and *happily ever after*. We are familiar with the structure, the beginning, middle and end in which we experience a temporal unfolding. Stories are inextricably linked to memory, which is a privileged view based on the teller's knowledge of the outcome. While this unfolding happens in one direction in time for the listener, Paul Ricoeur reminds us it happens backwards in time for the teller.[2] The *story* in fact offers the possibility of multiple time-frames and distortions as well of multiple voices and perspectives. The listener's trust in the telling of a story is that there will be a *dénouement,* where motivations will be made clear, and secrets revealed. However, the great power of stories, the endurance of the form and the compulsion to tell them suggests that telling stories is not merely an entertainment, an optional extra which we can choose to engage with or not, but a fundamental aspect of being. We tell stories to construct, maintain and repair our reality. When we were conceived, when the sperm met the egg, we were not there, but there is a second self-conception which is our own. We conceive ourselves in our minds and then through the speech-act of our stories, we are born. The telling of stories is more than an individual process, through our stories we form relationships; our family stories bind us to those with whom we have shared experiences and our collective stories become our tribal, regional or national identity. These stories are performed and performative; they do not leave us unchanged but can in fact motivate us to fight and be willing to die for an ideal or a belief.

Stories are not merely about things that have happened, but are about significant events that change us. Through our stories we demonstrate that we not only have had experiences but that those experiences have become part of our knowledge. The etymology of the term *experience* suggests that it is a form of authority based on trial, experiment and observation, which is opposed to theory.[3] One of the overarching themes of *Theories and Criticism* is the possibility that if we combine experience, observation and the authorial presence in the form of the story-telling, we can move beyond a preconception of what constitutes theory to achieve a new form of authority.

Stories are a contract and their existence requires another, a listener, to complete the event that is telling, even if that listener is oneself or an imagined other. Derrida describes the stories told to the self as "*auto*-biographies," in his discussion of Nietzsche's declaration "I will tell myself my life story," in *Ecce Homo*.[4] The relationship between the author/teller and the listener is fundamental to the writing of Peggy Phelan who emphasises not only the relationship between narrative story-telling and performance but that this form addresses the "persistent separation between the critical imagination and creative imagination." [5] Phelan also does not shy away from the emotional communicative potential of narrative. In *Unmarked: the politics of performance,* she expresses the wish to bring to critical theory "a certain affective emotional force." [6]

My interest is in knowledge and how we communicate knowledge to others. Regardless of what the knowledge relates to—how to wire a plug, what it is to be afraid, a theoretical understanding of experience—how we communicate that knowledge to others will determine how that knowledge is received. Different relationships between knowledge and the means of its communication is demonstrated in this collection by an exemplary variety of forms, all of which reflect the complex interrelation between form and content, between teller and context, and teller and listener/reader. Knowledge, communicated in the form of a story, may appear to lack veracity because of the association with childhood story-telling. However, looking for a literal truth in a story may both miss the point and misunderstand the form. The connection between fact and fiction, and the shifting sand that is truth and lies, is explored in this section through ideas, theories and images, suggesting the possibility that stories offer a different form of truth, be it poetic, metaphoric, psychological, theoretical or critical. In recent years there has been a re-conceptualising of the function and possibility of narrative, suggesting that the underlying structures of story-telling, which is associated with invented accounts, is identified as intrinsic to recounting non-fictional information. This turn to narrative and story-telling in disciplines beyond literature is the focus of this section on *Theories and Criticism.*

Notes

[1] Walter Benjamin, In *The Storyteller: Reflections on the Works of Nikolai Lesion* (London: Fontana, 1992), 89.
[2] Paul Ricoeur, *Time and Narrative: Volume 1* (Chicago: The University of Chicago Press, 1984), 42-43.
[3] Martin Jay, *Songs of Experience: Modern American and European Variations on a Universal Theme* (California: University of California Press, 2005), 10.
[4] Derrida refers to Friedrich Nietzsche's *Ecce Homo* (New York: Vintage Books 1969) p.221 in Derrida, J.*The Ear of the Other: Octobiography, Transference, Translation* (Nebraska: the University of Nebraska Press 1988) p.43-44.
[5] Peggy Phelan, *Unmarked: the politics of performance* (London: Routledge, 1993), 297.
[6] Ibid.

CHAPTER ONE

THE SETTING:
PARADISE LOST (AND REGAINED)

JANE RENDELL

In this essay I argue that the concept of the psychoanalytic setting is indispensable for exploring the spatial and textual relationship between critic and work. This is precisely the project I have been investigating in my *Site-Writing* project which develops an understanding of art criticism's spatiality by writing essays informed by the frame and process of the psychoanalytic setting, and its combination of analytic and associative modes.[1] Here I consider the main characteristics and activities at work in the psychoanalytic setting such as association, attention, construction, conjecture, interpretation and invention as devices adopted to tell stories, and explore these through my engagement with an artwork by Rosa Nguyen entitled *Petites Terres* (2008).

Following Sigmund Freud, in psychoanalysis the main conditions of treatment include "arrangements" about time and money, as well as "certain ceremonials" governing the physical positions of analysand (lying on a couch and speaking) and analyst (sitting behind the analyst on a chair and listening).[2] Freud's "rules" for the spatial positions of the analytic setting were derived from a personal motive—he did not wish to be stared at for long periods of time, but also from a professional concern—to avoid giving the patient "material for interpretation." [3]

> I insist on this procedure, however, for its purpose and result are to prevent the transference from mingling with the patient's associations imperceptibly, to isolate the transference and to allow it to come forward in due course sharply defined as a resistance.[4]

In a discussion of Freud's method, psychoanalyst D. W. Winnicott distinguishes the technique of psychoanalysis from the "setting in which this work is carried out." [5] In his view, it is the setting which allows the reproduction of the "early and earliest mothering techniques" in psychoanalysis.[6] Italian psychoanalyst Luciana Nissin Momigliano describes how Winnicott "defined the 'setting' as the sum of all the details of management that are more or less accepted by all psychoanalysts," [7] while Argentinian psychoanalyst José Bleger redefined Winnicott's term setting to include the totality of the "psychoanalytic situation." Bleger argues that the process includes what is studied, analyzed and interpreted and the non-process or frame provides a set of constants or limits to the "behaviours" that occur within it.[8]

Contemporary French psychoanalyst, André Green, who uses both Freudian and Winnicottian concepts in his work, considers how the analytic setting "corresponds precisely to Winnicott's definition of the transitional object." [9] Winnicott's idea of a transitional object, following on and developing aspects of both Freud and Melanie Klein's work, is related to, but distinct from, the external object—the mother's breast, and the internal object—the introjected breast. For Winnicott, the transitional object or the original "not-me" possession stands for the breast or first object, but the use of symbolism implies the child's ability to make a distinction between fantasy and fact, between internal and external objects.[10] This ability to keep inner and outer realities separate yet inter-related results in an intermediate area of experience, the "potential space," which Winnicott claimed is retained and later in life contributes to the intensity of cultural experiences around art and religion.[11]

According to Green, the position of the consulting room between inside and outside relates to its function as a transitional space between analyst and analysand, as does its typology as a closed space different from both inner and outer worlds. "The consulting room," he writes, "is different from the outside space, and it is different, from what we can imagine, from inner space. It has a specificity of its own."[12] Michael Parsons, in a commentary on Green's work draws attention to his understanding of the analytic setting not as a static tableau, but as a space of engagement, not as "just a representation of psychic structure," but as "an expression of it." [13] Parsons explains that for Green: "It is the way psychic structure expresses itself, and cannot express itself, through the structure of the setting, that makes the psychoanalytic situation psychoanalytic." [14] In Green's work the setting is a "homologue" for what he calls the third element in analysis, the "analytic object," which is formed through the analytic association between analyst and analysand.[15] Green argues:

> The analytic object is neither internal (to the analysand or to the analyst), nor external (to either the one or the other), but is situated between the two. So it corresponds precisely to Winnicott's definition of the transitional object and to its location in the intermediate area of potential space, the space of 'overlap' demarcated by the analytic setting.[16]

This overlap consists of the relation between the psychic processes of transference and counter-transference, whose roles Green describes as creating an "analytic association." [17] Psychoanalyst Christopher Bollas connects the relation between transference and counter-transference in the interaction between analyst and analysand to the interplay between free association and evenly suspended attentiveness.[18] Bollas has noted that Freud's clearest account of his method, outlined in "Two Encyclopaedia Articles: A. Psycho-Analysis," [19] suggests that psychoanalysis takes place if two functions are linked—the analysand's free associations and the psychoanalyst's evenly suspended attentiveness.[20] For Freud, in including rather than excluding "intrusive ideas" and "side-issues," the process of association differs from ordinary conversation.[21] Bollas defines free association as that which occurs when we think by not concentrating on anything in particular, and where the ideas that emerge which seem to the conscious mind to be disconnected, but are instead related by a hidden and unconscious logic.[22] He explains that evenly suspended attentiveness can only be achieved when the analyst also surrenders to his own unconscious mental activity; and does not reflect on material, consciously construct ideas or actively remember.[23]

In his later writings Freud went on to distinguish between construction and interpretation as different forms of analytic technique:

> "Interpretation" applies to something that one does to some single element of the material, such as an association or a parapraxis. But it is a "construction" when one lays before the subject of the analysis a piece of his early history that he has forgotten ... [24]

Green also proposes the term "conjectural interpretation" to define the constructive mode of analytic interpretation.[25] And psychoanalyst Ignes Sodré, in a conversation with writer A.S. Byatt, asserts that in "offering the patient different versions of himself" the analyst operates as a story-teller suggesting an inventive aspect of interpretation.[26]

As both the site framing the encounter between analyst and analysand, and created through the technical procedures of transference and counter-transference, the setting is clearly a space of engagement both emotional and intellectual, which involves the psychic processes such as attention and association, interpretation and construction, active in criticism as well as psychoanalysis. While the frame, or the non-process based aspect of the setting, brings into play the material sites in which the critic encounters the work, the mental interactions which reverberate between analyst and analysand influence the production of different ways of writing the interaction between critic and work.

Literary critic Mary Jacobus has described "the scene of reading" in terms of the relation, perhaps a correspondence, which exists between the inner world of the reader and the world contained in the book.[27] Taking up this insightful observation I suggest that criticism involves a movement between inside and outside: works take critics outside themselves offering new geographies, new possibilities, but they can also return the critics to their own interior, to their own biographies. This double movement suspends what we might call judgement or discrimination in criticism, and instead constructs a series of interlocking sites—settings if you like—between critic and work.

Paradise Lost (and Regained)[28]

Out of my front door, along the access corridor, past the cawing of dishevelled rooks on the mobile phone masts. Next the piss-drenched lift, then the snarling streets of London, trying to ignore the clogged drains, the overflowing rubbish bags, the pavements dotted with cigarette butts and chewing gum, the incessant scream of power saws slicing up tarmac, anxiously avoiding the aggression-fuelled vehicles—vans, buses, taxis. Then the unnatural crushed silence of the tube, until finally I reach the Euro-cool oasis of St Pancras Station. I slip thankfully into my seat, the Eurostar takes me to Paris, the TGV to Toulouse, and then on to Boussens. Finally my clattering thoughts begin to recede, and I am able to actually "see" the landscape, as it shifts from forested slope into pastures, and meadows lush with springs. My heartbeat slows, my mind stretches and thoughts float into inter-connected patterns.

Between two grand but slightly rusty iron gates, across a lush grass courtyard and around its majestic cedar tree, I enter the pale stone loggia fronting the building and leading to the central stairwell, lit from a window high above. Elegant steps wind up to the first floor, presenting a view back down to the original source. The scene below is of a checkerboard inlaid with circles: bright green tufts in dark brown soil ringed with blue enamel are laid on marble squares of black and white. This enhanced pattern is made of lids from antique nineteenth-century jars. The usual function of a lid is to hold tight the contents of a container, to prevent their escape or the ingress of other unwanted conditions or particles. Yet these lids have been over-turned and used as the basis for growing. In their interiors a series of gardens have been planted. The new grass seed springs lithely up towards the light defying the earthbound logic of the lid to hold things down in the dark—goose fat, ashes, even seeds.

Beyond the stairwell three rooms with identical windows overlook the entrance. In one a landscape of plates float off the floor. Glazed white with petalled edges, each one contains a small garden. The gardens refer to one another; they are variations on a theme combining earth and gravel, two materials from the site, variously planted with a range of seeds—grass, radish, and lettuce. The plates have been made in traditional moulds from the ground on which the building stands. The live earth is burnt, transforming nature into culture; the firing kills one life but engenders another. Here the plates, which usually contain food—vegetables and animals—cut from the soil and culled from the land, are returned to nature, and become life givers, coming alive as a seedbed for plants. The floating position of the plates between ground and table reflects the setting these miniature gardens offer: between nature and culture, life and death, freedom and containment.

The three rooms along the building's front are flanked by two larger exhibition spaces. The one to the right displays its wares on the floor, an arrangement of various plates, bowls, jugs, and fragments of vessels, sorted according to colour, bringing to mind Tony Cragg's *Spectrum* (1983), which ordered found items by their colour on the gallery floor, and Richard Wentworth's *Spread* (1997), a collection of ceramic plates laid out in a circle. Delicately balanced on the ceramicware are tiny vessels, glazed in the region's traditional blue, each one nurturing a new sprouting seedling, re-awakening the frame of this still-life.

On the wall of the exhibition space to the left, a tile collection, comprising traditional patterns from the region, is arranged in a grid. They remind me of the work of Adriana Varejão, the Brazilian artist who paints tiled interiors associated with various psychic states—phobias and anxieties—in works such as *O Obsceno* (2004) or *O Obsessivo* (2004), as well as *Azulejaria Verde em Carne Viva* (2000) and *Parede con Incisao a la Fontana 3* (2002), where the tiled exteriors of ceramic structures are threatened by the bursting out of fleshy life-forms held captive by the rigid rectilinear geometry.

The pattern of evenly spaced squares can also be associated with the layout of cultivated nature: fields separated by hedgerows, the distinct but fine lines between paddy fields, vegetable gardens with their evenly spaced rows of onions, carrots, and lettuces dissected by troughs. Although there are precedents—the kitchen, cottage, medieval herb and walled garden—we are less acquainted today with considering the working garden and the growing of food as an aesthetic location and meditative act.

The representation of nature in gardens is traditionally associated with paradise, with the absence of labour. Paradise gardens have a spiritual rather than a pragmatic function—they are places removed from the everyday—sanctuaries often used for reflection. While the Japanese dry garden forms a symbolic analogue to nature, the rugs of the middle-east follow the sanctity of water in dry lands and depict walled gardens with dancing fountains at their centre, exemplified in the design of religious architectural complexes, such as those built in Seville, Granada and Córdoba. In the west we have tended to separate the productive use of irrigated land for farming and agriculture, from the contemplation of nature in its various romantic forms, the untamed sublime of the wild and its domesticated and more comforting picturesque equivalent.

The sealed and self-contained world of the garden is a particular kind of setting one which could be described as a "heterotopia"—a place with a different ordering system.[29] Unlike paradise, the "no place" of the perfect world depicted by utopia, the unique logic of the garden also has a material physical location. The tiny and perfect verdant worlds contained in the lids and plates invite us to imagine new ways of life.

Petites Terres (2008) is a new installation by ceramic artist Rosa Nguyen where domestic ceramic-ware—pots and plates—finds new life through its support and containment of vegetal growth. The site-specific work is set within in a gracious nineteenth-century thermal spa building, built in 1857-1858 at Barthete on the river Louge in the foothills of Pyrenées. It is situated at a hot spring, whose waters, like those of the other such establishments in the area, have been enjoyed for health treatments from the Roman period onwards. The baths closed in 1926, and were used as a summer camp until the 1980s, after which Barthete laid empty for a number of years, part of pattern of decline in the popularity of spas across the region. It has been brought "back to life" by a museum, which houses a collection of 1500 pieces of pottery from the immediate vicinity, from France, as well as further afield: Algeria, Germany, Italy, Morocco, the Netherlands, Portugal, Spain, and Tunisia.[30]

Rosa Nguyen, *Petites Terres* (2008)

The museum project is the creation of its two curators, Claude Lege, an artist from the Ariege, and Suzanne Danis Lege, an art historian originally from Canada. Their collection of earthenware reminds us of the close association between agriculture and pottery in the ancient Comminges region. This area has a long history in the craft production of ceramics. The process used clay and limestone mined in the area, metal for the tin oxide glazes—blue, green, yellow, red, and violet, even the kilns were fired by wood from the surrounding forests.[31] The early production of *faience* ceramics in this area was an interconnected enterprise in close harmony with its context. However, with the changes brought by industrialization across Europe, came the pressure to transform to practices that were more polluting and drew on the unsustainable use of resources. Although this situation may not have been perceived as problematic at the time, current knowledge shifts perspective.

Today we face different problems. The beautiful hills, streams and forests of this region seem, for a visitor, like a pristine natural paradise. Yet this is a working landscape, much of the land is needed for farming, and with the impending global food crisis no doubt this will increasingly be the case. Maize is grown for human consumption, but also for animal feed, plastic bags, and more recently "biofuel." The frequent reliance on chemical fertilizers and pesticides draws life out of the earth but also discharges poison into rivers. The increasing use of water for domestic, industrial and agricultural purposes in Southern Europe, combined with the lack of rain and snow caused by climate change, have resulted in the damaging of aquifers and the drying-up of natural springs. With a future of drought predicted, it may be that spas will be rejuvenated. Public bathing may come back to life, and for functional uses—washing clothes and bodies—not just for leisure.

Rosa Nguyen, *Petites Terres* (2008)

Petites Terres draws together opposite principles, not in order to cancel out their meaning, but to entice one entity with the transformational potential held by its reverse, life out of death. This theme is strong in Nguyen's previous works, where she has brought live and vibrant natural elements into close proximity with the burnt earth of ceramic forms. A residency in Japan stimulated an interest in Ikebana, the art of flower arrangement, which, based on schematic principles connected with life forces, has developed out of the Buddhist practice of offering flowers to the dead. In Ikebana the potential offered by the container forms a key element in the composition. Here at Barthete, Nguyen's hybridized artefacts, ceramic containers brought to life by sprouting seeds, fed by spring water, respond to the attitude and methods of display that govern the curation of the collection. This museological code works against convention preferring to organise according to a desire to combine whole forms and fragments, and consider the sensual appeal offered by visual taxonomies of colour and pattern rather than the more usual regime of geographical origin, date or style.

The *nature morte* of the display ceramic is reactivated by its new use, while the motifs of artificial nature in the decorative patterns of the tiles and plates are reanimated with the fronds of living matter. In such a force field, *Petites Terres* makes adjustments to our understanding of the delicate balance between nature and culture, life and death. The paradise we believe we have lost is based on a state of not knowing. Once knowledge is gained, paradise as the bliss of ignorance really has gone.

Petites Terres could be understood in a number of ways, but for me these miniature perfect worlds are not simply vegetal scenes presented for our delectation, in which we can safely contemplate paradise lost. Rather they draw attention to the incompatible co-existence of what they contain—seemingly perfectly-balanced microcosms fed by spring water, and what contains them—the parched and polluted imperfection of the world. To consider *Petites Terres* as a setting where inner imagined and outer reality exist in tension, in a state of unresolved overlap, is to acknowledge that the difficult task of recognizing the loss of paradise is accompanied by the desire to escape that recognition and instead to dream of that which has been lost.

Notes

[1] See Jane Rendell, *Site-Writing: The Architecture of Art Criticism* (London: IB Tauris, forthcoming 2009). See also Jane Rendell, "Architecture-Writing," in *Critical Architecture,* ed. Jane Rendell special issue of the *Journal of Architecture,* 10, 3 (June 2005): 255–264 and Jane Rendell, "Site-Writing: Enigma and Embellishment," in *Critical Architecture* ed. Jane Rendell, Jonathan Hill, Murray Fraser and Mark Dorrian (London: Routledge, 2007), 150-162.

[2] Sigmund Freud, "On Beginning the Treatment (Further Recommendations on the Technique of Psycho-Analysis I)" [1913] *The Standard Edition of the Complete Psychological Works of Sigmund Freud, Volume XII (1911-1913): The Case of Schreber, Papers on Technique and Other Works,* translated from the German under the general editorship of James Strachey (London: The Hogarth Press, 1958), 121-144, 126 and 133. For a detailed description of Freud's consulting room, see Diana Fuss and Joel Sanders, 'Berggasse 19: Inside Freud's Office', in *Stud: Architectures of Masculinity* ed. Joel Sanders, (New York: Princeton Architectural Press, 1996), 112–139. For an extended discussion of the frame or scene of psychoanalysis in relation to contemporary art practice, see Mignon Nixon, "On the Couch," *October* 113 (Summer 2005): 39-76.

[3] Freud, "On Beginning the Treatment," 134.

[4] Freud, "On Beginning the Treatment," 126.

[5] D. W. Winnicott, "Metapsychological and Clinical Aspects of Regression Within the Psycho–Analytic Set-Up," *International Journal of Psycho-Analysis* 36 (1955): 16-26, 20.

[6] Winnicott, "Metapsychological and Clinical Aspects of Regression," 21.

[7] Luciana Nissin Momigliano, "The Analytic Setting: A Theme with Variations," in *Continuity and Change in Psychoanalysis: Letters from Milan* (London and New York: Karnac Books, 1992), 33-61, 33-34.

[8] José Bleger, "Psycho-Analysis of the Pscho-Analytic Frame," *International Journal of Psycho-Analysis* 48 (1967): 511-519, 518.

[9] André Green, "Potential Space in Psychoanalysis: The Object in the Setting," in *Between Reality and Fantasy:Transitional Objects and Phenomena* ed. Simon A. Grolnick and Leonard Barkin (New York and London: Jason Aronson Inc., 1978), 169-189, 180.

[10] D. W. Winnicott, "Transitional Objects and Transitional Phenomena —A Study of the First Not-Me Possession," *International Journal of Psycho-Analysis* 34 (1953): 89–97, see in particular 89 and 94. See also D. W. Winnicott, "The Use of an Object," *The International Journal of Psycho-Analysis* 50 (1969): 711-716.

[11] Winnicott discussed cultural experience as located in the "potential space" between "the individual and the environment (originally the object)." In Winnicott's terms, for the baby this is the place between the "subjective object and the object objectively perceived." See D. W. Winnicott, "The Location of Cultural

Experience," *The International Journal of Psycho-Analysis* 48 (1967): 368-372, 371. See also D. W. *Winnicott: Playing and Reality* (London: Routledge, 1991).

[12] André Green and Gregorio Kohon, "Dialogues with André Green," in *The Dead Mother: The Work of André Green,* ed. Gregorio Kohon, (Routledge, London, published in association with the Institute of Psycho-Analysis, 1999), 10-58, 29.

[13] Michael Parsons, "Psychic Reality, Negation, and the Analytic Setting," in *The Dead Mother,* ed. Kohon, 59-75, 74.

[14] Parsons, "Psychic Reality," 74.

[15] André Green, "The Analyst, Symbolization and Absence in the Analytic Setting (On Changes in Analytic Practice and Analytic Experience) – In Memory of D. W. Winnicott," *International Journal of Psycho-Analysis* 56 (1975): 1-22, 12.

[16] Green, "Potential Space in Psychoanalysis," 180.

[17] André Green, "Surface Analysis, Deep Analysis," *International Review of Psycho-Analysis* 1 (1974): 415-423, 418.

[18] Christopher Bollas, "Freudian Intersubjectivity: Commentary on Paper by Julie Gerhardt and Annie Sweetnam," *Psychoanalytic Dialogues* 11 (2001): 93-105, 98.

[19] See Sigmund Freud, "Two Encyclopedia Articles: (A) Psycho-Analysis" [1923] *The Standard Edition of the Complete Psychological Works of Sigmund Freud, Volume XVIII (1920–1922): Beyond the Pleasure Principle, Group Psychology and Other Works,* translated from the German under the general editorship of James Strachey (London: The Hogarth Press, 1955), 235-254.

[20] Bollas, "Freudian Intersubjectivity," 93.

[21] Freud, "On Beginning the Treatment," 134-135.

[22] Christopher Bollas, *Free Association* (Duxford, Cambridge: Icon Books Ltd., 2002), 4-7.

[23] Bollas, *Free Association,* 12.

[24] Sigmund Freud, "Constructions in Analysis" [1937] *The Standard Edition of the Complete Psychological Works of Sigmund Freud, Volume XXIII (1937-1939): Moses and Monotheism, An Outline of Psycho-Analysis and Other Works,* translated from the German under the general editorship of James Strachey (London: The Hogarth Press, 1963), 255-270, 261.

[25] André Green, "The Double and the Absent" [1973] in *Psychoanalysis, Creativity, and Literature: A French-American Inquiry* ed. Alan Roland, (New York: Columbia University Press, 1978), 271-292, 272-273, 274.

[26] Rebeccca Swift, ed., *A. S. Byatt and Ignes Sodré: Imagining Characters: Six Conversations about Women Writers* (London: Chatto & Windus, 1995), 245.

[27] Mary Jacobus, *Psychoanalysis and the Scene of Reading* (Oxford: Oxford University Press, 1999), 18.

[28] John Milton's *Paradise Lost* is an epic poem in blank verse. It was originally published in 1667 in ten books and concerns the Judeo-Christian story of the Fall of Man: the temptation of Adam and Eve by Satan and their expulsion from the Garden of Eden. Later in life, in 1671, Milton wrote the much shorter *Paradise Regained,* charting the temptation of Christ by Satan, and the return of the possibility of paradise.

[29] See Michel Foucault, "Of Other Spaces: Utopias and Heterotopias," in *Rethinking Architecture* ed. Neil Leach, (London: Routledge, 1996), 348-367. Even for Foucault who coined the phrase, it is not clear whether the different orders expressed by his examples of heterotopias, from floating brothels to prisons, are to be held up as shining ideals to aspire to, or as options to avoid.

[30] For more information about Barthete see http://www.barthete.com/thermes.php (accessed 10 April 2008).

[31] For a discussion of the history of ceramics in this region see for example Penny Collet, "Faiences Françaises and Martres Tolosane," *Craft Culture*. See http://www.craftculture.org/World/pcollette1.htm (accessed 10 April 2008).

CHAPTER TWO

NOT YET THERE:
ENDLESS SEARCHES
AND IRRESOLVABLE QUESTS

EMMA COCKER

> An artist might advance specifically to get lost, and to intoxicate himself in
> dizzying syntaxes, seeking odd intersections of meaning, strange corridors
> of history, unexpected echoes, unknown humors, or voids of knowledge …
> but this quest is risky, full of bottomless fictions and endless architectures
> and counter-architectures … at the end, if there is an end, are perhaps only
> meaningless reverberations.[1]

The list unfolds like chapters or episodes from a Paul Auster novel: the
blind following of another's footfall, the retracing of an already failed
endeavour, journeys with guidebooks whose content is obsolete, global
expeditions at the request of tree fanatics, a tragic sea voyage in search of
the miraculous, the hunt for angels.[2] Looking towards examples within
artistic practice, I am interested in how the notion of an irresolvable quest
might be reclaimed from the vaults of Romanticism and redeployed as a
strategic research methodology or framework for critical enquiry. As a
model of practice the irresolvable quest can be understood as a particular
process-based or performance strategy at the heart of a piece of work
where the process itself is valued above the object of its endeavour. This
could involve the artist undertaking a journey or task in pursuit of an
outcome that could seem to be improbable, ambiguous or arbitrary, or
alternatively they might appear locked into a form of quest or task that
remains endless, is wilfully thwarted or somehow strategically fails.
Whilst the method of a traditional quest narrative might be adopted, the
notion of the *telos* is often rejected or sabotaged in favour of a redeemed
or strategic form of anti-climax or deferral where the indeterminate or
latent potential of being *not-yet-there* is privileged above the finality of
closure.

Working against the dominant teleological grain of Western epistemology, the paradigm of an endless or impossible quest can be framed as a critical and conceptual approach for exploring meaningful non-productivity or irresolution, where it functions as a device for creating desirable states of aporia and conjecture. Performed according to an ephemeral, unfolding logic, it is a model of enquiry whose findings emerge through constant (r)evolution, where observations remain in transitional flux or interminable disarray. The search will always remain pleasurably unfulfilled and unrewarded, or return only with the most peripheral or unforeseen discoveries. The irresolvable quest enables a framework for tangential and transitory practices of meaning making. It offers a way of encountering and understanding the world and our place within it, that retains rather than eradicates the potential for uncertainty and disorientation, and that emphasises rather than disables the interplay between facts and fictions or between reality and the imagination. Using the practice of artists Heather and Ivan Morison as a point of reference, the intent is to explore the critical potential of the irresolvable quest as a form of non-rationalist knowledge construction and meaning making where irresolution and contingency, subjectivity and transitivity, partial truths and telling stories are redeemed alongside more empiricist methods of exploration.

The notion of an irresolvable quest is central to the work of Heather and Ivan Morison where their staging of grand, episodic adventures or global expeditions appears to produce outcomes that are slight or dematerialised, idiosyncratic or obscure, or else highly personal or anecdotal. In 2003, for example, they proposed to undertake a year long period of research, which would take the form of an irredeemably impossible *Global Survey* across the Baltic States, Russia, Western Siberia, Mongolia, China and New Zealand, where akin to "a pioneering exploration there (was) no end destination, only points to navigate by." [3] Chance encounter and opportunity were adopted as the critical decision making processes, whilst random meetings and conversational exchanges plotted the route taken or determined the direction for each episode of the adventure. The actual motivation for the journeys themselves often remained undeclared or arbitrary, or alternatively seemed nonsensical or absurd, or even poetic or purposeless. At times the object of their search functioned akin to Hitchcock's *Macguffin,* where it became a tactic for creating points of arbitrary focus from which to explore resultant peripheries or tangential narratives. It operated as a ruse or foil through which to undertake an alternative trajectory of enquiry. [4]

Recalling a folkloric order or logic, the artists' quests often appear marked by a particular task, challenge or performed ritual. At times, their journey was motivated by the process of fervent searching for, or collection of rare objects or sounds, whilst on other occasions they followed directions obtained from some strange or eccentric conversation

Fig. 1. Heather and Ivan Morison, *As his spaceship* Divine Vessel *enters orbit, Chinese astronaut Yang Lewei gazes down at earth,* image from *Chinese Arboretum,* 100 images of Chinese trees for billboards, 2003/2004. Courtesy of the artists and Danielle Arnaud Gallery

with a stranger met along the way. In the *Still Life* series of radio broadcasts for Resonance 104.4 fm, Heather and Ivan Morison presented recorded conversations from their various meetings and encounters, which included their discussions with an astronomer and an ornithologist *(Still*

Life #1), a collection of sounds gathered during a long, slow journey across various continents *(Still Life #4)* and an audio recording beginning with the sounds of a house band aboard a ferry crossing the Baltic Sea and ending in a Lithuanian flower shop *(Still Life #5)*. In *Divine Vessel* they attempted to write a science fiction novel based upon the onboard events witnessed during the isolation of a one-month sea voyage from Shanghai, China to Auckland, New Zealand. In *Chinese Arboretum* they followed the guidance of tree fanatics as they searched for rare trees, at times travelling thousands of miles across China to record a single specimen. Resulting in over one hundred photographs of trees, the titling of each image locates the geographical position of each discovery, but also makes reference to the highly personal dramas or daily events of individuals living nearby.

Operating in a realm that is neither wholly fact nor fiction, these various projects are characterised by a form of reportage or storytelling. LED announcements broadcast the artists' oblique messages from remote locations, whilst local radio stations transmit their intermittent conversations from distant lands. Newspaper insertions offer small glimpses from the poles of both humour and horror, by presenting fragmented narrative revelations of both prosaic and poetic proportion. A thousand limited edition mailed cards recount the artists' anguish at the demise of the Siberian larches, whilst from Beijing the same neatly typed signature informs selected postal recipients that, "Heather Morison is haunted by the horrific death of her two beautiful Java Sparrows .... Ivan is not so upset." [5] In other work, publicly sited billboards present their reportage through more democratic though no less ephemeral offerings.

These brief, curious forms of correspondence serve to reassert the experiential and negotiated lived space of the artists' travels. Heather and Ivan Morison recuperate the notion of a subjective itinerary or tour. They return value to the lost narrative that has arguably been eclipsed by the dominance of the objective or panoptic map.[6] Rather than trying to present a substitute for the actual experience of their journeys, their documentary residue offers only random, fractured clues or evidence from which an audience must draw their own individual conclusions. They issue a form of makeshift narrative emerging at the interstice between fictional, autobiographical and documentary perspectives. For theorist Michel de Certeau such "stories about places" are always provisional and incomplete, where they operate within what he describes as an "order (that) is everywhere punched and torn open by ellipses, drifts, and leaks of meaning: it is a sieve-order." [7]

Heather and Ivan Morison's accounts are separated and fragmented by pauses, gaps and blank spaces in transmission; we tentatively await their next postal offering or latest update on the LED screen. This gesture of

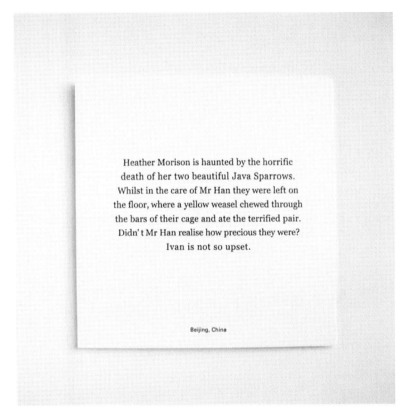

Heather Morison is haunted by the horrific
death of her two beautiful Java Sparrows.
Whilst in the care of Mr Han they were left on
the floor, where a yellow weasel chewed through
the bars of their cage and ate the terrified pair.
Didn' t Mr Han realise how precious they were?
Ivan is not so upset.

Beijing, China

Fig. 2. Heather and Ivan Morison, Edition of 200 printed and mailed cards, 2003. Courtesy of the artists and Danielle Arnaud Gallery

spacing further ruptures any coherent sense of either spatial or temporal continuity. Such spacing performs in a similar manner to the grammatical procedure of *asyndeton*, which is a disruptive break in syntax that Michel de Certeau describes as an act that, "Opens gaps in the spatial continuum" and "retains only selected parts of it that amount almost to relics." [8] Asyndeton is spatially performed, he argues, during the act of walking as the walker "condemns certain places to inertia or disappearance and composes with others spatial 'turns of phrase' that are 'rare,' 'accidental' or 'illegitimate'." [9] Heather and Ivan Morison's partial and idiosyncratic form of communication similarly retains and values the subjective experience of place, whilst challenging or discarding more established, accepted methods of spatial inscription. Travelling or walking become the vehicle of ritualistic rejuvenation, a means of disturbing the structure of the map or *text* in order to reintroduce the possibility of other realities in the gaps and pauses. Within Heather and Ivan Morison's practice the wandering or irresolvable quest is redeployed as a tool of resuscitation whose *telos* is no longer an object or a distant land, but rather a process or ritual through which to attempt to reinvigorate the conditions of existence with the possibility of chance and fortune, uncertainty and doubt, myth and legend. [10]

Heather and Ivan Morison capture the temporal experience of walking or travel where, contrary to the impervious stasis of the map, they resist "something that lasts, [in favour of] something that happens." [11] Emphasising the value of *presentness* as opposed to *presence*, their model of working can be read as offering an analogous experience to that of the novel for as Claudio Guillen asserts in *The anatomies of roguery: the origins and the nature of picaresque literature,* (1987):

> There seems to be something novelistic about every work of art which suscitates the sharing of a process rather than the observation of a conclusion ... the contact with a novel escapes us when we finish it ... the substance of a novel lies only in the gradual experience of it. [12]

Their practice could thus be contextualised as part of a literary tradition of *telling stories*, where the novelistic or essayistic manner of their work might be framed within a broader genealogy of literary quests or tales of wandering. The literary origins of the irresolvable quest are themselves diverse and wandering, emerging from both mythic and prosaic beginnings. On the one hand it can be witnessed in grand, heroic or chivalrous adventures such as those of Arthurian legend or alternatively as a roguish model of *sauntering* undertaken by "mere idlers and vagabonds." [13] It can then be traced through different trajectories as these traditions later bifurcate into the form of the Romantic quest for the sublime or the picaresque quest-as-mad-adventure. [14] Whilst a closer analysis of such literary parallels might reveal shared languages and intentions, it is essential to note that Heather and Ivan Morison's form of storytelling functions primarily within an artistic practice as a method or device through which to reiterate or reanimate the experience of their travels.

Located in the realm of the performed, the quest tradition is thus invoked or inhabited rather than extended strictly in literary terms. Its narratives offer a form of script or structure that can be borrowed or appropriated as a found set of instructions or rules of the game, where the artists challenge or test out the logic of the original by disrupting and re-contextualising traditional elements to create new readings and possibilities. The narratives of a quest tradition are thus opened out as a space of conceptual experimentation or critical form of role-play. A quest is adopted or inhabited as a framework for ludic wandering where the strategic or *logical* deployment of an illogical or archaic construct becomes a means of transcending or disrupting conventional rationality, or alternatively operates as the catalyst for a game of chance.

Counter intuitively perhaps, conceptual practices might borrow the language of the Romantic quest as a game or set of rules through which to play. In this context the conditions of irresolvable action or of endless deferral can be seen as part of a vocabulary of open-ended system or instruction-based actions, serial processes or even of durational performance.[15] The model of an irresolvable quest offers a site of endlessly repeatable exploration and enquiry that defers the demands for closure in favour of an eternally returnable narrative (pre)text; a voluntary paradigm of Sisyphean absurdity and resistance ensues. The notion of the quest is then inhabited as a game or followed as a set of rules that might be endlessly reiterated. For philosopher Roger Caillois, the model of an infinitely repeatable (yet also potentially pleasurable) pursuit or action operates at the heart of play. He argues that, "The possibilities of ludus are almost infinite …. it is common knowledge that what to begin with seems to be a situation susceptible to indefinite repetition turns out to be capable of producing ever-new combinations." [16] In his writing on games and gaming, Caillois describes how play can be understood as a resolutely unproductive gesture: it is "an occasion of pure waste." [17] He asserts that:

> The game's domain is therefore a restricted, closed, protected universe: a pure space. The confused and intricate laws of ordinary life are replaced, in this fixed space and for this given time, by precise, arbitrary, unexceptionable rules that must be accepted as such and that govern the correct playing of the game.[18]

When the irresolvable quest is deployed strategically within an artistic practice, it is similarly brought into action in a repeatable or ritualistic manner beyond the causal logic of everyday actions. It is performed or enacted freely according to certain rules or instructions, or through a form

of role-play or doubling that is "accompanied by a special awareness of a
second reality or of a free unreality, as against real life." [19] Operating
outside the frame of individualistic determinism and delimited by a time
frame that has often been fixed in advance, the nature of the quest in
practices such as Heather and Ivan Morison's is always resolutely
uncertain allowing, "Some latitude for innovations being left to the
player's [or artist's] initiative." [20] The quest often remains unresolved or
unproductive for at the end (if there is an end) the "situation [is] identical
to that prevailing at the beginning." [21] It has not resulted in the production
of an outcome beyond a dematerialised, ephemeral or highly partial form
of documentation. As Caillois asserts, "At the end of the [quest], all can
and must start over again at the same point." [22]

Caillois' analysis of play is a useful structure through which to
consider the practice of the irresolvable quest, because it has the capacity
to allow a form of critical conceptualism to be momentarily reconciled and
co-exist with the possibility of a *fall* from rational logic. In play, one
inhabits an immersive space where unlikely coalitions arise, and where
rational logic is temporally suspended or replaced by another set of rules.
Here, play can be seen as a means of escape or fall. It is a strategy for
desirable disorientation or vertiginous disruption that transports the
individual into some other fictional zone or psychological state of mind. In
play, the boundaries between the familiar and the improvised, or between
events of reality and those of the imagination can become wilfully
disturbed. Caillois' criteria of mimicry (simulation), chance (*alea*) and
vertigo (*ilinx*) enable a form of play through which to escape from the laws
of everyday reality, into a space of a heightened or delirious, experiential
register where uncertainty and the unknown become the dominant
characteristics.

For Caillois the gesture of role-play evident in both mimesis
(simulation) and make-believe is a means by which, "One can also escape
himself and become another." [23] Role-play opens up a space of liminality
where one must abandon the reality of one's habitual everyday, in order to
temporarily encounter the world from a fresh and unfamiliar perspective. It
is a space that exists within and yet beyond the parameters of rationalism,
a place where impossible propositions cannot be truly refuted and where
meaning emerges at the interstice between reality and the yet imagined.
The appropriation of another's motive or of an existing narrative (in the
physical following of instructions or retracing of another's steps) thus
creates the conditions for detour and disorientation where the quest

becomes less about finding the *object* of the search as about getting lost or abandoning ownership of one's direction. Heather and Ivan Morison abandon responsibility or control for their individual direction and action in favour of random and arbitrary rules, the capriciousness of chance and fortune, or the instructions or will of another. Alternatively they immerse themselves in the lives of others as they become absorbed by the passions and fascinations of various traditions and individuals. They adopt the role of the explorer, the collector, the amateur botanist, and the sci-fi novelist. They mirror and inhabit the practices of the florist or the beekeeper, and share the daily rituals of the astronomer or the ice fisherman.

Whilst play might articulate a *fall* from instinctual or rational models of behaviour, it simultaneously has the capacity to assuage the desires of empiricism by presenting a space of *meaningful inhabitation* or experimentation where *real* questions or hypotheses might be proposed and tested out. Whilst some forms of appropriation or mimicry can be seen as the empty occupation of a gesture or idea in order that it might be critiqued or even discredited, the act of repetition or mimesis involved in play is done with genuine investment or through a form of immersion in the activity involved. Play requires the suturing of the self into the space of the game. The irresolvable quest offers a place for strategic *playing out* or trial where the artist adopts a character or appears as a *double,* whose encounters with the world might be partially fictionalised or imaginary but are none-the-less irrevocably and experientially real. The character escapes the world of rational logic to inhabit a reality that is open to alternative and provisional meanings, or that is governed by a different order. The nature of role-play allows for the empathetic inhabitation of other positions and experiences, where they become embodied and tested out at the liminal zone between fact and fantasy, hovering at the threshold between the real and not-quite real, between how things are and how they might yet be.[24] Thus whilst play is, as Caillois argues, a separate and distinct practice to the everyday, it is still a site where meaningful questions might be (for a fixed duration) positioned and interrogated.

Roger Caillois' analysis of play and games can be used as a construct through which to explore the irresolvable quest as a gesture of *ludic* repetition or wandering, at the same time presenting a conceptual framework allowing oppositional ideas to be momentarily reconciled. The form of the irresolvable or endless quest within practices such as Heather and Ivan Morison's *Global Survey* can be redefined as a site of paradoxical conflation. In their work, a romantic tradition collides with a form of ludic conceptualism, as dispassionately rule-based instructions are undercut by highly subjective and contingent interpretations, and meaningful experimentation appears punctured through by random acts of chance or risk. The irresolvable quest can thus be conceived as a paradigm of strategic deferral or resistance that has the dual capacity to subvert or critique the logic of rational systems and ideologies, whilst at the same time reasserting a critical value for wilfully indeterminate, unproductive action. The notion of an unresolved, incomplete or endless action, or even of a failed, thwarted or repeated gesture could be seen as a form of *inexhaustible* or Sisyphean performance—a task without telos or destination—which assuages the need to perform whilst deferring the arrival of any specific goal or outcome. By rejecting completion in favour of a redeemed form of anti-climax or deferral, such practices remain suspended in a loop of open-endedness and of what could be. The irresolvable quest is reclaimed as a temporal site of rehearsal and infinitely repeatable permutations, a protected space for exploring the potential of "bottomless fictions" and "meaningless reverberations."

Notes

[1] Robert Smithson, "A Museum of Language in the Vicinity of Art," *Art International,* (March 1968), in Lucy Lippard, *Six Years: The Dematerialization of the Art Object from 1966-1972 ...* (Berkeley and Los Angeles: University of California Press, 1973/2001), 44.

[2] The examples evoked here include: 1. Sophie Calle's *Suite Vénitienne* (1979) or Vito Acconci's *Following Piece* (1969). 2. Tacita Dean's *Disappearance at Sea I and II* (1996 and 1997) and *Teignmouth Electron* (1999). 3. The Situationists' use of maps for other cities to find their way around Paris or Lucy Harrison's projects *Guided Tour; Riga* (2005) and *Detour* (2004). 4. Heather and Ivan Morison's *Chinese Arboretum (2003/4).* 5. Bas Jan Ader's *In Search of the Miraculous (Songs for the North Atlantic: July 1975).* 6. Sophie Calle's *Where are the angels?* (1984) or even Tim Brennan's *Museum of Angels.*

[3] See http://www.globalsurvey.org

[4] A MacGuffin features in a film, play or book, as something that starts or drives the action of the plot but later turns out to be unimportant.

[5] See http://www.morison.info

[6] For one definition of the difference between *space* and *place,* and an account of the historical shift from *itinerary* to *map,* see Michel de Certeau, *The Practice of Everyday Life,* trans. Steven Rendall, (Berkeley and Los Angeles: University of California Press, 1984). A broader geographical context for this debate is explored

in Phil Hubbard, Rob Kitchin and Gill Valentine (eds.) *Key Thinkers on Space and Place* (Sage Publications, 2004).

[7] De Certeau, *The Practice of Everyday Life*, 107.

[8] Ibid., 101.

[9] Ibid., 99.

[10] De Certeau suggests that, "walking about and travelling substitute for exits, for going away and coming back, which were formerly made available by a body of legends that places nowadays lack. Physical moving about has the itinerant function of yesterday's or today's 'superstitions'." See De Certeau, 1984, 107.

[11] Claudio Guillen, The Anatomies of Roguery: The Origins and the Nature of Picaresque Literature, (Garland Publishing, 1987), 17.

[12] Ibid., 435.

[13] Henry David Thoreau describes the act of sauntering performed by wandering scoundrels who adopted the guise of a pilgrimage in order to maintain their peripatetic lifestyle, in Henry David Thoreau, *Walking*, (Harper Collins, 1994), 2.

[14] See Robert Fraser in *The Victorian Quest Romance*, (Northcote House Publishers Ltd, 1998); Gustavo Pellon and Julio Rodriguez-Luis, (eds.) *Upstarts, Wanderers or Swindlers: Anatomy of the Picaro,* (Rodopi Publishing, 1986); Claudio Guillen, *The Anatomies of Roguery: The Origins and the Nature of Picaresque Literature* (Garland Publishing, 1987), Stuart Miller, *The Picaresque Novel*, (Cleveland, 1967).

[15] This connection between conceptual practice and Romanticism has previously been discussed by Jörg Heiser, "Emotional Rescue," *Frieze*, 71, (2002); in the exhibition *Romantic Conceptualism* curated by Jörg Heiser (Bawag Foundation, Vienna, 2007) and accompanying catalogue Jörg Heiser et al., *Romantic Conceptualism* (Kerber Verlag, 2008), and Jan Verwoert, *Bas Jan Ader: In Search of the Miraculous*, (Afterall, 2006). See also Johanna Burton, "Mystics Rather than Rationalists" in *Open Systems. Rethinking Art c.1970,* ed. Donna de Salvo, (Tate Publishing, 2005).

[16] Roger Caillois, *Man, Play and Games*, trans. Meyer Barash, (University of Illinois Press, 1958 / 2001), 30.

[17] Ibid., 5.

[18] Ibid., 7. For a full list of the characteristics of play see Caillois, 1958/2001, *Chapter 1, The Definition of Play*.

[19] Ibid., 10.

[20] Ibid., 9.

[21] Ibid., 10.

[22] Ibid., 5.

[23] Ibid., 19.

[24] There is also a connection here to a form of appropriation explored by Alison Landsberg in *Prosthetic Memory: The Transformation of American Remembrance in the Age of Mass Culture* (New York: Columbia University Press, 2004).

CHAPTER THREE

DON'T SAY YES – SAY MAYBE!
FICTION WRITING AND ART WRITING

MARIA FUSCO

Here is an arrow whose flight would consist in a return to the bow: fast enough, in sum, never to have left it; and what the sentence says – its arrow – is withdrawn. It will nevertheless have reached us, struck home; it will have taken some time – it will, perhaps, have changed the order of the world even before we are able to awake to the realisation that, in sum, nothing will have been said, nothing that will not already have been blindly endorsed in advance. And again, like a testament: for the natural miracle lies in the fact that such sentences outlive each author and each specific reader, him, you and me, all of us, all the living, all the living presents. [1]

The bridge between fiction writing and visual art making is a wide one, too broad in fact to traverse with any real surefooted assurance. Increasingly, I've become interested in fiction that positions anti-suspense and polyphonic narrative structures as its primary creative arcs, and how this type of writing may be utilised to probe readers' attitudes towards the *accuracy* of contemporary critical art writing.

Such anti-suspense may be described as a response to, or break from traditional narrative structures where the reader/viewer experiences a beginning, middle and end—in that order. Because such stories are propagated around us on a daily basis, we have specific expectations and anticipations that are redolent of narrative form itself. We assume there will be characters and action that will involve themselves with one another. We expect a series of incidents that will be connected in some way and that the problems or conflicts arising in the course of the action will achieve some final state; either that they will be resolved, or at least a new light will be cast on them. So then, we as spectators come prepared to make a narrative reading of any creative encounter, and I would suggest that this is as true of reading fiction as of *reading* art, in that we consistently attempt to make a whole out of sometimes dislocated or unhinged fragments.

Causality, that is to say, quotidian cause and effect, and its experiential relationship to time are central to looking at and making sense of almost anything. Here I am considering *time* as the chronological space that looking takes place within. Both in terms of the personal time spent in the act of *reading* and the historic timeline or literary lineage within which a work is placed, suggesting temporal compression, through looking as an activity in itself.

Criticism is one part of this process—the reflective component—where the vocative honesty of the complete object is generally favoured over the idea of a *leaky* object. An object that encourages the viewer/reader to "cruise" [2] (as Roland Barthes so admirably suggested in *The Pleasure of the Text*) its bitty nature in whatever combinations prove to be the most satisfying, useful and most importantly *precise* at any given reading, are vital if we are to adhere to Ezra Pound's assertion that: "Fundamental accuracy of statement is the ONE sole morality of writing." [3]

By utilising the analytic precision that *relief from plot* can create in fiction writing, let us consider then the potential for such fiction to intervene in visual art criticism, investing the textual object with a new life or critical trajectory. A more profound cathectic critical immersion: in which the spectator is encouraged and facilitated to be always in the midst of the action rather than wondering what will happen at the end.

Thus the independent experiences of fiction and visual art writing—as creative practices—could together potentially gain the ability to produce non-sequential narratives which reintroduce the reader/viewer to closer looking; calling for the readers' presence in the present, where inherent readability simultaneously determines the exact location of the addressee and an axiomatic relationship to their correspondent.

Umberto Eco has observed in a recent collection of his essays *On Literature*,

> ...Let us try to approach a narrative work with common sense and compare the assumptions we can make about it with those we can make about the world. As far as the world is concerned, we find that the laws of universal gravitation are those established by Newton, or that it is true that

Napoleon died on Saint Helena on 5 May 1821. And yet, if we keep an
open mind, we will always be prepared to revise our convictions the day
science formulates the great laws of the cosmos differently, or an historian
discovers unpublished documents proving that Napoleon died on a
Bonapartist ship as he attempted to escape. On the other hand, as far as the
world of books is concerned, propositions like 'Sherlock Holmes was a
bachelor,' 'Little Red Riding Hood is eaten by the wolf and then freed by
the woodcutter,' or 'Anna Karenina commits suicide' will remain true for
eternity, and no one will ever be able to refute them…There is little respect
for those who claim…that Superman is not Clark Kent. Literary texts
explicitly provide us with much that we will never cast doubt upon, but
also, unlike the real world, they flag with supreme authority what we are to
take as important in them. [4]

Utilising Eco's observations about the irrefutable veracity of fiction, as
a *fixative* of meaning, we can further progress and examine the dissolution
or again dissemination of the absolute object (as previously outlined)
through non-sequential narrative structures, and its attendant questioning
of the authorial voice. An excellent example of this is to be found in the
work of Irish author Flann O'Brien, particularly in *The Third Policeman*,
cited in many sources as the first postmodern novel.

The Third Policeman is O'Brien's second novel, produced quickly as
an entire work in 1939. O'Brien infamously wrote furiously, without pause
or correction on a typewriter perched at a shaky desk of his own
design—he submitted it to his English publisher Longmans, who had
recently published *At Swim-Two-Birds*. Their subsequent rejection letter
read, "We realise the author's ability but think that he should become less
fantastic, and in this new novel he is more so." [5] Disheartened, O'Brien
shelved the manuscript, claiming that it had been lost, and so it remained
until one year after his death in 1966, when it was posthumously
published.

The Third Policeman is an ontological tale, which tracks the plight of
its unnamed narrator, who, with his scheming accomplice John Divney,
has brutally battered old Mathers to death for his box of cash. We follow
the narrator on a surreal, cyclical journey, largely played out in an
absurdist rural police station, regulated by Sergeant Pluck, Policeman
MacCruiskeen and the eponymous third Policeman Fox. Throughout the
text, the narrator is taunted by his perceptive conscience Joe, and
counselled by the erroneous teachings of his idol, philosopher de Selby. At
the end of the novel, we discover that the narrator has been dead
throughout the book, and that his ghastly adventures are a metaleptic hell

that he has earned for the killing of Mathers.

Whilst the body of O'Brien's fiction works such as *The Third Policeman* and *At Swim-Two-Birds* are the obvious literary successors to the self-conscious tradition of *Tristram Shandy*, which also questioned the primacy of the author (though not in my opinion with such self-reflexive, thematic consistency), it is O'Brien's energetic repudiation of the author as central signifying presence that is a useful tool in the consideration of critical art writing, for it displaces the *site* of the writing past the object it is considering, persuasively enacting Richard Sheppard's assertion,

> Those critics who see the essential feature of postmodernism as its *acceptance* of postmodernity with its decentred plurality, ephemerality, fragmentation, discontinuities, indeterminacy and depending on one's point of view, chaos, seem to me to have got it precisely right. [6]

The narrator's lack or forgetting of his name in *The Third Policeman*, "…the next time I was asked my name I could not answer. I did not know."[7] is a clear indicator of O'Brien's scepticism of authorial supremacy. In this exchange between the narrator and Sergeant Pluck, the policeman is trying to identify his suspect:

> 'What is your pronoun?' He inquired.
> 'I have no pronoun,' I answered, hoping I knew his meaning.
> 'What is your cog?'
> 'My cog?'
> 'Your surnoun?'
> 'I have not got that either.'[8]

O'Brien's inventive use of language is notable here (as is its placement within a broad frame of culturally references), in terms of fusing together the *functionary* naming of words such as *noun* together with an instinctive understanding on his reader's part of what he is trying to convey; i.e. that I as reader understand that Pluck is asking for the first and second names of his suspect. Keith Hopper observes,

> The most interesting phrase is Pluck's use of 'cog' as a synonym for name…Presumably 'cog' is a clipped form of cognomen (a nickname or surname), though it also suggests a cog in a machine (a character in a literary text), a bicycle cog…[and] Cartesian 'cogito' (*cogito ergo sum*).[9]

"Cruiskeen Lawn," O'Brien's column in the *Irish Times* that ran from 1940-1966, shared the same concerns and linguistic playfulness as his fiction,

Front cover of *The Happy Hypocrite* (2008). Courtesy of Book Works

> Readers may recall that, when writing about NAMES some weeks ago, I revealed that there was a very queer, not to say vowellent, one to be found at the back of the Latin dictionary, namely (!) AEAEA.[10]

This fusion of metaphoric or expressive language, set within an albeit satirical newspaper column, has been very supportive to me in terms of my own thinking about the bumpy terrain of critical art writing. At first, I found my art writing at odds with my fiction writing, understanding of course that they perform different functions, but at the same time feeling a need to rationalise or at least satisfactorily settle in some way the *leakage* between the two. O'Brien's application of his analytical and creative skills are an excellent example of the potentiality of writing across genre and subject, in order to determine a more exact destination of meaning.

Derrida has written of Nietzsche's work that it is "Future Producing,"[11] and so too is *The Third Policeman*'s. Its very own material syntax is meta-critical, referring to its own knowledge (and non-knowledge) by shuffling the order of our narrative world, even before we are aware that nothing will have been told to us, that we have not already *blindly* endorsed in advance, through agreeing to read the text, in the first place.

In addition to O'Brien's actual writing output, (both fictional and factual), his questioning of the author is also established by O'Brien's battery of *noms de plume* including: birth name Brian O'Nolan/Brian Ó'Nualláin; fiction writer Flann O'Brien; *Irish Times'* columnist Myles na gCopaleen; occasional correspondence George Knowall and the anonymous editor of his student journal *Blather* which when seen together make it virtually impossible to catalogue and therefore *fix* O'Brien's work within a single writerly methodology or genre. This expansiveness opens up for me a very intriguing rhizomatic textual experience, by which I mean that O'Brien's rebuttal of authorial supremacy allows me as writer and reader (and of course other readers), to traverse his work more thoroughly by increasing the amount of entry and exit points by which it may be interpreted. This is useful to bear in mind in regards to interpretation or extrusion of the meaning of art objects through the act of writing.

I feel that for art writing, there is much to be garnered from the *transformative* quality of fiction both in terms of being exact, and in terms of re-looking at material. O'Brien's *second* policeman MacCruiskeen's long-term compulsive hobby, of manufacturing increasingly tiny chests,

Inside spread of *The Happy Hypocrite* (2008).
Courtesy of Farhad Ahrarnia and Book Works

requires that in order for him to actually make the chest, he must also make minute tools so that he can do the job more *precisely*. Here, again, I am thinking of course, of Ezra Pound's assertion about the "fundamental accuracy of statement" [12] and its intrinsic relationship with methodology,

> Six years ago they began to get invisible, glass or no glass [magnifying glass]. Nobody has ever seen the last five I made because no glass is strong enough to make them big enough to be regarded truly as the smallest things ever made. Nobody can see me making them because my little tools are invisible into the same bargain.[13]

This hunt for transformation is neatly expressed in Maurice Blanchot's quote at the beginning of his 1940 book *Thomas the Obscure* (itself often cited as the first postmodern novel),

> …making no distinction between the figure and that which is, or believes itself to be, its centre, whenever the complete figure itself expresses no more than the search for an imagined centre.[14]

The "imagined centre" here is an elusive one for the art writer, and in my case, I feel that I can only access it through the *figure* of writing that is somehow self-conscious, in that it is demonstrating, or again, interrogating its very form.

The Third Policeman's construction directly encourages its readers to be pro-active in an obvious way, and it is this very clear, non-sequential, anti-suspense direction that may be considered as an analogue to the experience of art writing, in that the reader must decide on the meaning or partial conclusions of their own reading, both of the actual artwork and also its attendant critical writing.

The problematic of this notion is that form cannot of course be challenged or even put into practice in any forum: if one has been commissioned to write an eight-hundred word review of an exhibition or a book, it will probably not be appropriate to write it in *haiku* form. So, therefore, critical art writing does at times involve a considerable amount of occlusion. What I am really interested in discussing here is the potentiality for more precise forms of writing production (through the medium of fiction), which can be applied topically at appropriate moments.

To this end, I have founded *The Happy Hypocrite*, a new journal for and about experimental art writing. It is hoped that this bi-annual publication will encourage, test and build a constituency for divergent forms of *writing*, addressing the lack of legroom for art writers to write away from the form of the traditional review. The journal is themed by methodology rather than by subject: issue one is *Linguistic Hardcore*, issue two *Hunting and Gathering*, and issue three *Volatile Dispersal: Speed and Reading*, with an aim to cluster and aggregate forms of practice together in a hopefully *inappropriate* manner.

Just as O'Brien's use of footnotes in *The Third Policeman*, (which describe de Selby's fallacious philosophical theories in relation to an incident in the preceding text), threaten to mutiny the main text towards the end of the novel by taking up most of the page, so too might *The Happy Hypocrite* mistake the weight of words—and this I would suggest is a positive creative force. The narrator's reliance on de Selby's take on the world, is in direct contrast with his scepticism about his conscience. Joe's observations, which although much more insightful, are not expressed in academic language, and are therefore discarded by the narrator as being less authoritative. It is interesting to consider this in relation to the critic's use of theoretical texts.

Contemporary art criticism then, may be observed to be assembling an inauthentic absolute object or teratological corpus, through rationalist grafting of interpretation from scrappy parts—criticism demanding to be read of itself, whilst simultaneously calling for a reading or comprehension of something which is outside of itself. The meaning of that outside reading, can of course never be proved, just as O'Brien's world of words is open to constant reinvestment depending on "how you look at it."

So, if all voices and their creators are posited with the same authority, then just whose voice should we listen to? And more importantly, whose voice should we write with? If we remind ourselves of the two fundamental presuppositions of postmodernist fiction writing (as demonstrated in *The Third Policeman*): first, the belief that the world consists of a random assortment of disconnected elements and that any attempt to discover an order in this chaos is necessarily an act of fiction-making and, secondly, the assumption that a text is ultimately a self-referring structure, an entity without significant connections with the external world. Obviously, these two presuppositions are closely intertwined, since the maker who doubts the very possibility of knowing the world, who questions the category of *reality* itself, will naturally come to believe that the only certain reality is the reality of its own discourse.

This is a good thing. And a necessary thing to keep in mind in relation to an art writing practice (the practice of writing one's own work) that must at all times be vigilant, playful, quick-witted and exact.

And so we return to the beginning:

> Here is an arrow whose flight would consist in a return to the bow: fast enough, in sum, never to have left it; and what the sentence says – its arrow – is withdrawn. It will nevertheless have reached us, struck home; it will have taken some time – it will, perhaps, have changed the order of the world even before we are able to awake to the realisation that, in sum, nothing will have been said, nothing that will not already have been blindly endorsed in advance. And again, like a testament: for the natural miracle lies in the fact that such sentences outlive each author and each specific reader, him, you and me, all of us, all the living, all the living presents.[15]

Notes

[1] Jacques Derrida, "Loving in Friendship: Perhaps – the Noun and the Adverb" in Jacques Derrida, *Politics of Friendship*, trans. George Collins (London & New York: Verso), 1997, 31.

[2] Roland Barthes, *Pleasure of the Text* (New York: Hill and Wang), 1975, 4.

[3] Cited in Raymond Carver, *Call If You Need Me* (London: Harvill), 2000, 88.

[4] Umberto Eco, *On Literature* (London: Vintage), 2006, 5.

[5] Mike Collins.
http://corkuniversitypress.typepad.com/cork_university_press/2006/02/surreal_bic ycle.html (accessed April 22 2008).

[6] Richard Sheppard, *Modernism-Dada-Postmodernism*, (Evanston: Northwest University Press), 2000, 358.

[7] Flann O'Brien, *The Third Policeman* (London: Flamingo), 1993, 21.

[8] Ibid., 58.

[9] Keith Hopper, *Flann O'Brien: A Portrait of the Artist as a Young Post-Modernist*, (Cork: Cork University Press), 1995, 123-4.

[10] Flann O'Brien *The Hair of the Dogma*, (London: Grafton), 1987, 147.

[11] Derrida, *Politics of Friendship*, 31.

[12] Ibid.

[13] O'Brien, *The Third Policeman*, 76.

[14] Maurice Blanchot, *Thomas the Obscure* (New York: David Lewis), 1973, 3.

[15] Derrida, *Politics of Friendship*, 31.

CHAPTER FOUR

TALKING THEORY

YVE LOMAX

The word *event* was on the lips of many and hearing this I had to ask: what exactly constitutes an event and how can it be said of a still photographic image? Having asked the question I knew what was demanded of me: I had to do some theorizing, and in time a book became written.[1]

Now, in addressing the question of what constitutes an event, I most certainly wanted to say something about the nature of an event; however, it was soon realised that with an event I could not take it as given that a *something* was there, was there awaiting theorisation, awaiting something being said about it. For sure, I was listening out for theories of the event, yet in trying to do some theorising there was no recognisable object to which I could point my index finger and say, "there it is, there it is." Indeed, there was no object that I could observe and contemplate and gain an understanding of and get my hands upon.[2] In my endeavour I had to consider that with a stone an event could be going on; yet, with an event, I could not take it as given that there was a *something* that could be looked over, looked at attentively, viewed closely.

Going back to the Greek word *theoria* you can find that it is rooted in meaning *to look at something attentively, to look over, to view closely*, yet when *theoria* becomes translated as *contemplatio* what becomes emphasised, in this act of looking, is an act of division—something is partitioned off into a separate sector and enclosed therein. However, through listening out for theories of the event and attempting to do some theorising, what I became enabled to do was to ask: is the *something* that theory is partitioning off and enclosing fabricated in and by the very act of partitioning and enclosing?

What must a theory first and foremost do? The philosopher Isabella Stengers answers: it must distinguish its object. When it is demanded of a theory that it must distinguish its object there is, in that demand, a call for an act that judges what is to be taken into account "as of essence" and what is to be excluded as anecdotal or mere background noise. For sure, in judging what is to be taken into account and what is to be excluded there is an act of partitioning off and enclosing. However, what Isabella Stengers asks us to consider is that in such judging and partitioning there has been the "fabrication" of an object. And it is a fabrication because in judging what is to be included "as of essence" a theory has already drawn up a set of ideas that have been determined to give shape and outline an object— how else would it know what is "of essence" and what can be excluded and ignored? [3]

So, what am I trying to say here? Well, what I am trying to say is that, in theory's distinguishing of its object, a partitioned off and enclosed part of that which transpires in the world is having imposed upon it a set of ideas—a shape and outline—that are not only predetermined but also drawn up externally to it. Indeed, what I am trying to say is that, in distinguishing its object, a theory not only fabricates an object but also constructs, what the political philosopher Antonio Negri calls, *exteriority*.[4]

In the act of partitioning off and enclosing, theory constructs an inside, yet it also produces an outside, an exterior position. And saying this leads to a question that I really want to ask, which is: *do you see theory as that which sets itself up in an exterior position?* And to ask this question is, at heart, to ask: *when exactly do you hear theory talking?* Or to rephrase the question: *what presuppositions do you hold concerning theory?*

Of late, I have had cause to turn my attention towards presupposition. I have had my head turned, and I cannot look away. But it is not love that holds me there, keeps me there, keeps me looking. And what is it that I have seen happen when presupposition happens? I'll not beat about the bush: what happens when presupposition happens is the establishment of a *before* and a *beneath*.

Let me elaborate. With presupposition there comes a *pre*, which establishes anteriority and antecedence; then there comes the *sup-position*, which sets down a place that is beneath or, in other words, hidden below. Through establishing anteriority and antecedence, presupposition leads me to believe that something is already there and as such can be taken as given. Indeed, pre-supposition gives me a before in time; however, it also puts into position a realm beneath that is concealed from me.

In addressing the question of what constitutes an event and listening out for theories of the event, what I found thrown into question, time and time again, was the presupposition that (a) *something* is standing there before the befalling of an event. I also found that what posits this presupposition is the subject-predicate distinction, which continues to settle in many a language, many a sentence.

The subject-predicate distinction distinguishes a primary position and this is where the subject is placed. Being placed in the primary position the subject thus stands as what comes first, and standing as first readies the assumption that *something* is standing there before the befalling that is, so the dictionary tells me, "the action of a verb; an occurrence, an event." [5]

> ◆Have you heard theory talking here, here where words have been speaking of presupposition? Perhaps you have, perhaps you haven't. However, in hearing the talking that has been happening here have you presupposed the existence of language?

An awkward silence is just about to be broken; a public lecture is just about to be written; a declaration of intent is on her lips; and in advance of a word being spoken or written has it been presupposed that language *is*? Two people are chatting; they are talking about this and that; but, is their experience of language one of presupposition? When I come to say something, say something about something, which is what some would call meaningful discourse, do I take it as given that the taking place of language has already happened? But this is precisely what presupposition makes me do. Once presupposition cuts in, the taking place of language is not only deemed to have already happened *before* the utterance of meaningful discourse, no matter how meaningless or trivial this may be, but is also forced to "go to ground," that is to say, go down to a place *beneath* and become hidden.

Through presupposition, the taking place of language is put in the position of being both before and beneath, and when that happens the taking place of language becomes placed beyond meaningful discourse; or, to put it the words of the philosopher Giorgio Agamben, "the event of language always and already transcends what is said in this event." [6] And when the event of language is always and already in the position of *before* and *beyond*, language is torn apart and suffers a scission that divides it into two separate planes: on the one hand, the taking place of language and, on the other hand, the plane of meaningful discourse, which corresponds to what is said within this taking place.

For Giorgio Agamben, the scission of language into two irreducible planes permeates all of Western thought, from Aristotle, up through to the duality of *Sage* (saying) and *Sprache* (speaking) in Heidegger or between *showing* and *telling* in Wittgenstein.[7] It can also be found in modern linguistics when a distinction is made between *parole* and *langue*.

Now, I am not saying that the aforementioned philosophers unthinkingly presupposed the existence of language, far from it. However, what holds me captive is the thought that when the taking place of language is presupposed (unwittingly or not) language suffers a splitting and something of itself becomes separated and concealed from itself. I speak of the taking place of language, but this could be equally the taking place of myself.

Again let me ask: Have you heard theory talking here, here where words have been talking of the presupposing of the existence of language?

My attention has been turned toward presupposition, and I cannot look away. And what I see is not only the taking place of language being presupposed but also how, in saying something about something, a presuppositional structure takes hold of the very words I utter.

Let me say more. As I was entreated to leave infancy behind, my education insisted upon and persisted in teaching me the importance of saying something. Stand up and say something about something! And as I diligently did, I learned to make predicative assertions; but, what no one told me was that in learning to say something about something I was also learning to presuppose. In learning to say something about something, what was handed down to me was the subject and predicate relation: first of all there is the subject—let's say, "morning"—and then, secondly, the words by which something is said of it—"brings daylight." Behold: "Morning brings daylight." However, in order to say "brings daylight," and for these words to be meaningful, I had to take "morning" as already given; indeed, if I did not presuppose it then I could never have accomplished saying something about it. Yes, what my education handed down to me was presupposition.

As that child how could I *not* presuppose? For sure, I could have stood up and just said "brings daylight" or indeed "remains suspended", but what was handed down to me, on "good authority", was that language must speak about something—I must do more than merely repeat names and say "morning" over and over again. Indeed, my education was insisting that I speak those words by which something is said about something. However, for these discoursing and predicative words to be meaningful, I had to learn that the existence of a name has to be presupposed—a predicative assertion only becomes possible through taking a name, such as morning, as already given.

Some would say that the infantile vocation of language is to name.[8] And there you are, an infant delighting in saying the word that names. And you are delighted because you are discovering that the name-giving gesture is an experiment with language. But then (it seems so sudden) the insistence comes that you begin to say something about something. And now you become the child who in encountering the world has, beyond names, something to say of it. And as you become that child, and enter the world of discourse, you are instructed that names are what you receive. Quite simply, you are to learn names and, equally, learn that names are what are handed down to you—it is an historical transmission. For language, and yourself, to speak about something, the existence of names must be presupposed.

As you learn to say more and more things, what you find out is that discourse always predicates something of something whereas the name tells you nothing about that which it calls—the name only makes an announcement and asserts nothing. Indeed, as you learn more names, you find out that the meaning of a name has to be explained—passed on—for you to understand it. Then you find out that, for discourse, there is something unsayable within the name: it can predicate something of the named but it cannot say what the name names. And this is why, so you are told, the name and the named can only be presupposed by discourse. And here, as presupposition takes hold, what emerges, again, is a fracture of language itself. A split has occurred: the name and discourse occupy realms that are separate from each other. For sure, names can enter into the world of discourse and, indeed, endless definitions can be placed next to every name, but what is said in discourse can only be said thanks to the presupposition of names. Giorgio Agamben puts it like this:

> ... the fracture between name (*onoma*) and defining discourse (*logos*) ... traverses all of language ... Discourse cannot say what is named by the

name. What is named by the name is transmitted and abandoned in discourse, as untransmittable and unsayable. The name is thus the linguistic cipher of presupposition, of what discourse cannot say but can only presuppose in signification. Names certainly enter into propositions, but what is said in propositions can be said only thanks to the presupposition of names.[9]

Discourse presupposes the name and, moreover, presupposes what is named by the name. Indeed, discourse presupposes the name "morning" in order to say something of it and, at the same time, what is named by the name is posited on the basis of a presupposition, which sets the scene for taking it as given that the named occupies a realm that is beneath and anterior to language. I cannot deny it: the presupposition of the named sets the scene for a vision of something that is, in all senses of the word, *beyond* language.

> ❖And yet again I will ask: Have you heard theory talking here, here where words have been talking of what becomes presupposed when we say something about something?

Discourse cannot say what is named by the name, it can only say something about it; the only way for the named to enter language is for it to become a subject that has been presupposed by the words that say something of it. Indeed, the only way for the named to enter language is through presupposition. The words that say something about morning most certainly bring morning into the light of day; however, through presupposition that which is named by the name "morning" will be banished to a realm that is separate from and dark to the world of discoursing words.

Through presupposition what is named by the name is brought into "defining discourse"—*logos*—but as this happens it is also placed outside and excluded from it. Discourse asks me to take as given that something is there prior to the words that speak about it; however, with this presupposition what is produced is a world of *somethings* that are a world of something-other-than-language. And what there is to experience here is a division that divides the linguistic from the non-linguistic. Indeed, what is to be experienced is a world that bears a division that separates the taking place of things in the world from the taking place of the word. A division is made and what comes with it is a vision of *something* that stands outside of language. Behold morning, but beholding it through presupposition is to see a vision of some non-linguistic thing that has been included in language only on the condition that it has been excluded from it. And seeing this vision leaves me saying that, in truth, such a non-linguistic thing that only can be conceived of in language. The non-linguistic only can ever be found in language; it is, as Giorgio Agamben will say, "nothing other than a presupposition of language." [10]

How can I experience, in speaking and writing, language without presupposing the existence of it? But, as Giorgio Agamben asks, "what can an experience of this kind be?" [11] How can there be, with language, experience not of this or that signifying proposition but, rather, of the pure fact that one speaks, that there is language? What is more, how can I speak without presupposing that of which I speak? Indeed, how can language be without presupposition operating with in it? In the writing and thinking I have been doing of late, these are questions that I have been unable to ignore—they have held me, passionately. [12]

It is undeniable that within language a presuppositional machine operates (do we not learn to presuppose through language?) However, something of late has been forcing me to see through the presuppositional structure of language and catch sight of the taking place of language—and the world—free of presupposition. A first move has been that of seeing how presupposition produces and maintains division between the event of language and what is said in this event, between the name and defining discourse and, finally, between the "linguistic" and the "non-linguistic." However, a second move has been that of attempting to see when, in language, the presuppositional machine becomes inoperative. And this is precisely what the philosopher Giorgio Agamben bids us see, and this "*vision of language itself*" is not without political implications. [13] To see the presuppositional machine becoming inoperative in language is to have apprehension of living a life that has nothing other than its own living at stake within it, that is, of existing without presupposition—for some, this constitutes "happy life." [14]

◆Again I will ask: Have you heard theory talking here, here where words have been asking if they can speak without presupposition?

I have asked if two people talking have presupposed the existence of language. And now I want to ask if these two people have, in their chatter, taken it for granted that their lived experience is antecedent to language. Imagine that you are one of these people. You are talking to a friend and relating something that happened at 3.45pm the previous day and then, out of the blue, a stranger comes up and asks: "What can you say?" The question isn't asking you what you can say about this or that; on the contrary, it is merely asking *What?* For a moment your mouth gapes. You don't know what to say, and so say to yourself: *What can I say?* And still your mouth gapes.

In the moment your mouth hangs open such that all manner of small winged creatures have the opportunity to fly in and out, you could, in sheer desperation, speak of your life and experiences. Maybe you would speak of that time when, as a child, you were run over. A sports car it was, travelling fast through a village that rarely saw cars but frequently had children tearing across its single, straight, road. Or perhaps you would speak of that first time in hospital when tonsils had been taken out and jelly was going down in lumps as tears were battled against as parents were departing and leaving you there for yet another night.

Tales of lived experience are falling from your tongue; but, as the words fill the air, have you supposed that your lived experience, happy or sad, is antecedent to and distinguishable from the words that bring it to life? Let's say you respond to the question by saying that the words that speak lived experience are what bring it to life ... *life is made in speech and remains indistinguishable from it.*

Hearing these words that do not fear life living in speech, you cannot deny that what is lived—your life—is not immune from fable. (Hasn't fable, *fabula*, got something to do with speech?) Indeed, with life being made in speech and remaining indistinguishable from it, you cannot deny that you could construct your lived experiences on the basis of a fabulous invention. And then speaking of your life and experiences as a way to answer the imperative of the question of what can you say, perhaps you would speak of that person who betrayed a friendship and did underhand deeds. Or maybe you would speak of those terrible times when you were subjected to a war that had insidiously incited an insurrection that caused cherished ones to be profoundly silenced and have taken from them the life that breathes in the word.

Maybe you would not speak of this life that had had its heart ripped out but, rather, gather words to have word, world and life remaining tight together. And maybe you would do this so as to say that the words that speak of your life and experiences do not minister to the biographical paradigm that in modern times bends ears and sells books. Was not biography, autobiography formed by a catastrophic separation that tore life from its ties to speech and made it become so-called real life?

In a short essay called "The Dictation of Poetry," Giorgio Agamben produces a wonderful telling of how the tight unity between life and speech, which is announced in the prologue to the Gospel of John, suffers a drastic rupture whereupon life has its ties to speech broken and becomes so-called real life.[15] In the theological tradition that emerges from the Gospel of John, lived experience and poeticized experience—that is to say, life and speech—are interlaced, but this life-language relation "run in precisely the opposite direction from the convention dominating the modern concept of biography"; when lived experience becomes biography it "inexorably departs from speech, and becomes a real fact." [16] And with this departure, lived experience assumes a position that is antecedent to language.

Biography, autobiography, would have us believe that real life always and already precedes the words that speak it; however, what here is believed in, so-called real life, can only be believed in because the ties between life and speech have been broken. Autobiography "it is nothing living."[17] So-called real life does not truly live, it can only require that it is said to live; departing from speech, it does not live in speech; on the contrary, it becomes a fact that speech is required to report ... *she lived in the poor part of town.*

What does biography do? Answer: it makes us believe in a self that has its lived experiences antecedent to language. What does autobiography do? Answer: it makes the *I* that speaks itself presuppose itself, which is, precisely, to take itself as preceding the event of language. However, as Giorgio Agamben is keen to remind us, Émile Benveniste's studies on pronouns tells us that *I* is "a term that can only be identified within an instance of discourse ... The reality which it invokes is the reality of discourse." [18] When *I* speak or indeed write, I do not stand separate from or behind language but, rather, appear *through* it. In other words, *the words that speak lived experience are what bring it to life.*

Is it presupposition that gives the *I* of autobiography the notion that it is there before it pronounces itself, its life, in language? I'll answer: yes. For sure, presupposition gives the *I* a before in time, which means I can take myself as already given; but, let me hasten to add, presupposition also makes something of this I remain below itself; indeed, something remains hidden and separated from it. And what is hidden and separated from me is my linguistic nature. In presupposing itself, *I* does not have access to itself; to the contrary, its linguistic nature becomes estranged from it.

Each time an *I* is uttered—by me or you or whomever—there is, although we may not think it, the event of language. Language hasn't already taken place; it is happening there and then. And this is precisely what Benveniste's theory of enunciation shows.[19] Pronouns such as *I* indicate an instance of discourse; indeed, *I* (or *you*) indicates that the existence of language is taking place. But in presupposing itself, in taking itself to be antecedent to language, *I* presupposes the very existence of language. And again the question returns that, of late, has been holding me passionately: *How can I, in speaking or writing, experience language without presupposing it?* Responding to this question perhaps you would simply say: *I am never anywhere but in saying* I. In saying these words there quietly comes a refusal to have life and language separated, and with this refusal something of the presuppositional machine has been jammed; for, neither life nor language are presupposed.

◆And yet again I am going to ask if you have heard theory talking here, here where there has been talk of lived experience and the taking place of language?

Let me be direct: has it made you happy to hear of the interlacement of life and speech? Moreover, has it made you happy to hear of the presuppositional machine becoming jammed and inoperative?

Happiness. So often we say yes to something for the sake of something else—I'll do it because of … (whatever). But with happiness there is no such because. We say yes to happiness for its own sake, which is to say that happiness is its own because; it is, as Aristotle would say, "self-sufficient." [20] When happiness appears in our world, what appears is precisely that which doesn't lack anything and is founded only upon its taking place. In other words, happiness is that which has nothing hidden below or behind it. Simply put, there is no presupposition. And with this said there immediately comes the question: is there a chance for happiness to happen when we—you and me—take care to find out what is presupposed in whatever we are doing, living, thinking? Is there *happy life* to be had in exposing presupposition? But wait, isn't exposing presupposition exactly what critical activity demands of us? What does critique mean? I'll answer: to not take anything as given, to not presuppose?

If critical activity were to take the criticized as given, it would presuppose it before a word was said of it, and to presuppose the criticized is to make it substantive, which is precisely to make it a definite, which is to allow the criticized to be taken, unquestionably, as *is*. However, critical activity—*critique*—has to question everything: it cannot take the criticised as given; it cannot take the critic as given; and, moreover, it cannot take itself as given. In other words, it has to be total.[21] But hearing these words said makes me hesitate and wobble before saying anything; indeed, they make me want to cry out: *What can I say? What can I say?* However, what I can say is that if critical activity is to take place it cannot be for the sake of something else.

If critical activity is to take place it cannot be "I'll do it because of ..." which would mean that critical activity is put in the service of something that lies beyond it and escapes its activity. But embracing what is said here takes me—and critical activity—to an "extreme place." [22] And it is an extreme place, for in taking place, the activity of being critical has to bear the radical insecurity of questioning everything, including itself and any *cause* that lies beyond it.

Critical activity cannot take place for the sake of something else; it can only go toward its taking place, yet in this movement it has to bear the insecurity of taking place without presupposition. However, in bearing this insecurity, critical activity has the chance to become its own because and have nothing below it, behind it or beyond it; and with that happening there comes a chance for happiness to appear, which is, precisely, its own because.

> And for one more time I must ask: Have you heard theory talking here, here where happiness has not been shunned in the critical activity of exposing presupposition? Have you?

Notes

[1] See Yve Lomax, *Sounding the Event: Escapades in dialogue and matters of art, nature and time* (London and New York: I.B.Tauris, 2005).

[2] Ibid., 45.

[3] Ibid., 47-54.

[4] "There is no exteriority to fall back upon, on any occasion." Antonio Negri, *Time for Revolution*, trans. Matteo Mandarini (New York and London: Continuum,

2003), 49. Following in the footsteps of Spinoza, Negri says, time and time again, that there is no exteriority or, in other words, no transcendence.

[5] See Lomax, *Sounding the Event*, 96.

[6] Giorgio Agamben, *Language and Death: The Place of Negativity*, trans. Karen E.Pinkus with Michael Hardt (Minneapolis and Oxford: University of Minnesota Press, 1991), 86.

[7] Ibid., 85.

[8] See Giorgio Agamben, *Idea of Prose*, trans. Michael Sullivan and Sam Whitsitt (Albany: State University of New York, 1995), 97.

[9] Giorgio Agamben, *Potentialities: Collected Essays in Philosophy*, trans. Daniel Heller-Roazen (Stanford, California: Stanford University Press, 1999), 107-8.

[10] See Giorgio Agamben, *Homo Sacer: Sovereign Power and Bare Life*, trans. Daniel Heller-Roazen (Stanford, California: Stanford University Press, 1998), 21 and 50.

[11] Giorgio Agamben, *Infancy and History: On the Destruction of Experience*, trans. Liz Heron (London and New York: Verso, 2007), 6.

[12] This is a reference to my forthcoming *Passionate Being: Language, Singularity and Perseverance.*

[13] Giorgio Agamben will draw our attention to a vision of language that lets the "unpresupposed" appear. See *Potentialites*, 47.

[14] . See Giorgio Agamben, *Means without End: Notes on Politics*, trans. Vincenzo Binetti and Cesare Casarino, *Theory out of Bounds*, Volume 20 (Minneapolis and London: University of Minnesota Press, 2000), 8-9 and 109-118.

[15] See Giorgio Agamben, "The Dictation of Poetry," in *The End of the Poem: Studies in Poetics*, trans. Daniel Heller-Roazen (Stanford, California: Stanford University Press, 1999).

[16] See ibid., 70 and 85.

[17] Hélèn Cixous, *The Book of Promethea*, trans. Betsy Wing (Lincoln and London: University of Nebraska Press, 1991), 19.

[18] Quoted by Giorgio Agamben, in *Infancy and History*, 53.

[19] See Agamben, *Death and Language* for more on this theory, 23-5.

[20] Aristotle, *The Nichomachean Ethics*, 1176 b 5, trans. W.D.Ross, in *The Basic Works of Aristotle* (New York: The Modern Library, 2001), 1102.

[21] See Gilles Deleuze, "Critique," in *Nietzsche and Philosophy*, trans. Hugh Tomlinson (London and New York: Continuum, 2005), 89-90.

[22] Ibid., 110.

CHAPTER FIVE

TALK: TURBULENCE

SISSU TARKA

This text is based on a written conversation between Sissu Tarka and one of her collaborators. It was presented at the symposium *Telling Stories: Theories and Criticism* in the format of letters. The notes and references that fundamentally structure the mode and content of Tarka's writing here are included in the publication. The reading of a mail conversation rather than a more traditional paper at the symposium allowed Tarka to address the distribution of otherness, agency and conviviality inherent in the text in its performative nature: I am telling you … a story. The text interweaves the complexities of animation and its discourse, in particular animation *as* "minor" discourse, with ideas around the *active work*, and its application to animation, more explicitly, interactive animation. Inherent to animation, Tarka suggests, is its multiple discourse, expressed in an open and active dimension of the moving image/text.

***

Excerpts from a mail conversation, January – April 2007

Date: Tue, 16 Jan 2007 14:36:12 -0000
Subject: blackboard
You asked me to respond to your ideas you sent a while ago, about issues of collective action. Before anything else I want to describe my interest in animation, in its spacing and incomplete image, which for me relates to a vital need to process multiple modes of knowledge production. This multiplicity, questioning the linear and finite, was necessary as I felt uncomfortably confronted with an institutionalised, canonised, and limited language during my research on moving images and moving image culture. The decision to search for a specific place that animation can occupy, created new conditions for my work and research. I found that this

is comparable to what Deleuze & Guattari develop as a "minor literature,"[1] which they attribute to Kafka's work, for example. Characteristically this is a deterritorialised language, appropriate for strange and minor uses—a language cut off from the masses in which everything is political and takes on a collective value.[2] This literature, operating from the margins, is critical and doubtful by its nature. If an individual is speaking with such deterritorialised language, the voice is also already that of the community in which s/he is speaking. That is, what is spoken by someone, expresses the voice of more than one, and it constitutes solidarity among a particular collective. As a site, this language is capable of maintaining its obscurity and subversion and suggests an animation practice as a form of a minor discourse belonging to technical and film theoretical orientation. As such it neither hides itself nor interferes with other media, but remains marginal and essentially displaced. Its character of subversion and only occasional appearance gives the semblance of a virtual entity: non-linear, elusive, and not always actualised. Here linearity is understood as a prescribed or, if you will, inscribed or predetermined trajectory. The paradox of animation's elusive amorphousness is that the animated drawing comes into being precisely as the very trajectory of a line, the tracing of an outline, of a firm boundary. This concept of "minor" animation is intrinsically linked with its relation to the past, where animation manifests itself as essentially historical. The use of the latest technical means, supporting this point of view, suggests that the temporality integral to this historical entity—animation's power of non-linearity—connects animation to the social. Indeed, technologies and their processes can never be established if they exclude people's experience and imagination of how to use them. Without the varying and transforming experience of new instruments under changing social conditions, animation loses its essence of addressing a collective/individual imaginary and thus loses its essence as a subversive image.

In contextualising animation and discovering its images and signs, in particular within the digital (as you know, this is the medium I choose to work with), I revealed however a second site that it occupies. This is an approach that dominates animation practice today in both non-commercial and commercial imagery, and contrasts with conceiving animation as a minor discourse. It searches for an essentially plural experience in animation projects and an ambiguous relation to subversion and obscurity. This second site, which suggests animation as an omnipresent image, constitutes a sort of thickness in visual culture, to the extent that it punctuates the very mechanism of the visual. From this point of view animation can exceed its determined identity associated with film and history. Animation's second site of discourse is linked to contemporary artwork that is characterised by an excess, a beyond, or a "hyper-." [3] These two intrinsically linked views have increasingly become a confrontational issue for artwork informed by new technologies. When neither the first nor the second view entirely maps the imaginative, paradoxical, and (inter)active concepts that animation gives rise to, the combination of the two views manifests another, a third site, if you like. This is a dimension where contemporary animation claims a crossover that puts into question the two differing views.

Grounding my writings to you in this twofold dynamic of animation, my text connects theory, a voice and a movie: I have posted you an animation, a digital movie that deals with some issues I am talking about. My work at this time feels like a turbulent net, and needs, I think, some ordering—some time.

Best

Date: Wed, 31 Jan 2007 22:57:42 +0000
Subject: [ACTIVE]]]]

Thanks for your remarks on minorities and movie-making. Let me for now continue with my thoughts on animation and how they are linked to an open dimension of the image and its discourse. It is a link, as I want to suggest, related to *active works* where the role of passive observing is transformed into the role of *active viewing*. I should explain to you, that when I talk about viewing here, I mean the engagement with an artwork in a wider sense, including an audience of a performance for example, or the interactive user of the computer generated image. Turning backwards first, in the formation of what Umberto Eco describes as the "open work," [4] a work potentially remains without a definite conclusion; it is infinitely variable according to its elementary source components, or units. It is open in that the performer, of a music piece for instance, actively intervenes in its production by organising the components in the order s/he chooses them to be heard. This example demonstrates the possibility of a multiple reading or interpretation of a work with no single unequivocal line of establishing meaning. Interesting to me here is the role of the work's openness, which is not to create an autonomous performer or audience, but to interrupt the order of communication by posing new communicative situations; the work shifts in parallel with the complexities (specificities, etc.) of the changing contexts. Another détournement brings into play an explicit social dimension in active viewing. Jacques Rancière provocatively describes *art as service*, where artists, in recognising lack of connections in the social bond, attempt to repair these connections.[5] He refers to Nicolas Bourriaud's idea of "relational aesthetics" (you are familiar with it, I know), which suggests artwork as re-establishing, and being re-established by, interactive relations and a generative power re-created each time it is shown.[6] The forms emerging out of this programme are seen as products; they are temporary images, or fleeting constellations, constituted by collective behaviour.[7] The installations that artists create are then sociable environments co-constructed and produced by inter-human relations, by people's behaviour in relation to each other and in a particular setting.

Calls in current discourses for a return to Eco's "open work," and the critique of Bourriaud's "relational aesthetics," are perhaps symptomatic of a confusion and a collapse of the sensual non-political dimension of artwork with the emergence of communicative networks, its implications for the establishment of communities, and the demand for the political in today's art. The insistence of a participatory element in contemporary practices, explicitly delivered in forms of spaces of inter/action (e.g. performative spaces, interactive installations using creative software), provide a space for multiple meaning and works as multiplicity. However art is also concerned with a de-politicisation in the sense of insisting to some degree on its autonomy and singularity. By singularity here I mean an autonomy of art—when art is not merging with politics for example, when it keeps a certain *being itself*, a single entity in a way. It interests me what Rancière, in his text *Problems and Transformations of Critical Art,* describes as a kind of displacement of the political in relation to art, so uncertain of its politics. He is talking about the effects of a shrinking public space, where mini-demonstrations of artists, their mechanisms of interaction, and their provocations *in situ* or elsewhere, possibly adopt a substitutive political function.[8]

I am waiting to hear from you

Date: Wed, 21 Feb 2007 11:50:38 +0000
Subject: Re: antagonisms
Yes, several questions arise: what do the notions of participation, or interactivity, exemplify in our varying relations to contemporary artwork

informed by new technologies? How are antagonistic relations, fundamental for a fully functioning society, articulated in work? Does all artwork become, to some degree, political? Who is political, and what does it mean to be political in relation to the image? And, what kind of subjects are we dealing with?

Claire Bishop addresses this set of issues in her article "Antagonism and Relational Aesthetics." [9] We have briefly talked about this before; I became interested in Bishop's writing while programming interactive work and identifying in Bourriaud's formulations of interactive relations a number of relevant connections to digital animation. Bishop's critique on Bourriaud—this was around 2004—paralleled my critique on the "relational" for its ignoring, for instance, that an audience might not identify with a work and as such does not co-produce it. Bishop notes that the economy of "relational aesthetics" leads to a restriction in terms of the act of viewing, because such interactive installations miss some important aspects. This restriction consists of reducing the viewer to a collective, physically present participant, without taking into account the optical contemplation of an object or that the work possibly involves a non-identification. When Bishop refers to today's viewer as a fundamentally divided and incomplete subject, it is in order to suggest that the task of the contemporary work is to expose the relations this subject has to the world. Pointing out that a harmonious community (involving a *collective* agreement) is fictitious, Bishop advocates a shift, from the emphasis on interactive relations between work and viewer, to re-assessing where the active process actually resides. Active viewing is reinforced not through literal inter-action, but by *partial* identifications: in practice, through work whose forms are defined by how difference is incorporated within them. There is an antagonism at play, understood as a positive, generative concept, describing an absence of the closure needed to constitute a functioning society.[10] For Bishop, the tensions and asymmetries that antagonism brings along are obligatory for social and democratic communication. They are realised in a discomforting work of art and are opposed to the interpersonal, interactive experience of a *common interest*, as in a work typified as "relational aesthetic." [11] At stake is the activity of the artwork that manifests this experience of diversity, discomfort and tensions, and echoes the boundaries of communities.

Date: Thu, 15 Mar 2007 13:18:47 +0000
Subject: Re: more animation
You ask me to write about my practice a bit more, and my experience of animation while making work. Over the last few years I have made a number of movies based on line drawings and on still images which, when put into motion, express a peculiar economy of movement. Animation to me means the dynamic state of an image, with a surface that actualises a particular state at a particular moment in time. In addition, animation works—I mentioned this in a previous mail—articulate the capacity to express a lack of completion, and thus are, by their nature, processual and unfinished. Thereby, animation as an infinitely transforming form, exceeds the idea of an image constituted in relation to a definite period of time. Animation's images are mobile, unforeseen, paradoxical, non-linear, interruptive, operating in the present—its forms are yet to come.

The antagonism underlying *interactive* animation—you remember I was very interested in work by jodi (http://wwwwwwwww.jodi.org)—is shown in the peculiar relation one has to its images, which manifest an experience of a spacing, of a limit or an obstruction in which the one who engages with the work is faced with the conflicting situation of partial or full identification, or perhaps with none. This sort of work makes a statement of a divided subject position rather than aiming for a unified, harmonious community. The work, Bishop describes, is active when it brings to light what is repressed in maintaining social harmony.[12] The interactive image here includes, by its nature, discomfort, political engagement, and tension on the side of both its production and consumption. Animation, with its claim for a deliberately incomplete image that often resides in a site of the political, of ambiguity and subversion, has perhaps always suggested such a space. Along Bishop's lines, the active engagement required by interactive animation, repositions the viewer as a political, divided, and incomplete subject.

Date: Fri, 6 Apr 2007 23:26:58 +0000
Subject: Re: Fwd: Re: Multiple multiple
I am returning to the practice of animation and its discourse. If animation is inherently linked to social-economical structures, which in turn are undergoing perpetual modifications, digital animation is perhaps most effective when conceived as the opposite of the marginality attributed to animation thought of as minor. I ground this thinking in (digital) animation's potential for manifold appearance and site. But perhaps it is

precisely the dynamic of animation, of work that complicates discourse, and resists easy categorisation, that interrupts in terms of its spacing image and its uncertain discourse/text that it de-territorialises: it effectively provokes or undoes what has been established, it escapes a *proper territory*, it is not oppositional but appropriate for strange uses. In doing so, its discourse expresses itself as a multiplicity in parallel with the plurality of a subject within contemporary society. One might call this an open and active dimension of the (moving) image/text.

Best and hopefully see you soon

block 104
block 105
block 326
block 325
~~block 333~~
~~block 091~~

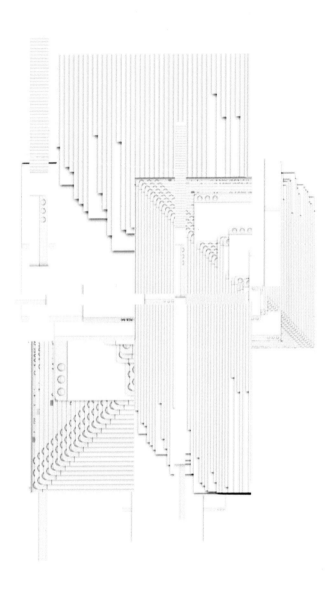

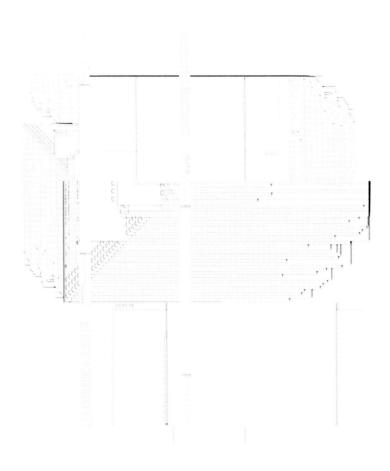

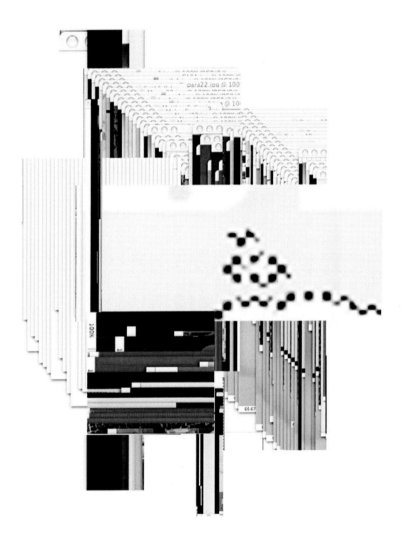

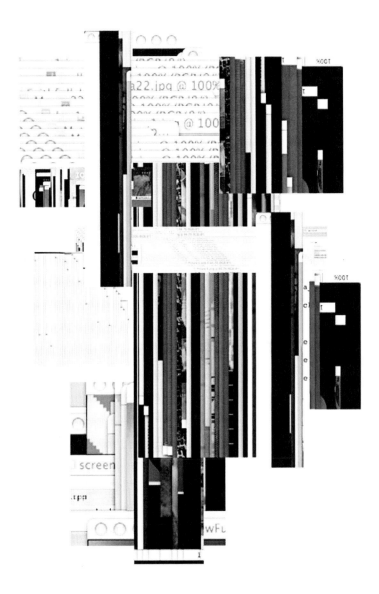

Notes

[1] Gilles Deleuze & Félix Guattari, "What is a Minor Literature?" in *Kafka: Toward a Minor Literature* (Minneapolis, London: University of Minnesota Press, 1986), 16-27.

[2] Deleuze & Guattari, *Kafka*, 16-17.

[3] See Mario Perniola on the "hyper-mystification" (2004:49) of the artwork and its discourse transformed by economic operations, "The Third System of Art" in *Art and its Shadow* (London: Continuum, 2004), 44-54.

[4] Umberto Eco, *The Open Work* (Harvard: Harvard University Press, 1989)
On Eco: Trebor Scholz, "On Open Work by Umberto Eco":
http://distributedcreativity.typepad.com/reading_group/2005/10/post.html
(consulted May, 2008).

[5] Jacques Rancière (2004), "Problems and Transformations in Critical Art" in Claire Bishop ed., *Participation* (Cambridge, Massachusetts: MIT Press, 2006), 90.

[6] Nicolas Bourriaud, *Relational Aesthetics* (Dijon: Les presses du réel, 2002)
The key passages in Bourriaud I refer to are in the subsection "Technology as an ideological model (from trace to programme)," 68-71.

[7] Bourriaud, *Relational Aesthetics*, 83.

[8] Rancière, "Problems and Transformations," 92.

[9] Claire Bishop ("Antagonism and Relational Aesthetics" *October*, No.110, Fall 2004: 51-79). The following paragraphs refer to Bishop's text as a whole and concern questions of viewing: concepts of collectivity, community, and antagonism, read in Bourriaud's concept of "relational aesthetics."

[10] The basis for Bishop's argument is an understanding of a fully functioning social residing in Ernesto Laclau and Chantal Mouffe's (*Hegemony and Socialist Strategy: Towards a Radical Democratic Politics*. London, New York: Verso, 2001) notion of antagonism. Bishop (2004) on this antagonism: 65-70. In a critique on Bishop, Liam Gillick ("Contingent Factors: A Response to Claire Bishop's 'Antagonism and Relational Aesthetics'" *October*, No.115, Winter 2006: 95-106) reminds us of Mouffe's understanding of a "paradox of liberal democracy, which concerns the recognition of the antagonsim suppressed within consensus-based models of social democracy, not merely a simple two-way relationship between the existing sociopolitical model and an enlightened demonstrations of its failings."

[11] Bishop, "Antagonism and Relational Aesthetics," 68. For other critical reflections on political art and relational aesthetics, see for example: Jonas Ekeberg & Ole Slyngstadli eds., *How to look at Art Talk, Aesthetics, Capitalism*. Verksted #2/3 (Oslo: Office for Contemporary Art Norway, 2004).

[12] Bishop, "Antagonism and Relational Aesthetics," 79.

CHAPTER SIX

THE METHODOLOGY OF MAILMEN: ON DELIVERING THEORY

CRAIG MARTIN

The multiplicity, the dangerous flock of chaotic morphologies, is subdued.[1]

In one of his essays on the changing nature of contemporary spatiality the geographer Nigel Thrift has pointed out that "the nomadologic of movement becomes the natural order of thought." [2] This image of a vibrating multiplicity will be familiar to many people; it pervades much intellectual work of the past two decades. In a text published in the same year, Thrift puts forward a concern: that this world seen as tumultuous, in constant movement, turbulent, and complex is reduced by attempts to try and capture this, to represent it, *to write it* in conventional form. Instead Thrift posits other means that, for example, embrace the pre-cognitive dimensions of experience. Similarly, Brian Massumi, in his book *Parables for the Virtual,* has discussed the issue of "movement." [3] In terms of finding a *position* within a nexus of possible sites, Massumi argues that the desire to *locate* the individual (the subject) leads to a loss, that is, a loss of movement, and thus the potential that movement suggests in the Bergsonian sense. Instead, this positioning creates an overly stabilised image of the world and so reduces movement.

The present paper comes out of just such a problematic of stability and *location*. It sets out to explore the condition of writing in relationship to *position* primarily in terms of "situation" as a way of locating and so controlling meaning, of situating the text in relation to pinning it down. Michel Serres, whose work permeates this entire argument, has spoken of his disdain at the limitations of a singular means of speaking or writing. Instead, he believes in a reservoir of voices, of multiple means of speaking, be they anecdotal forms or indeed academic ones.[4] Using Thrift's notion of the *non-representational*, the argument concerns not so much the pre-cognitive affect of the body as a perceiving membrane, for example, but rather the means through which writing can *dis*locate both itself and the reader, opening those other voices. These questions emanate from debates on aspects of movement and mobility, especially the concept of the *in-between*, both in theoretical and geographical terms, but specifically in relation to the elusive *location* of the in-between. Whilst the notion of such a geographical *site* is clearly problematic in that it rests upon a utopian discourse, the imaginative geographies of writing such a space into existence are central to the present work. How can we write *of* movement, about movement in all its process, in its unpredictability, in its non-linearity, without overly ordering or controlling it, without *placing* it?

I aim to consider how modes of theoretical and critical writing appear to tame the complexity of thought, in part through a process of rationalisation. The overall drive is to explore how a possible *alternative* form of academic writing has emerged through the work of French philosopher Michel Serres. I will initially look at Nigel Thrift's concept of *non-representational* theory outlining his unease at the tenor of contemporary modes of academic writing. This investigation will by necessity be at the methodological level but, as will be argued, this cannot be dissociated from the context of Serres' work, and from the premise of writing itself. The overarching focus will be on the cast of *operators* that Serres utilises in his work, alongside the mythical narratives that propel these operators. In doing so the intention is to propose that such methodological devices offer potential means of reinvigorating the modes of academic writing.

Within the field of social and cultural geography there has been much recent debate on Thrift's conception of what he terms *non-representational* theory. At its core, Thrift's *problem* is one of reduction, or more specifically, the reductionist tendency within academic writing. One of the limitations of the interpretative frameworks that exist presently within academic writing is that overall they are determined by the legacy of Enlightenment thought. Namely, its *singularizing* world-view that has produced imperialistic impressions of the world. In this scenario there is one way of looking at the world, that is both determined and determining. "It is fair to say," Thrift argues "that Euro-American cultures are naturally perspectivist, that is they try to make the whole world the singular object of the viewer's vision." [5] In doing so he believes that this form of academic thought is "mechanistic." Michel Serres has suggested something very similar—in his conversations with Bruno Latour, Serres points to certain universalising ways of looking at the world such as Marxism, psychoanalysis, semiotics and so on.[6] These, he believes, offer only limited potential, in that they provide a universal passkey which is believed to fit all doors; as Serres states, this denies the lack of complexity and difference that abounds. Instead, we require more localised ways of looking. A situation arises—one of multiplicity rather than homogeneity. There are many viewpoints, rather than simply one viewpoint. There can also be many ways of writing. This, in part is where Thrift's conception of non-representational theory launches itself. He sets in place "a challenge to the dominant theoretical model which still attempts to set up a stable picture of what the world is like."[7] A complexity of thought and a layering of writing are called for, rather than the need to assert a unified, flattened picture of the world that does not reflect the tangled messiness of it. It is about "changing the ethos of engagement."[8] Overall, the spirit of Thrift's entanglement is to question how we can understand the multiplicity of the world and *picture* it without reducing this snapshot to a deadened, or tamed version. How to do this then? This is the methodological crux, if you like. Such modes of writing are, Thrift would argue, process-based, thus enabling us to see practice and thought as ongoing, dislocated and never fixed. There is the wish "to value openness, to create new degrees of freedom,"[9] and to constitute a way of thinking that harnesses the energies of experiment, demonstration and dynamism.

The writing of Michel Serres evokes some of the spirit that Thrift calls for. However at the same time I want to contend that Serres' work travels beyond Thrift's desire for a process-based approach to writing. The main reason I argue this is due to the play between complexity and simplicity that pervades his work. With specific regard to this the subjects tackled by Serres are vast in their scope, but they are handled with a lightness of touch and a familiarity of tone that dismantles this complexity. On first reading, the work of Michel Serres is far from simple; the reader is taken on an encyclopaedic journey through the natural sciences, through literature, through philosophy. The works are daunting in the range of their references and the speed at which he moves between disciplines and discourses. The writings constantly reveal new avenues, as well as fresh fissures and cracks in thought that one had missed in previous readings. William Paulson, one of Serres' translators, has maintained that, "Serres's books are notoriously resistant to summary, mainly because they are saturated with multiple levels of image, metaphor, concept, story, and argument."[10] In my view, these layers are an attempt by Serres to disassemble the *rightness* of writing, a phrase that he uses to consider the notion of power and truth in the context of scientific method and thought.[11]

Serres is concerned with communication. Although decidedly limited when looking at the entire gamut of his work, the roles of communication and connection begin to elucidate his project, particularly in terms of a methodological approach. Movement is ever-present in Serres' work, manifest in part through the multiplicity of images that weave through the various books; the figure of Hermes in his five volume collection *Hermes*; global communication space in his book *Angels*; communicative noise in his book *Genesis*; educational knowledge and learning in *The Troubadour of Knowledge*, societal bonds in *The Natural Contract*; communicative relations through his concept of the quasi-object; and finally the role of spatial topology which pervades all of his work. He has been accused of using methods of *free association* and *comparitivism* to connect concepts and disciplines that in the eyes of the *academy* are incompatible. The boundaries of thought are seen as almost sacred. Serres disputes this. For him these boundaries are there to be broached, just as numerous thinkers have done before. These disciplinary borders are "less a juncture under control" Serres claims "than an adventure to be had."[12] Bruno Latour considers that one of the problems readers have with Serres' work is methodology: "How does he proceed?" they ask.[13] How does he reach those plains of thought the reader eventually encounters? The criticism appears to be that the methodology employed is too fast, alien to the normal procedure of academic writing in particular. By no means downplaying the content of Serres' work, the current work challenges those detractors who target his style, his methodology, as a means of criticising how he actually travels between disciplines and concepts. Instead, I wish to argue that the power of Serres' entire output lies at the intersection where his content meets his methodology; that they are inextricably bound together in the sense of the topological fold.

Where his critics have claimed that Serres' style is overly poetic, too quick, and lacking in explication, the reverse is evident; the *lack* of explication in his book *Genesis*, for example, is determined by the very subject of the book – noise. In the classic model of communication, noise is the unwanted element in the journey. Noise, for Serres, is the clamour of multiplicity and as such the prose beckons forth noise and lack of explication:

Sea, forest, rumor, noise, society, life, works and days, all common multiples; we can hardly say they are objects, yet require a new way of thinking. I'm trying to think the multiple as such, to let it waft along without arresting it through unity, to let it go, as it is, at its own pace. A thousand slack algaes at the bottom of the sea [...] Background noise is the ground of our perception, absolutely uninterrupted, it is our perennial sustenance, the element of the software of all our logic. It is the residue and the cesspool of our messages.[14]

The nature of Serres' project within *Genesis* is demonstrated here by: "to let it waft along without arresting it through unity." [15] There is an appositeness of style, a marrying of form to content. With passages such as this, the opacity Serres is accused of is far from the case; instead there is an aptness of method. On the surface, whilst many of the *objects* that Serres employs as narrative tropes in his work may seem obscure, they actually serve as explanatory devices, but mechanisms and constructions that require time and work. As noted above, where Serres' work is concerned with the passage between disciplinary boundaries—most notably his own wanderings between the hard and soft science—one of his devices for demonstrating the complexity of this movement is that of the Northwest Passage, from his fifth book in the *Hermes* series:

The passage is rare and narrow ... From the sciences of man to the exact sciences, or inversely, the path does not cross a homogeneous and empty space. Usually the passage is closed, either by land masses or by ice floes, or perhaps by the fact that one becomes lost. And if the passage is open, it follows a path that is difficult to gauge.[16]

This quote is an evocation of difficulty, of the task at hand for Serres in moving between disciplines. By utilizing the structure and complexity of the topographical features of the Northwest Passage he is on the one hand simplifying the image of thought, but at the same time challenging the reader to set out on an edifying exploration of their own; to look at the richness of this geographical feature in order to grasp just how difficult such an intellectual movement is. As a way of working then, such mechanisms could clearly be seen as metaphors, but Serres has described this in even clearer terms as a form of *shortcut*—it is concerned with speed of travel, efficiency of method, but also geographical *distance*. This speed of movement that might be said to typify his methodology is developed out of Serres' background in mathematics and in particular topology. He argues that philosophical thought is characterized by slowness, by "intermediate steps." [17] Instead, his desire is to move quickly, which is given form through the speed of mathematics and the shortcuts that it offers. There is "a speed accompanying mathematical thought that plays with amazing shortcuts." [18] For Latour, it is mathematics above all that offers Serres the ability to move quickly and, as I would argue, to avoid location. This gives Serres the means to draw the maximum result from the minimum amount of effort, or rather from the "minimum number of suppositions." [19]

Whilst it is Serres as the authorial voice who is our ultimate guide through his work, he is recognized for his use of *operators* as a means of taking these shortcuts. As with the example of the Northwest Passage, the operators utilized, be they characters or objects, are our guides through individual books themselves but also through Serres' entire corpus. These operators take an array of forms: statues, angels in *Angels: a Modern Myth*, sensations in *The Five Senses*, the harlequin in *The Troubadour of Knowledge* or the earth in *The Natural Contract*. Like the stylistic relevance of the prose in *Genesis*, so the operators employed are appropriate to the task at hand, they are, as Serres has discussed a form of localized solution—the solution grows from the circumstance, it is immanent in the object. By this he indicates that the operators he uses are there out of necessity, in order to guide the reader in their passage through the book. Serres has stated:

> You have to invent a localised method for a localised problem. Each time you try to open a different lock, you have to forge a specific key, which is obviously unrecognisable and without equivalent in the marketplace of method. [20]

In this case we are observing the use of localised method as a means to get as close as possible to the object at hand. Serres' most seasoned operator is the figure of the Greek god Hermes. His employment is founded upon Hermes' place as the messenger god and as the god of travellers and boundaries. He travels *with* Hermes, following him in his movements and journeys. As such, Hermes is the key operator in relation to how the movement between and across disciplines is instituted in Serres' work. Serres talks of the need to "imagine how Hermes flies and gets about when he carries messages from the gods." [21] The flitting, fidgety character of Hermes sets the text in motion, dislocating it. As with Hermes, so with the harlequin. In *The Troubadour of Knowledge* Serres begins with a tale involving the harlequin's coat, this patchwork fabric becoming the repository of experience—it is "zebrine, tigroid, iridescent, shimmering ... lashed, spotted like an ocelot." [22] The coat is taken up and worn by the reader; it *clothes* the reader in the context of the book.

These operators are set within a system of everyday language, a language of storytelling, myth and narrative. Paulson argues that he "does not equate the abstract concept with the abstract word," [23] instead the mode of storytelling for Serres is very important. Again, for Paulson "Serres is a philosopher arguing that stories are more fundamental than arguments." [24] The mythical story in Serres' hands is once more a means of delivering his ideas with speed and agility. Stretching his own lineage back to Plato, Serres notes how Plato used myth as a form of describing complex ideas—storytelling in this sense has a commonness and familiarity of form that communicates knowledge in a different way to the normative methodologies of academic writing. The existence of myth and mythical characters in Serres' work are shadow-like, they are always there—just as he has argued that even within science itself myth is ever present, reason may have tried to evacuate myth but "everything takes place as though science is waiting in stones and myths at the same time that it is in conflict with them." [25] Myth and difference were repressed in Euclidean space, measure triumphed according to Serres, but the shadows were immanent, waiting to be rediscovered, a task that he has set himself: "In an aged Europe asleep beneath the mantle of reason and measure, mythology reappears as an authentic discourse." [26]

At the close of his book *The Natural Contract*, Serres introduces the narrative device of several short tales under the overall title of "Casting Off." These stand as a final attempt to guide us (through the vehicle of storytelling), toward the *dénouement* of his argument—the role of the bond, the contract between humankind and the earth. Each of them deals with an image of this *natural* contract—the first through the quasi-mythological use of Adam and Eve. In his tale "The Port of Brest," Adam and Eve have been separated as Adam embarks on a sea journey. Eve is left on the shore and throws him a red apple; as the boat pulls away they begin to throw the apple back and forth to one another, taking a bite every time,

> The engines pick up the pace; the boat heads for the mouth of the harbor. The apple, getting smaller, passes from sea to land once again. Adam and Eve are no longer laughing; far from it, they're in a hurry. Toss, wait, catch, bite, throw back. Seated astern, I watch the couple's little game, which started out just like that but has become hurried, urgent, difficult, and I'm losing count. Tracing ever-longer arcs as it gets smaller, and as the boat, getting up steam, heads away sounding its horn, the apple soars ever more majestically.[27]

Although a web-like network is produced through the throws of the apple, the bond constructed between ocean and shore, between Adam and Eve, is finally broken. "At that distance, no one can recognize anyone else's body." [28] In terms of method alone, through the familiar language of mythical narrative, this story is an attempt to illuminate to an even further degree the preceding arguments in the book. One could argue that this technique provides the reader with a distance, a space in which to formulate the relationship between this story and their preconceived ideas of theoretical writing. Rather than a sequential, logical *denouement* to *The Natural Contract,* Serres deploys the interruptive, but familiar trope of the story. In part, the story has the power to produce a rupture in our thought, to surprise us in its simplicity of form. This is where we might say that the moment of *surprise* offered by the storytelling device leads us back to Nigel Thrift's non-representational theory. For Serres' use of "more and more, everyday language" [29] holds to at least one of Thrift's aspirations for non-representational theory—that it differs from "the dominant theoretical model."[30]

That the work of Michel Serres is too complex and diverse to be shoehorned into a convenient catch-all term such as non-representational theory will come as no surprise. Whilst in itself a laudable quest on Thrift's part, his use of term actually serves to reduce the complexity of the debate. Rather than embrace the spirit of non-representational theory wholeheartedly, I wish to suggest that specifically in terms of methodology we can investigate the strategies of Michel Serres' writing as a way of "changing the ethos of engagement" as Thrift put it.[31]

So, what is the actual potential of this for contemporary writing practice? My overarching assertion is that this depends primarily on the condition of content, not all contexts will demand a reconfigured form of academic or critical writing. Having noted some of Serres' working methodologies it is clearly the case that Serres' style is determined by the very context and content of his *investigations.* As Serres has argued at length there is a need to understand the suitability of the tools in a local context as the openness that Thrift calls for may not be appropriate to all contexts. With Serres' work in particular the *aptness* of his operators, the characters and objects, those narrative devices, have always been apparent. Overall, I question whether the practice of academic writing can ever ultimately achieve what Nigel Thrift hopes for. As Serres has already demonstrated, the historical and contemporary power of academia is such that many impediments are in place. To return to his discussions with

Latour—on his use of the operators Serres asks; "how can we let them be free to live, and to come and go?" [32] We can ask ourselves a similar question of critical and academic writing. It is necessary to follow Serres, to go with him, to recognise how his use of myth or the operators such as Hermes challenge the fixity of writing in the sense of it being overtly stabilised. We can learn much from Serres' practice, in particular, that the language of the everyday, those commonplace *characters* that are often overlooked in the drive to cloud theoretical writing in a haze of wonderment, can be used as a means of opening up this form of writing to vibrancy and dislocation.

Notes

[1] Michel Serres, *Hermes: Literature, Science, Philosophy* (Baltimore: John Hopkins University Press, 1982), 53
[2] Nigel Thrift, "Movement-Space: the Changing Domain of Thinking Resulting from the Development of New Kinds of Spatial Awareness," *Economy and Society*, Vol. 33, No. 4, (2004): 590
[3] Brian Massumi, *Parables for the Virtual: Movement, Affect, Sensation.* (Durham: Duke University Press, 2002), 3
[4] Michel Serres, "Literature and the Exact Sciences," *Substance*, Vol.18, No.2, Issue 59 (1989): 3
[5] Nigel Thrift, "Summoning Life," in *Envisioning Human Geographies*, ed. Paul Cloke and Philip Crang (London: Arnold, 2004), 83
[6] Michel Serres and Bruno Latour, *Conversations on Science, Culture and Time* (Ann Arbor: University of Michigan Press, 1995), 91
[7] Nigel Thrift, "Summoning Life", 82
[8] Ibid.
[9] Ibid., 83
[10] William Paulson, "Swimming the Channel," in *Mapping Michel Serres*, ed. Niran Abbas, (Ann Arbor: University of Michigan Press, 2005), 31
[11] Michel Serres, "Literature and the Exact Sciences", 4
[12] Michel Serres and Bruno Latour, *Conversations on Science, Culture and Time,* 70
[13] Ibid., 43
[14] Michel Serres, *Genesis*, (Ann Arbor: University of Michigan Press, 1995), 6-7
[15] Ibid.
[16] Josué V. Harari and David F. Bell, "Introduction: Journal à Plusieurs Voies" in Michel Serres, *Hermes: Literature, Science, Philosophy*, (Baltimore: John Hopkins University Press, 1982), xi

[17] Michel Serres and Bruno Latour, *Conversations on Science, Culture and Time,* 68

[18] Ibid.

[19] Ibid., 96

[20] Ibid., 92

[21] Ibid., 64

[22] Michel Serres, *The Troubadour of Knowledge*, (Ann Arbor: University of Michigan Press, 1997), xiv

[23] William Paulson, "Swimming the Channel," 26

[24] Ibid., 35

[25] Michel Serres, "Literature and the Exact Sciences," 12

[26] Michel Serres, *Hermes: Literature, Science, Philosophy*, (Baltimore: John Hopkins University Press, 1982), 53

[27] Michel Serres, *The Natural Contract*, (Ann Arbor: University of Michigan Press, 1995), 98

[28] Ibid., 99

[29] Michel Serres and Bruno Latour, *Conversations on Science, Culture and Time,* 72

[30] Nigel Thrift, "Summoning Life," 82

[31] Ibid.

[32] Michel Serres and Bruno Latour, *Conversations on Science, Culture and Time,* 74.

CHAPTER SEVEN

NEVER WORK WITH ANIMALS, CHILDREN AND DIGITAL CHARACTERS

MARY OLIVER

Just as the good story-teller can transport the listener to a liminal plain of experience, so the performer, whether on or off screen, has the ability to transcend the physical and psychological gap of pretence. This is still true when a live performer appears alongside their recorded double. Once engaged in dialogue, logically we know they cannot both exist, but they simply do. The "liveness" of a performer does not depend on their physical proximity to a spectator but rather the ability to communicate their presence.[1] A good digital double act is often described as having a magical quality, one in which the audience can immerse themselves in the uncanny spectacle of fake repetition. We do not have to believe in the existence of both parties to enjoy the interface. The dominance of screen based imagery however, means that we are probably more accustomed to seeing performers on screen and, rather like being upstaged by a cute child or fluffy puppy, often a struggle ensues between the real and recorded self for the attention of the viewer.

Neither twin nor doppelganger, the digital self is a reminder that we are moments away from becoming the gods of our own universe and these seemingly simple comedic works point to a darker desire to create the perfect human.[2] Bill Viola observes "that with each new step in the evolution of technology, we take a step closer to our ideal of higher and higher quality, which actually means creating things that look more and more like nature itself."[3] Having not quite succeeded in the creation of the cyborg, for the moment we must trick the spectator, by using the filmic text as a device with which to disguise the fact that there is really only one performer.[4]

Despite the wonders of recording and the ingenuity of the writer, the digi-self can only work in a limited fashion. Rather like working with performing animals that only have a set number of tricks, once scripted and recorded the digital performer is limited. In addition we cannot always control the machines on which we present these characters, sometimes leading to unpredictable and embarrassing performance moments. Maintained in her cryogenic state the digi-self lives only at the point of performance, but with each exhalation the live performer is moving further away from the moment of creation thus making this relationship both extraordinary and ultimately futile.

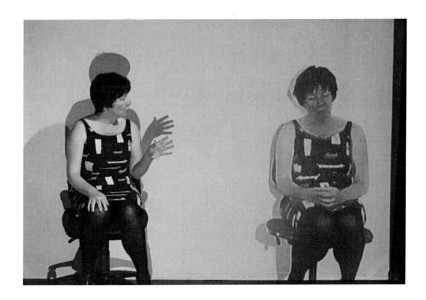

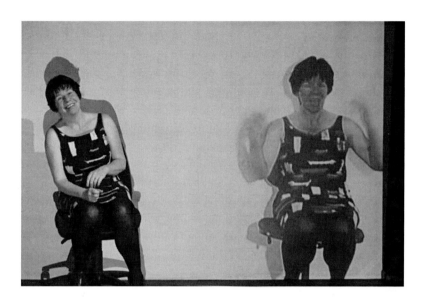

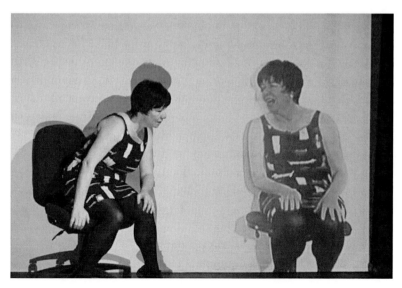

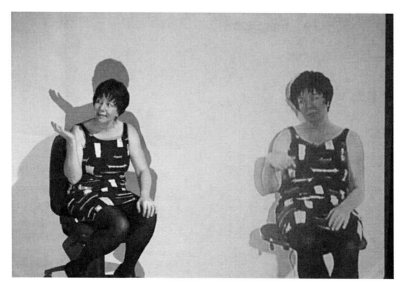

Notes

[1] I refer to Philip Auslander's use of the Roberts Blossom article "On Filmstage," *TDR: Tulane Drama Review* 11, 1 (1966): 68-72, to suggest that in the presence of the screen the live performer will always have the presence of a "fifty watt light bulb." In Auslander, *Liveness: Performance in a Mediatized Society*, Routledge, second edition 2008. 41-42

[2] "Behind the development of advanced technologies is the age old desire to extend the body in space and time (through machinic, communications, and biotechnological tools) and thus to transcend it (to become "God")" Amelia Jones, *Body Art: Performing the Subject*, (University of Minnesota Press, 1998), 205.

[3] Bill Viola, *Reasons for Knocking at an Empty House: The Visionary Landscape of Perception* (Thames and Hudson, 2005), 220.

[4] I refer to Robert Altman's description of the film maker as impostor and conjurer, cited in Erik Barnouw, *The Magician and the Cinema* (OUP, 1981), 112.

PART II

OBJECTS AND NARRATIVE

INTRODUCTION:
OBJECTS AND NARRATIVE

GILLIAN WHITELEY

We think with the objects we love; we love the objects we think with.[1]

We find, lose, covet and hoard objects, investing them with meaning, memories and value. The loss of possessions, through war or natural disaster, can be traumatic as they are tied up with our identity, histories and culture. Martin Landy's purposeful destruction of all his things in *Break Down* (2000) was an audacious exercise carried out by a privileged Western artist but it left him bereft and raised broader ethical questions about material accumulation and emotional attachment. What precisely is the nature of our relationship with objects? How important are different kinds of knowledge and experience to an understanding and interpretation of them? Just how do objects *tell stories*? How are stories told, performed, encountered and experienced through objects?

As individuals, we bring our subjectivities to our encounters with objects. The particularities of experience, social class, culture, ethnicity, gender and sexual orientation inform our readings of texts and all manner of cultural production, including our encounters with material culture and the built environment. We invest objects with ourselves and construct our own stories around them. In her book, *Evocative Objects*, Turkle explores our diverse relationships with objects through a series of short autobiographical essays in which "scientists, humanists, artists and designers" address things that matter to them as each selects an object that connects them to ideas and people. Her book reveals how object narratives undergo metamorphosis. As she remarks, "Objects have life roles that are multiple and fluid." [2]

We desire, consume and fetishize objects and weave our own stories and memories around them, fearing their *uncanny* properties, revering religious relics, treasuring heirlooms and the human traces they possess. Objects are metonymic: they stand for something else. Susan Stewart has written eloquently on our *longing* for objects of all kinds and scale from the miniature, to the gigantic. On the souvenir, she remarks that it displays the "romance of contraband," it speaks to

> ... a context of origin through a language of longing, for it is not an object arising out of need or use value; it is an object arising out of the necessarily insatiable demands of nostalgia. [3]

In *Design and Order in Everyday Life*, first published in 1991, Mihaly Csikszentmihalyi also addressed the meaning and significance of everyday objects and souvenirs. In Csikszentmihalyi's view, the classification and categorisation of things - whether functional objects or artistic production - is socially constructed, with critics and interpreters taking a key role. He examined how people respond to art objects and design qualities in the domestic environment, concluding

> Visual values are created by social consensus, not by perceptual stimulation. Thus art criticism is essential for creating meaning, especially in periods of transition when the majority of people are confused about how they should be affected by visual stimuli. Art critics believe that they are discovering criteria by which they can reveal natural esthetic values. In reality they are constructing criteria of value which then become attached to visual elements. [4]

From seventeenth-century *cabinets of curiosity* to the Museum of Corn-temporary Art in Chicago,[5] particular objects are endowed with *significance* by individuals and institutions. Museums, galleries, department stores and *ebay* all classify and categorise objects based on some kind of constructed value system. Importantly, as Ella Shohat and Robert Stam [6] have suggested, these value systems are not only to do with cultural origins but they relate directly to epistemologies and ideologies and to the institutionalisation of hierarchical systems of valorisation that give primacy, for example, to art over craft and design and treat the functional with ambivalence.[7] They reflect back a particularly Western, Eurocentric view of objects that is tied up with capitalist economics and the lowliness of labour – something which, in Britain, is rooted in the industrial revolution and the evolution of a particular set of discourses related to social class, structures and institutions. Indeed, the collecting policies of national museums and galleries both reflect and helped form the *nation-state,* a persistent but increasingly problematic entity within a global and increasingly cosmopolitan culture.

Neil Cummings and Marysia Lewandowska unpicked some of these value systems in *The Value of Things*, a project which focused on the collection and exchange of objects as commodities in both the museum and the department store. They view material culture as a complex set of competing "product narratives" which dispute ownership, contest interpretation and disagree on value, arguing that

...in a seemingly homogenised mass of consumables, nothing has a verifiable 'essence' or legitimate 'history'...[8]

Of course, artists have worked with objects for centuries—creating, depicting, manipulating, presenting and re-presenting them, investing domestic and manufactured objects with new meaning, [9] re-visiting the *readymade*,[10] opening objects up to fresh interpretations. Artists, designers, makers and critics invest objects with narratives—but objects have a certain resilience too. Can objects tell their own stories? Do they have agency? Do they, to borrow a phrase from Arjun Appadurai, have a *social life* —indeed, can objects *act*?[11]

In the flotsam and jetsam of contemporary culture, objects are lost and mourned, whilst found objects undergo resurrection. Salvaged objects embody potentiality for renewal and for a *re-telling*. The essays in this section address objects and narratives in a wide range of contexts and settings. The artefact, the souvenir, the art object is here, as are objects that are lowly, discarded, quotidian, domestic, manufactured, collected, remembered and forgotten. Above all, these ruminations are presented as things through which we might think.

Notes

[1] Sherry Turkle in *Evocative Objects: Things We Think With,* ed. Sherry Turkle (Cambridge, Mass/London: MIT Press, 2007), 5.
[2] Ibid., 6.
[3] Susan Stewart, *On Longing, Narratives of the Miniature, the Gigantic, the Souvenir, the Collection* [first published 1984], (Durham/London: Duke University Press, 1993), 135.
[4] Mihaly Csikszentmihalyi, "Design and Order in Everyday Life," *Design Issues*, Vol. 8, No. 1, Fall 1991, 33.
[5] See Victor Margolin and Patty Carroll, *Culture is Everywhere* (Chicago: Museum of Corn-temporary Art/Prestel, 2002).

[6] Ella Shohat and Robert Stam, "Narrativising Visual Culture – Toward a Polycentric Aesthetics" in *The Visual Culture Reader*, ed N. Mirzoeff , (London: Routledge, 1998), 27-47.

[7] See Richard Sennett's recent examination of this relationship in *The Craftsman* (London: Allen Lane, 2007).

[8] Neil Cummings and Marysia Lewandowska, *The Value of Things* (Birkhauser: Basle, 2000), 38.

[9] Arthur C Danto has explored this extensively in, for example, *The Transfiguration of the Commonplace (*Cambridge, Mass: Harvard University Press, 1981).

[10] See John Roberts, *The Intangibilities of Form, Skill and De-skilling in Art after the Readymade* (London/New York: Verso, 2007).

[11] See Arjun Appadurai, *The Social Life of Things*, (New York: Cambridge University Press, 1986) and, on the idea that "objects too have agency" see Bruno Latour, *Reassembling the Social: An Introduction to Actor-Network Theory*, (Oxford: Oxford University Press, 2005), 63-87.

CHAPTER EIGHT

INTERCONTINENTAL DRIFT, OR FRANCIS ALŸS AND THE SAINT OF THE REPLICA

MARTHA BUSKIRK

Salon-style hanging seems to be making a comeback, and the show that opened at the Hispanic Society in New York in fall 2007 was no exception. Wall after wall in the wood-panelled rooms usually devoted to the society's nineteenth-century collection were densely reinstalled with paintings belonging to a single individual. By a certain measure it is a collector with eclectic tastes, since the works vary greatly in the levels of skill and ambition they demonstrate. More striking, however, is the degree of sameness, since all depict an identical subject. With the exception of a few quite literal reversals, all portray a single female head, painted in left-facing profile and draped with a red head covering, in front of a neutral, dark background. Numbering nearly three hundred, all are hand-made copies based on reproductions of a nineteenth-century painting of a fourth-century saint known as Fabiola. The unusual assembly undoubtedly presented a bit of a puzzle to the few visitors who came across it without forewarning. Most, however, would have known that they were encountering a project by the artist Francis Alÿs, in an exhibit co-sponsored by the Dia Art Foundation—even though this information is itself far from sufficient to account for the issues raised by Fabiola's proliferation.[1]

 Branching out from his early identification with the role of tourist, Alÿs has moved between outsider and participant, combining observation and intervention. He plays the reception side of the equation through his emphasis on various kinds of accumulation – ranging from the random assortment of small metal objects that attached themselves to magnetized shoes worn in Cuba and a pull toy he dragged through the streets of

Mexico City, to his ongoing Fabiola collection. Harvested from flea markets around the world, the Fabiolas provide inescapable evidence of popular traditions, even as the descent into the second-hand marketplace has stripped the individual objects of much of their specific history. To the extent that they are now more closely associated with Alÿs than with their

Francis Alÿs: Fabiola. Installation view from Dia at the Hispanic Society of America, New York, September 20, 2007–April 6, 2008. Photo Cathy Carver. Courtesy the artist and Dia Art Foundation, New York

original makers, however, these second-hand paintings raise the question of how much space really separates the traditional medium of painting from the twentieth-century legacy of the readymade. Then there is the issue of the intersection of production and reception, since both everyday objects and works of art are subject to shifting uses over time.

"Every object tells a story." Or at least that's the claim made by an on-line project co-sponsored by the Victoria and Albert Museum that encourages members of the public to post anecdotes about their own prize possessions. Look a little further, however, and that assertion becomes immediately murky, given that it seems to be subjects rather than objects doing the talking. There is a lot to be learned from things, as anyone involved in the study of material culture can readily attest, but they can also be remarkably mute when it comes to specific associations that may have been attached, but not permanently affixed, during episodes of use. While initial production and distribution can themselves be difficult to pin down, information about subsequent use is even more elusive, dependent as it is on quickly changing contexts and potentially forgotten memories.

Common objects also abound in contemporary art practices—as any stroll through the galleries will readily attest. The classic line is that their transformation into art is linked to being taken out of use. Yet is the act of claiming an object as art so very different than the other ways that emotional associations accrue to people's possessions? Both are performed upon already extant objects, at some point after the moment of initial manufacture, and both have the potential to alter the significance of the article without drastically changing its physical characteristics. Given that a great many non-art objects are acquired for reasons that go beyond the strictly utilitarian (unless one defines the display of symbolic status markers as a need), it becomes increasingly difficult to sustain the idea of a categorical shift from use to non-use as the basis for the readymade in its many recent permutations.

Caught up in these considerations are the differing readings of the readymade's significance. At one end, there is the challenge to definitions of art, including issues of originality and the importance of the artist's statement of intent. But there is also the link to the world beyond the gallery or museum walls, via objects themselves, rather than their mediated representation. The way artistic use may prompt attention to other histories of an object is suggested by, among other things, the rather remarkable energies devoted to tracking down the manufacture details of the urinal Marcel Duchamp used for his 1917 *Fountain*, with more than one art historian having spent a surprising amount of time scrutinizing the early twentieth century catalogues of the J. L. Mott Iron Works in a still elusive attempt to pin down exact details regarding the urinal model Duchamp rather off-handedly purchased. When an everyday object does become firmly identified as a work of art, then one could say that the claim made by the artist in question has taken a certain priority, yet other readings, associations, or projections are hardly precluded. Readymade objects are not unique with respect to the shifting associations brought by different audiences, yet they throw into sharper relief questions about what qualities could be considered inherent to the physical object itself, and what has been brought by later users, including artists.

There is another complication, in the similarities between artistic claims associated with already extant objects and the provenance histories for works of art in general. While such histories have an instrumental function in supporting attribution claims, they also provide hints regarding a work's shifting cultural value—and in that sense its use for different owners. But of course a readymade requires a provenance almost by definition. Those stories about discovering a remarkably valuable work of art in a dusty second-hand shop depend upon recognizing inherent evidence of an object's status, and particularly the artist's hand (in contrast to an everyday object declared art on the basis of an external claim). Yet there are also plenty of obviously hand-made objects in such settings where the original author started out obscure and is forever destined to remain that way. The possibility that a painting might therefore be subject to the same sort of operation as a readymade, taking on new associations through the subsequent attentions of another artist entirely, is one of the implications of Alÿs's collection of multiple painted copies of Fabiola. Finding large numbers of paintings of the same subject in widely dispersed locations, however, also tends to draw attention to what the multiple appearances of this object can reveal about the relevant circulation systems themselves. In this way as well, the object takes on subsequent functions that could scarcely have been anticipated at the time of its initial creation.

Ducks on a Beach

Sometime during late summer in 1992, beachcombers in the vicinity of Sitka, Alaska noticed that they were being inundated by rubber duckies floating in on the tides. Or at least that's how the story was reported, once it hit the media circuit. Actually it was a combination of turtles, ducks,

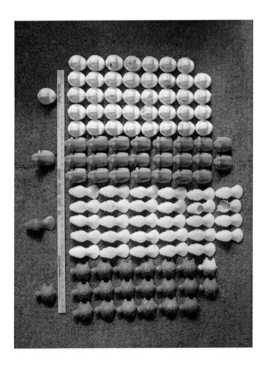

Floatees toys collected by Dean and Tyler
Orbison near Sitka, Alaska, 1993-2004.
Photo courtesy Dean Orbison.

beavers, and frogs, and the bath toys weren't made of rubber, but plastic. More significantly, they kept on coming, sending smaller invasion forces in two-to-four-year intervals. They also turned up along the Aleutian Islands, Japan, and elsewhere around the Pacific, in findings consistent with computer simulations of a 6,800 mile current loop known as the North Pacific Subpolar Gyre.

The toys were set adrift in January 1992 when a container ship on its way from Hong Kong to Tacoma, Washington lost part of its cargo in an ocean storm. 7,200 packages of bathtub toys, each containing a yellow duck, red beaver, green frog, and blue turtle, went overboard. Being designed to float, however, they managed to bob back up to the surface and continue their travels on their own. Produced in China for a Massachusetts company called First Years, the toys started out as a basically unremarkable example of global production trends. Once they began appearing on Alaskan beaches, however, their potential as markers for a different form of intercontinental circulation attracted the attention of an oceanographer named Curtis Ebbesmeyer, who has used the flotsam from container mishaps, including an earlier spill of 80,000 Nikes, to gather data on ocean currents. In turn, Ebbesmeyer relies on scouting reports from an international network of beachcombers, alerted by his web site and newsletter to be on the lookout for these escaped indicators.[2]

Something about this particular bit of flotsam also provided a hook for media attention. As Donovan Hohn, the author of a lengthy feature in *Harper's Magazine* suggests, the emphasis on the ducks, at the expense of their fellow travelers, and their misidentification as rubber can be attributed to the breakout popularity of Ernie's rubber duckie song during the first season of *Sesame Street* in 1969-70, though the species already had a certain pull with children due to the popularity of Robert McCloskey's 1941 book *Make Way for Ducklings*. There is a convergence of these factors in Eric Carle's *10 Little Rubber Ducks*, a 2005 children's book inspired by newspaper accounts of the floating toys, viewed through the grid of the specific subspecies popularized by Ernie, which tells an uplifting and therefore somewhat fanciful story about a journey from production by happy, artisan-like workers in an unnamed country to ocean-going adventure.[3] Finally, a display associated with a 2006 exhibition at the Tacoma Art Museum based on the art from this children's book became the occasion for at least a small number of the floating toys to reach their initial destination.

While these tub toys are not going to tell many stories themselves, there are various different narratives that might be built around them. Some relate to what could be described as the intentional history of the object. One could use the toys as an example of patterns of production and consumption in a global economy, or they can be connected to evolving childhood rites and practices as they have intersected with the luxuries of modern-day plumbing. Their accidental second use was a radical redirect, essentially unconnected to their maker's intentions. Designed to float, and made from a remarkably resilient material, however, the toys happened to be capable of surviving years in open sea, and even remained buoyant after being punctured by animal bites and partially filled with water. Their convergence with the natural system of ocean circulation turned them into data points for mapping ocean currents, and already established popular culture associations helped propel this activity of a specialized beachcombing subculture into a media-worthy story.

There are also objects that have been thrown into circulation systems intentionally, with the idea that they will somehow be carried outward by the same currents that these floating toys helped track. One of the other categories on Ebbesmeyer's web site is *messages in bottles*, or MIBs in beachcomber parlance, and he serves as a clearinghouse for reported findings of that nature. These are communications intended for the ocean, even if their delivery is far from certain, and their recipient unpredictable. Yet they are also not the only example of an object set deliberately adrift, nor are the oceans the only kind of circulation system employed for such gestures. Alÿs has been interested in social rather than natural situations, responding as both observer and instigator. Having taken note of the persistent sifting and scavenging activities around Mexico City's trash, he created his own sculptural version of the MIB in the form of seven small bronze, snail-like sculptures painted different colors that he placed in garbage bags scattered throughout the city in February 1994. Since then he has kept on the lookout for them to turn up again in the city's flea markets, and has rediscovered two.[4] And he was also scouring the second-hand vendors to another end, in his pursuit of a specific painted subject whose appearance in these haunts was linked to a centuries-old chain of historic events.

Saints in a Flea Market

Despite the persistent hunt that Alÿs's large Fabiola collection now suggests, its origins were rather happenstance. In 1992, the same year when beachcombers started observing the flotilla of bathtub toys, Alÿs noticed an odd coincidence in a Brussels flea market. When he began his forays, Alÿs set out with the idea that he would assemble a nice group of major masterpieces through painted copies. Although he went in anticipating versions of the *Mona Lisa* and *Last Supper*, what he found almost immediately was two identical female profiles designated by the seller as Fabiola, and his quest was eventually redirected:

> Six months later I had acquired close to a dozen replicas of the veiled woman, whereas my masterpiece collection was still down to a couple of *Angelus* and a very laborious version of *Les Demoiselles d'Avignon.* Eventually I swapped the Picasso for another *Fabiola*. [5]

Part of what Alÿs found striking was this evidence of ongoing amateur interest in a work that was obscure by art historical standards. By 1994 he had acquired 28, which he exhibited at Curare, in Mexico City. Now, many more years since the initial impulse, the collection has grown to nearly three hundred examples, and certainly it could have been exponentially larger still if he had been willing to include prints and other forms of mechanical reproduction alongside the handmade replicas.

Like a lone toy in the sand, a single Fabiola might pass under the radar without difficulty, just one more female profile among numerous recognizable as well as unidentified portrait images. Nor is the rendering of her image likely to command attention, since many of these paintings are decidedly unremarkable, and indeed show clear evidence of amateur execution. Presented by Alÿs as a group in a Dia-sponsored exhibition which opened at the Hispanic Society in New York in 2007, before travelling to the Los Angeles County Museum of Art in 2008 and London's National Portrait Gallery in 2009, however, her proliferation forces attention to the various frameworks within which one might attempt to understand this project. One context is that of Alÿs the artist, whose interest in vernacular traditions of image production and use has included a different engagement with the copy enacted through a series of collaborations with sign painters in Mexico City. Another is the history of Fabiola, from her life in the fourth century to the interest that continues into the present after gaining new momentum in the nineteenth century. Then there is the matter of the image itself, which is striking for the remarkably consistent iconography, despite a reach that extends across multiple countries and even continents. The oft-repeated profile derives from a painting of Fabiola by the French academic painter Jean-Jacques Henner, which was exhibited in the Salon of 1885, though the multiplication also indicates the importance of reproductions in the dissemination of the image.[6]

Fabiola is, for starters, a somewhat unlikely saint. Although she was a Christian, her first husband was so abusive that she eventually disregarded church doctrine by obtaining a civil divorce, followed by a second civil marriage. After the death of her second husband, however, she repented, successfully sought the pope's absolution, and embarked upon a series of good works—selling all her possessions to fund charitable or religious institutions, including one of Rome's earliest hospitals. She also made a pilgrimage to Jerusalem that brought her into the circle of St. Jerome, helped establish a hospital in Porto, and was preparing to set sail for Jaffa at the time of her death. The context of her sainthood was therefore not the early Christian martyrs, but a slightly later wave of veneration accorded to ascetics and monks, following Constantine's 313 edict establishing religious tolerance for Christianity. Given the evidence of her ongoing appeal, it is also notable that this wealthy divorcée achieved her sainthood during the fairly long stretch of time prior to the pope's consolidation of this function in the tenth century, when saints were recognized through popular acclaim rather than centralized church authority.[7] There is also the importance of her hagiographer, since little would be known about her were it not for her association with St. Jerome, whose eulogy, following her death in 399 A.D., is a major source of information about this Roman patrician woman's life of sin and redemption.[8]

A later turning point in this history is the 1854 British publication of Cardinal Wiseman's *Fabiola, or the Church of the Catacombs*, and its subsequent translation into a number of other languages. This literary success took place in the context of the nineteenth-century Catholic revival in England, where Wiseman was already a well-known figure following his controversial papal appointment as first archbishop of Westminster, and where his novel was joined by other heroic tales of early Christian sacrifice, including Cardinal Newman's *Callista*. Yet here another irony surfaces, since Fabiola apparently enjoyed a surge of renewed popularity on the basis of a novel whose fictional protagonist shares very little with the life and times of the historical figure of the same name. The main action of Wiseman's novel is set in 302-303, nearly a century earlier than the life of the historic Fabiola, during one of the waves of Christian persecution under Diocletian.

The story told by Wiseman's novel is one of the gradual transformation and ultimate conversion of Fabiola, haughty daughter of Fabius, who is introduced to the subterranean religion by her slave Syra. Fellow characters include such recognizable figures as St. Agnes of Rome, a child martyr already celebrated in the fourth century, and St. Sebastian, whose martyrdom, begun with arrows and ended with clubs, did not attract widespread interest until the Renaissance. The Fabiola of the novel is a wealthy Roman patrician, but there the resemblance to the personage described by St. Jerome sharply diverges, since she remains a virgin heroine similar to Agnes, who refuses marriage other than her spiritual union with Christ. The widely translated book served in turn as the basis for her equally apocryphal reappearance in Italy in two movie treatments, a 1918 silent directed by Enrico Guazzoni, and a 1949 epic-length black-and-white version directed by Alessandro Blasetti, where cinematic conventions dictated the addition of a love interest for Fabiola, in the form of a young man who is falsely accused of the murder of her father (perpetrated by anti-Christian forces), along with a generous supply of martyrs, gladiators, and a climactic final victory delivered by the arrival of Constantine's army in Rome.

Fabiola's painted representation followed in the wake of her literary popularization, with the multitude of copies Alÿs has harvested all based on a canvas that Henner showed in Paris at the 1885 Salon. By the time he painted his profile view of Fabiola, Henner enjoyed a well-established academic reputation, starting with the awards he garnered during his initial period of study in Paris from 1846 to 1855, his eventual success in the Prix de Rome competition in 1858, which took him to the French Academy in Rome from 1859 to 1864, after which he returned to Paris to a life of official honors, including regular exhibition in the Salon starting in 1867, a series of increasingly important academic ranks starting with chevalier de la Légion d'honneur in 1873, the same year he became a member of the Salon jury, to grand officer in 1903, two years before his death in 1905. His output included numerous commissioned portraits, paintings of religious themes, and various nude idylls involving individual or grouped figures, the most famous and widely engraved of which was his 1871 *L'Alsace. Elle attend*, with its patriotic reference to the territory lost in the Franco-Prussian war. Subsequent copyists, however, have evidently also been drawn to *The Reader*, a reclining female nude perusing a book, which was shown at the Salon of 1883.

What is key in this account is the role of the copy, since Henner's painting of Fabiola disappeared from view in the late nineteenth century—though not before being recorded in a photograph, which was already the source for copies during Henner's lifetime. In his discussion of the work, Stephen Bann emphasizes the "productivity" of the reproduction, in the context of a wider visual culture.[9] Indeed, Fabiola's popularity as a painted subject seems to have proliferated entirely below the art-historical radar prior to Alÿs's attention. Although the assembly is not entirely consistent with respect to medium (including examples as various as needlepoint, ceramic, wood inlay and dyed legumes), the overall focus also provides evidence of the ongoing status of painting in the popular imagination, long after having been unseated from its position of default pre-eminence in the context of critically or institutionally valorized modes of contemporary art.

It hardly seems coincidental that a vernacular form of painting prompted Alÿs's own forays into the medium, when he took inspiration from the metal street signs he was seeing in Mexico City to create paintings that in turn became models as part of an elaborate back and forth collaboration with a number of the same sign painters. However, Cuauhtémoc Medina also ascribes Alÿs's decision to incorporate painting into a practice that had been more oriented toward performance actions and sculpture to his discovery of Fabiola, suggesting that these copies contributed to his recognition of painting as medium that has retained a wide currency, in contrast to a play with everyday activity that is paradoxically more likely to register with a relatively narrow audience.[10]

With his process of mining second-hand venues, Alÿs bears some resemblance to the archaeologist, sifting the junk heaps of a culture for clues about its lived dynamics—even as the appearance of the paintings in this context means that they are largely stripped of specific evidence of origin or historical use by the time they cross the artist's field of vision. The collecting also provides a partial index of Alÿs's activities in general, with the listing of places, dates, and prices paid serving as a record of the artist's movements as they were registered by his encounters with Fabiola's dispersed likeness. The numerous examples Alÿs has discovered in flea markets as widespread as Belgium, Mexico, France, the Netherlands, Austria, Germany, Sweden, Italy, Denmark, England, the United States, Spain, and Argentina demonstrate the reach of this image, as well as the more specific intersection of its dissemination and the far-from-systematic movement of Alÿs through that territory in conjunction with the travels associated with his international practice. Yet presumably he did not have time to visit flea markets or second hand shops in every place he has traveled in the last fifteen years, and of those he did visit, undoubtedly many did not yield up any handmade images of Fabiola. Alÿs has also further reduced their evidentiary value by leaving behind most of the associated frames in order to make them easier to transport, and by a somewhat haphazard record-keeping system that has left more than a third of the collection without acquisition information.

When it came to the Dia exhibition, it was not just a matter of putting the paintings on view, but also applying other aspects of museum protocol as part of their visit. The exhibition catalogue is the result of years of research, initially pursued by the artist himself, as well as assistants and collaborators who became somehow entangled in this collecting interest, and more recently by Dia's curatorial and conservation staff. In a sense the condition reports on individual objects and the meta-data on the group as a whole are simply standard procedure, art historical business as usual. There is, however, also the slight variation that the resultant catalogue raisonné concerns not the accumulated production of the artist whose name is associated with the project, but rather the work of multiple and frequently anonymous artists, collected and now loaned by Alÿs, who thereby handed over the work of care and assessment he initially appropriated in his guise as artist-collector.

Other things have happened along the way as well. Prior to the Dia exhibition, Alÿs had not shown the Fabiola paintings since 1997, mainly because of his desire to avoid confusion while involved with his other investigation of the copy in the collaboration with the sign painters. But 1997 was also the occasion of a large-scale, unplanned switch. That year, Alÿs displayed approximately sixty Fabiolas in an exhibition entitled "Antechamber" at the Whitechapel Art Gallery in London and then sent the same group to Estonia to be shown in the second Biennial of Saarema. When the group was returned from Estonia, however, half had been replaced with roughly executed acrylic substitutes. These faked versions of the artist's original copies have been retained, but in a supplemental section of the catalogue (in contrast to several other works that were removed from the collection entirely when Alÿs discovered that they had been painted specifically to be passed off as flea-market finds).[11]

"Instigator" is the term Lynne Cooke uses to describe Alÿs's collecting activity, emphasizing the way in which his actions open onto further investigations.[12] While much information has been lost regarding the individual Fabiola paintings in his collection, other conclusions can be drawn from the narratives already in circulation. The parallels are hardly exact between the floating toys, accidentally turned into flotsam that could be interpreted as evidence of ocean currents, and amateur paintings of saints, with their mute evidence of popular religious practices in the intersection of narrative fiction, the circulation of reproductions, and the ongoing significance accorded in such contexts to the medium of painting. They have in common the fact that neither the ducks nor the saints were intended for the circulation systems where they were eventually set adrift, and after being let loose in this fashion, both had the potential to remain largely unnoticed. Once observed as phenomena rather than isolated examples, however, both open onto many more points of significance than the objects would have suggested in their original or intended contexts.

Fabiola's journey is hardly a simple one, from contemporaneous eulogy to later popular fiction, from salon painting to mechanical reproduction to painted copy to second-hand marketplace to artist's studio, and now a sojourn in the museum. Many questions about her appearance are fated to remain unanswered, yet it is also striking how much information has been generated by the after-effects of Alÿs's chance encounter. In the same way that Alÿs has recognized the presence of a camera in the street as a catalyst, not simply a passive recording device, his pursuit of Fabiola's likeness has been destined to produce a ripple effect.[13] As his interest became known, friends started keeping their eyes out for examples, thereby extending the reach of his collecting activity. He has also inspired attention to Henner's nineteenth-century academic painting in previously unlikely quarters. There is the further likelihood that the dissemination of information about this project will inspire others to look for Fabiola paintings of their own, with this widening interest having an impact on price and availability that will in turn affect Alÿs's ability to continue his pursuit. And there is the final, appealing irony that paintings which might not have been thought of as art have secured that status in the hands of an artist whose works based on a play with everyday activities can run the risk of not being recognized as such.

Notes

[1] "Francis Alÿs: Fabiola" opened in New York at the The Hispanic Society of America in fall 2007. It subsequently travelled to the Los Angeles County Museum of Art, fall 2008, and the National Portrait Gallery, London, in spring 2009.

[2] See Curtis Ebbesmeyer's web site, Beachcombers' Alert! www.beachcombersalert.org.

[3] Donovan Hohn outlines this history of duck imagery in "Moby-Duck or, The Synthetic Wilderness of Childhood," *Harper's Magazine*. January 2007, 39-62.

[4] On this work by Alÿs, *The Seven Lives of Garbage,* see Cuauhtémoc Medina, "Fable Power," Medina, Russell Ferguson, and Jean Fisher, *Francis Alÿs* (London and New York: Phaidon, 2007), 90-93.

[5] Francis Alÿs, "Fabiola or the silent multiplication," in *Fabiola* (Mexico City: Curare, 1994), 4.

[6] For Jean-Jacques Henner's oeuvre, see Isabelle de Lannoy, *Musée National Jean-Jacques Henner: Catalogue des Peintures*, 2nd edition (Paris: Réunion des musées nationaux, 2003).

[7] See Lawrence S. Cunningham, *A Brief History of Saints* (Malden, MA: Blackwell, 2005), particularly chapter 1, "The Saint: Beginnings," 5-27.

[8] See Susan Laningham, "Painting Fabiola: The Hagiographer as Literary Artist," Francis Alÿs, *Fabiola: An Investigation*, ed. Karen Kelly and Lynne Cooke (New York: Dia Art Foundation, 2008), 28-29.

[9] Stephen Bann, "Beyond *Fabiola*: Henner In and Out of His Nineteenth-Century Context," in *Fabiola: An Investigation*, 40. See also note 2, p. 32, regarding the disappearance of the painting and its photographic reproduction.

[10] See Cuauhtémoc Medina, "Francis Alÿs 'Tu subrealismo' (Your surrealism), *Third Text* 38, Spring 1997, 43. Medina makes the related point about the potential obscurity of work based on the everyday in "Fable Power," 82.

[11] See Lynne Cooke, "Francis Alÿs: Instigator/Investigator," in *Fabiola: An Investigation*, note 7, p. 63. According to Cooke, "Wishing to conceal the fact that they had lost or otherwise appropriated his works, the Estonian organizers seemingly hoped to fool him into believing that the substitutes – the copies they commissioned of his copies – were actually works that he had collected."

[12] Cooke, "Instigator/Investigator," 72.

[13] Alÿs on the impossibility of observing a phenomenon without interfering with it, quoted in Medina, "Fable Power," 93.

CHAPTER NINE

CURATING THE CITY

ROBERT KNIFTON

For Walter Benjamin, history is read backwards from the ruins. From fragmented memorial traces of objects, a story can be reconstructed. Patched together in space and time, memory and myth, it is sewn through with the golden thread of narrative, connecting disparate elements into something larger and yet still circumstantial and incomplete. The principal site for such a practice of history, memory and storytelling is the city. The city is its object—what Jonathan Raban remarks upon as " the soft city of illusion, myth, aspiration, nightmare…" [1] whilst for Italo Calvino, the city immanently stores up such stories, awaiting those who would just scratch at its surface: "The city…does not tell its past, but contains it like the lines of a hand, written in the corners of the streets." [2] Treating the city like a curated object raises questions about the narratives hidden within: what exactly is the relationship between memory, history, narrative and the city? Can we walk cities like museums, and access the stories within—and if so, how? This essay aims to delineate such a practice by analysing theories of memory, history, narrative and the museum. Finally, by looking at Jeremy Deller and Paul Ryan's booklet on Brian Epstein's Liverpool we will see how art can bring together such stories.

Memory and *history* encompass alternating opposed and reconciled versions of narrative within the city. History is the sanctioned story, the official yet incomplete reconstruction of what happened and is no longer. Stored in the libraries and archives of the city it is present within urban discourse, yet at the same time curiously absent. Divorced from the original settings in which it gained meaning it is, in the typology of Pierre Nora, removed in order to atrophy. Nora contends that history is "how modern societies organize a past they are condemned to forget because they are driven by change." [3] History uproots memory and renounces its unofficial format, yet yearns for its absolute pervasiveness, immediacy, and presentness. Memory binds communities together and creates social identities in ways history cannot hope to: memory is the agent of the imagined community. Two features of its formulation aid it in such a task: firstly, it is crystallised in the streets, as a residual trigger seeped into sites—what Nora calls the "lieux de mémoire." Secondly, and as Mieke Bal remarks, "Memory is an act of vision of the past, but as an act it is situated in the memory's present." [4] Thus, unlike history, memory ties us to an eternal present, it links time and space, and through its application of narrative can sublimate between the two, so that senses of temporality and spatiality become fused and confused in the exploration of the contemporary city.

Andreas Huyssen comments that "One of the most interesting cultural phenomenon of our day is the way in which memory and temporality have invaded spaces and media that seemed among the most stable and fixed: cities, monuments, architecture and sculpture." [5] He advocates the model of urban palimpsests to study this process; the overlaying of multiple memory readings of time and space—a mapping not of clarification, but of over-complicated confusion—the effect akin to layering all the systems of the city from the subway sewers up to the airline flight paths onto one undeniable yet incomprehensible mesh. Thus the city we now imagine is not legible as a whole entity, as a body organism or social politic, but is an agglomeration of heterogeneous illegibilities, each expressed as a memory narrative adhering to a particular space and overlapping with a multitude of alternatives. The picture we have is of a vast, ungraspable multiplicity, and we might dismiss any attempt to understand it or explain such a phenomenon as futile. Yet something is retrievable from this palimpsestuous confusion. In Benjamin's words, "the intoxication of the city might provide a form of 'profane illumination', a momentary glimpse of the reality behind the myth." [6] The role of the artist might be to provide those momentary glimpses through the stories and narratives they attach to urban spaces through a process of cultural anamnesis.

Anamnesis is the recollection of things once forgotten. As a memory process, cultural anamnesis has two specific qualities: first, the form of its expression as culture means that it draws primarily upon collective memory as its source, the imagined memories of an imagined community. In this way it works counter to what Pierre Nora has termed the "atomisation" of memory, the move away from collective memory into version of private memory. Second, cultural anamnesis develops memory into a narrative. Nora notes, "Memory has known only two forms of legitimacy: historical and literary. These two have run on parallel tracks but until now have always remained separate. Lately the boundary between the two has blurred."[7]   An art project working as cultural anamnesis will include within its boundaries, and thus attach to the city, forms of lived history or *geschichte*, written history, and literary memory. Cultural anamnesis attached to the city becomes a form of literary psychogeography—stories which invest the urban fabric with an emotional affect. By constructing such literary psychogeographies, the city perceived through artistic means of recollection does not simply bring to the present visions of a collective past palimpsestually superimposed on its sites— what Calvino described as the city's "…relationships between the measurements of its spaces and the events of its past."[8]   Rather, "by defining the relation to the past, it shapes the future."[9] The emotional, affective landscape of the city as brought to recollection through the artistic imaging of a cultural anamnesis potentially alters fundamentally the inhabitant's relationship to the city—their understanding of present and future developments of that site.

On *literature* and *history*, Hayden White points out that whilst historical consciousness and fiction often appear to be diametrically opposed factions, they in fact share much similar structure. There is a narrative purpose to history that contains "an irreducible and inexpungeable element of interpretation." [10] History, like literature, draws upon emplotment and the historian carries with them pre-formed general notions of the kind of stories they might find within a particular event, site or object. White posits,

> …in general there has been a reluctance to consider historical narratives as what they most manifestly are: verbal fictions, the contents of which are as much invented as found and the forms of which have more in common with their counterparts in literature than they have with those in the sciences. [11]

For White, where the two diverge is that "in history…every representation of the past has specifiable ideological implications." [12] In literature, the evocation of the past serves emotive rather than ideological purposes.

The novels of W.G. Sebald are a good example of the type of cultural anamnesis with which we are engaged, as the following passage from his novel *Austerlitz* demonstrates,

Memories like this came back to me in the disused Ladies' Waiting-Room of Liverpool Street station, memories behind and within which many things much further back in the past seemed to lie, all interlocking like the labyrinthine vaults I saw in the dusty grey light, and which seemed to go on and on for ever. In fact I felt, said Austerlitz, that the waiting-room where I stood as if dazzled contained all the hours of my past life. [13]

In this passage, Austerlitz's recollection is at once personal and emotive and yet tied to the object of the city train station, a public shared place, and part of a wider collective past—that of wartime evacuations. Linda Hutcheon, in her study of the historiographic metafiction literary trope to which Sebald arguably belongs as a novelist, comments on the paradoxical contestation and adoption involved in narratives that address literary and historical forms in unison. She notes,

It is part of the postmodernist stand to confront the paradoxes of fictive/historical representation, the particular/the general, and the present/past. And this confrontation is itself contradictory, for it refuses to recuperate or dissolve either side of the dichotomy, yet it is more than willing to exploit both. [14]

Narrative forms of cultural anamnesis are continually telescoping through these dichotomous levels, engaged with them all but never constricted within the narrow confines of their boundaries.

A further method of investigating literary narrative is Bakhtin's chronotope. The chronotope is the literary alignment of time and space within a specific narrative that gives it its character. As a *time-space* it can function much like Nora's "lieux de mémoire." The chronotope however allows a certain fusion and confusion between space and time. Paul Smethurst remarks that in the chronotope, "the indicators of time and space tend to fuse, allowing different spaces to be represented by different times, and different times to be represented by different spaces." [15] This interpenetration of time and space typified by the chronotope make it the ideal model with which to view urban memory narratives, which share this spatial-temporal fusion. *Austerlitz* again provides a fine example of this: when Jacques views the Biblical illustration he associates it with another time-space, a displacement through memory and a refiguring based on his own personal narrative,

...I immersed myself, forgetting all around me, in a full-page illustration showing the desert of Sinai looking just like the part of Wales where I grew up, with bare mountains crowding close together and a grey-hatched background…[16]

However, Bakhtin's chronotope theory goes further—it allows for space/place to generate their own chronotopes, and thus their own narrative forms. Bakhtin contends, "a locality is the trace of an event, a trace of what had shaped it. Such is the logic of all local myths and legends that attempt, through history to make sense out of space."[17] Places contain the traces of historical events that have shaped them, meaning that urban environments themselves determine the kind of narratives in which they are implicated rather than having such stories thrust upon them. Thus the city becomes mobile, its stories free to cross districts, merge and shape themselves through the everyday interactions of its inhabitants. Like Benjamin and Lacis claimed, it is porous, so that "a grain of Sunday is hidden in each weekday."[18]

What of the art exhibition? Museums offer a prime example of the chronotopic fusion of time and space. They heterotopically represent a multiplicity of elsewheres and sometimes. Bataille was nevertheless correct when he noted that visitors rather than art constitute the true content of exhibitions. He proposed, "A museum is like the lungs of a city—every Sunday the crowds flow through the museum like blood, coming out purified and fresh."[19] It is impossible to understand display without reference to an audience; thus an exhibition can become the site where the narratives present in the streets are explicated, that is "caught in the ambiguity of the actualization."[20] The communicative possibility of the exhibition is to articulate cultural anamnesis. Museum display becomes a dialogue between an audience and an urban narrative in which the museum site is mediator. The problem, however, is that the exhibition display can only ever offer a kind of fabricated nostalgia, an *ersatz* memory or museal vision of the past. The version of the urban memory narrative it offers is hopelessly incomplete.

Andreas Huyssen predicts,

> Musealization itself is sucked into the vortex of an ever-accelerating circulation of images, spectacles, events, and is thus always in danger of losing its ability to guarantee cultural stability over time.[21]

There are two major issues contained within Huyssen's statement. Firstly, the circulation of images: inevitably the exhibition cannot hope to display all the narratives present in the urban environment, nor should it wish to.

Such a tactic would only lead to the illegibility of the palimpsestuous city being mirrored by a museal simulacra, like in Borges' tale, *On Exactitude in Science,* where a map created of a country is so precise in its detail that it covers the land with its likeness, veiled with verisimilitude. The museum needs to perform a contestation of dominant narrative forms. Rather than display a narrative of institutionalised heritage it ought to aspire to seek out the elided stories and liminal memories that subsist between such monolithic discourses.

Secondly, Huyssen's statement hints at a temporal struggle within museum display which draws us back into our discussion of memory and history. Didier Maleuvre contends,

> Art constitutes a caesura of history, hence of experience and of the subject: it cuts into the very concept of the subject of culture in a way that calls into question ideas of immanence, naturalism, and authenticity. [22]

Maleuvre views museums as essentially historical—engaged with the production of history. However, drawing on the definitions we earlier encountered it seems more persuasive to view the museum as mediating between memory and history, since, quoting Eugenio Donato, "The museum displayed history as an eternally present spectacle with transparent origins and anthropocentric ends." [23] In other words, the museum displays history as memory, most particularly as collective memory. We can see this tie between the exhibition and collective memory in the manner in which exhibitions possess the potential to offer society a narrative that binds together the imagined community. One such imagined community is that defined in Deller and Ryan's vision of Brian Epstein's Liverpool, to which we now turn.

Jeremy Deller and Paul Ryan produced the booklet *The Liverpool of Brian Epstein* as a new artwork for the Tate Liverpool exhibition *Centre of the Creative Universe: Liverpool and the Avant-Garde*[24]. Charting sites connected with the former Beatles' manager in his hometown of Liverpool, the booklet can be viewed as an artist-initiated process of cultural anamnesis that taps into urban memory narratives and palimpsestuously reconstructs a forgotten past onto the present. Epstein's multiple identities as band manager, dapper man-about-town, gay man at a time when it remained illegal and Jewish family shop-owner are addressed by the booklet. The memories Deller and Ryan draw upon are in part lived histories, as in the testimonies of Rex Makin and Joe Flannery. For example, Flannery's recollection of the bars he frequented with Epstein,

Jeremy Deller and Paul Ryan, *The Liverpool of Brian Epstein*, 2007
Copyright and courtesy of Jeremy Deller and Paul Ryan

> We went to the Magic Clock and the Bar Royal, as they were the in places
> to go to for male drinking. The Bar Royal was on a backstreet leading to
> the market where livestock was sold: dogs, cat and rabbits.[25]

In this example, and throughout the work, there is a particular chronotope in view—that of 50s Liverpool's gay subculture. By bringing this chronotope to the foreground, Deller's text and Ryan's drawings permit this elided, marginalised narrative to reclaim its position in the city, re-emerging in palimpsests overlaying the current city grid. Maps of the city included in the work reinstate long-demolished sites of the gay scene, allowing these narratives to once more gain a hold on the urban fabric. In his text, Deller explains how it was through the removal of objects, buildings and sites connected with such histories that these memories were, at least from official histories, erased during the 1960s regeneration of Liverpool city centre. He writes,

> The market in Queen Square went, as did Great Charlotte Street, to make
> way for a shopping centre. The planners' rationale for the development is
> in retrospect slightly suspect. Their aims were for:
>   1) A unified civic and social centre and legal precinct
>   2) Unification of ownerships
>   3) The removal of non-conforming uses from the area
> The last point refers to the crowded livestock market but possibly
> subconsciously refers to the gay scene that flourished there.[26]

History is read backwards from the ruins; the most potent theme in Deller and Ryan's booklet is of urban decay. In the first few pages we learn of the boarded-up terraces near Epstein's old Anfield home, bought by the football club in anticipation of development; Joe Flannery laments, "I've been living on a bombsite all my life. There have always been changes with people pissing around with the city…"[27] Paul Ryan's drawings linger over ruins such as the spectral remains of houses ghosting out of the Paradise Street development, or the burnt-out Dickie Lewis pub on the East Lancs. Road. Perhaps most strikingly there are the contrasting views of the Victoria Monument in Derby Square: as it is now, surrounded by the modern law courts, and in 1945, isolated in the post-Blitz rubble. This last pair of images in particular presents a palimpsest that spurs an act of collective memory. The overlapping urban visions the artists create are a vision of the past situated in present memory: a powerful profane illumination.

Paul Ryan, *Victoria Monument, Liverpool*, 2007
Copyright and courtesy of Jeremy Deller and Paul Ryan

Taken as a whole, Deller and Ryan's publication acts as a literary psychogeography of Liverpool, with the identity of Brian Epstein as the emotional affect at its core. The booklet is intended in one aspect to function as a practical guidebook: the narrative it follows is spatially expressed and offers up a number of locations which combine in a psychogeographic mapping of Epstein's identity, from the various clubs, bars and theatres he visited, through residences, to the Synagogue at which he was a member of the congregation. Further, in its creation Deller and Ryan undertook wanderings through the city, visiting the key sites already mentioned, but also allowing for a drifting, random association with the city fabric to emerge. This second aspect is crucial in permitting the artists to develop a sense of the city's fragmented strata and moving layers, the crystallised memories of the streets. In these wanderings, past and present are merged in the artists' chronotope, so that the Sixties' St. John's Precinct Development becomes imaginatively commingled with the present-day Paradise Street Development, and contemporary cabaret acts conflate with their preceding equivalents.

By defining the present's relation to the past, the booklet casts questions on the future. It is noted that the current Paradise Project is a Grosvenor Estates project, owned by the Duke of Westminster, whose £6bn portfolio makes him Britain's richest landlord. Deller wryly remarks that the development will feature "a Debenhams at one end of the street and the nirvana of a John Lewis at the other." [28] Yet this encroachment of big business is framed by reference to the earlier St. John's development, and the loss of small businesses it incurred, including one owned by the Epstein family,

> The NEMS shop on Gt. Charlotte Street was one of the outlets that made way for the shopping centre. Perhaps this was the beginning of the end for family businesses in the town as retailing became more corporate and "unified".[29]

In another, perhaps more positive, example of this relation of past and future, one of the sections of the booklet is entitled "Brian's Children." This chapter features images of performers, musicians, variety acts, that the artists met during their time in the city. Through their inclusion Deller and Ryan envisage them as heirs to Epstein's legacy, shaping the vision of Liverpool and how it is remembered in the future, the stories told about it.

Deller and Ryan's booklet deals not with one narrative of Liverpool, but with several: the fictive and the historical, the particular and the general, the present and the past. They focus on forgotten aspects of city narrative—the hidden gay subculture swept aside by regenerative reconstructions, the familial terms of commerce similarly under threat of erasure, the sublimated religious identity present in the city. These themes take the form of a series of urban palimpsests of difference layered on to the collective image of the city. They are like characters in a novel that has been woven through the buildings and monuments of the city, waiting to be discovered. In bringing to fruition their own city of text, the artists contest previous homogeneous texts of the city found in standard historical accounts. By undertaking such a project through an artistic framework of literary narratives and cultural anamnesis Deller and Ryan offer not a history of a faded, disappeared past, but a memorial to a present past.

The city is a landscape that evokes past time. It has a story, but it is a collapsed narrative, one under constant pressure to disintegrate. Further, it is filled with histories and memories once attached to objects but now in ruins. In this city history and memory have become liminally conjoined spaces. According to M. Christine Boyer it falls on us to make sense of the fragmented narratives the city proffers us. She writes,

> Since we have all become wanderers among the vestiges and debris of the city's fabric, it is these scattered images that carry us along a memory walk as either distracted tourists or sympathetic observers.[30]

A memory walk down memory lane. The literature in the footsteps of the crowds is a chronotope of urban life, a palimpsestuous proliferation of memory narratives. When walking such a confusing space the selectorial anamnesis of art and the art exhibition is a useful guidebook. Remembering to forget is as important as recollecting when choosing a route through the multiple urban narratives available. Mieke Bal writes that "the present is a museum in which we walk as if it were a city." [31] However, just as apt, the past is a city in which we walk as if it were a museum.

Notes

[1] Jonathan Raban, *Soft City*, (London: Harvill Press, 1994), 4.

[2] Italo Calvino, *Invisible Cities*, (London: Secker & Warburg, 1974), 11.

[3] Pierre Nora, ed., *Realms of Memory*, (New York: Columbia University Press, 1996), 2.

[4] Mieke Bal, *Looking In: The Art of Viewing*, (Amsterdam: Abingdon, 2000), 47.

[5] Andreas Huyssen, *Present Pasts: Urban Palimpsests and the Politics of Memory*, (Stanford: Stanford University Press, 2003), 6-7.

[6] Neil Leach, *The Anaesthetics of Architecture*, (London: MIT Press, 1999), 37.

[7] Nora, *Realms of Memory*, 20.

[8] Italo Calvino, *Invisible Cities*, (London: Secker & Warburg, 1974), 10.

[9] Nora, *Realms of Memory*, 11.

[10] Hayden White, *Tropics of Discourse: Essays in Cultural Criticism*, (London: John Hopkins University Press, 1978), 51.

[11] Ibid., 81.

[12] Ibid., 69.

[13] W.G Sebald, *Austerlitz*, (London: Penguin, 2001), 192-193.

[14] Linda Hutcheon, *A Poetics of Postmodernism: History, Theory, Fiction*, (London: Routledge, 1988), 106.

[15] Paul Smethurst, *The Postmodern Chronotope: Reading Space and Time in Contemporary Fiction*, (Amsterdam: Rodopi, 2000), 68.

[16] Sebald, *Austerlitz*, 77.

[17] Mikhail M. Bakhtin, *The Dialogic Imagination: Four Essays*, (Austin: University of Texas Press, 1981), 189.

[18] Walter Benjamin and Asja Lacis, "Naples," in *One-Way Street and other writings,* Walter Benjamin, (London: Verso, 1997), 171.

[19] Neil Leach, ed., *Rethinking Architecture: A Reader in Cultural Theory*, (London: Routledge, 1997), 22.

[20] Michel de Certeau, *The Practice of Everyday Life*, (Berkeley: University of California Press, 1984), 117.

[21] Andreas Huyssen, *Present Pasts: Urban Palimpsests and the Politics of Memory*, (Stanford: Stanford University Press, 2003), 24.

[22] Didier Maleuvre, *Museum Memories: History, Technology, Art*, (Stanford: Stanford University Press, 1999), 3.

[23] Eugenio Donato, "The Museum's Furnace: Notes Toward A Contextual Reading of Bouvard and Pécuchet," in *Textual Strategies: Perspectives in Post-Structuralist Criticism, ed.* Josué V. Harari, (London: Methuen, 1980), 237-238.

[24] *Centre of the Creative Universe: Liverpool and the Avant-Garde*, exhibition curated by Christoph Grunenberg and Robert Knifton, Tate Liverpool, 20 February – 9 September 2007.

[25] Jeremy Deller and Paul Ryan, *The Liverpool of Brian Epstein*, (Liverpool: Tate Liverpool, 2007), 10.

[26] Ibid., 17-18.

[27] Ibid., 10.

[28] Ibid., 18.

[29] Ibid., 18.

[30] M. Christine Boyer, *The City of Collective Memory: Its Historical Imagery and Architectural Entertainments*, (Cambridge: MIT Press, 1996), 374.

[31] Mieke Bal, ed., *The Practice of Cultural Analysis: Exposing Interdisciplinary Interpretation*, (Stanford: Stanford University Press, 1999), 5.

CHAPTER TEN

APPROPRIATED IMAGERY, MATERIAL
AFFECTS AND NARRATIVE OUTCOMES

MARIE SHURKUS

> To an ever greater extent our experience is governed by pictures, pictures
> in newspapers and magazines, on television and in the cinema. Next to
> these pictures firsthand experience begins to retreat, to seem more and
> more trivial. While it once seemed that pictures had the function of
> interpreting reality it now seems that they have usurped it. It therefore
> becomes imperative to understand the picture itself, not in order to recover
> a lost reality, but to determine how a picture becomes a signifying structure
> of its own accord.[1]

Thus Douglas Crimp stated the premise for the 1977 *Pictures* exhibition.
His curatorial essay explored how the featured artworks engaged
appropriated image fragments that invited viewers to invent narratives. In
a later version of this essay Crimp specifically located the source for this
narrative impulse in the frame. Pointing to Sherrie Levine's 1978 series,
Sons and Lovers—which featured pictures of women appropriated from
advertisements and collaged into hand-drawn silhouettes of the
presidential heads that appear on U.S. coins—Crimp argued that Levine's
compositions forced viewers to read the two images through the frame of
the other, namely female identity through economic currency.[2] Thus,
Crimp laid the groundwork for a critical interpretation of postmodern
appropriation as a strategic approach to representation that was specifically
designed to visually underscore the ideological content of imagery.
Building on Crimp's insights, Hal Foster would later define appropriation
as "recoding." [3] These semiotic analyses were further supplemented by a
Marxist interpretation of materiality in which exchange determines value
and meaning.[4] Accordingly, *rephotography* became defined as a strategy
that was specifically designed to demonstrate how media images
interpolated identity through the production of desire. Richard Prince's
work was exemplary in this regard: by appropriating the *Marlboro Man*

out from under the advertising text of Phillip Morris, Prince effectively revealed how seductively these cowboys called us to be like them and *light up*.   Largely as a result of the semiotic and Marxist analyses that developed around postmodern appropriation, the artwork was reduced to its image and the viewing experience was aligned with reading. Thus, for example, Foster wrote: "the artist becomes a manipulator of signs more than a producer of art objects, and the viewer an active reader of messages rather than a passive contemplator of the aesthetic or consumer of the spectacular."[5] Seen from another perspective, these analyses left both the viewer and the artwork disembodied.

The on-going development of digital technology is transforming our understanding of representation yet again.[6] The *new* digitized image no longer *represents* in the traditional sense, for it neither acts as an iconic mirror reflecting the world nor does it function as a mere symbolic reference. Rather, it has become a dematerialized form that mobilizes affect in the viewer. Expanding upon these insights, new media theorist Mark Hansen has argued that viewers do not stand outside of the image; rather they are imminent to it: "the image can no longer be restricted to the level of surface appearance, but must be extended to encompass the entire process by which information is made perceivable through embodied experience." [7] Accordingly, traditional notions of viewership that invoke a subject-object dichotomy no longer apply, for the boundaries of the viewer's body and the artwork have become enfolded. In this new conception of representation the viewer's body becomes the substrate through which an image *appears* or more precisely develops.

Hansen's description of the embodied viewer suggests a radical transformation of representation, one that has occurred in tandem with a general retreat from the semiotic analysis of imagery that once dominated the critical assessment of postmodern appropriation. Ultimately, this shift in our understanding of representation has reinstated the viewer's body, in fact positioned it at the centre of representation.   Nevertheless, the question remains: where does this leave the material body of the artwork? Taking up this question, this essay returns to the late 1980s, when new media's insights on representation were emerging through the "post-photography" debates.[8] Initially these debates positioned analogue against digital photography and thus described representation as shifting away from indexical inscriptions toward a more translational approach.[9] These critics leaned heavily on Roland Barthes' *noeme* of photography, namely photography's ability to capture "what has been" and preserve it.[10] In contrast, digital technologies translated imagery into malleable numeric codes. By the early nineties, however, this discourse had moved away from such comparative analyses of reproductive processes. Recognizing that in practice these realms often intersected, critics attended to the issue of representation, where they confronted the image, isolated as an incorporeal form "whose connection to the material world had lapsed." [11]

Alongside the insights generated through the *post-photography* debates a new but related direction was also developing in appropriation art. Beginning in the late 1980s, several artists—Jennifer Bolande, The Chapman Brothers, Jeff Koons, Sherrie Levine among them—began to appropriate images from two-dimensional sources and re-present them as three-dimensional sculptures. In these works the body of the sculpture provides the material substrate through which an appropriated image becomes visibly present. Like the Pictures Generation's use of rephotography, these appropriation artists did not alter the figuration of their source imagery. However, unlike rephotography, the expressive qualities of the physical materials that composed these artworks dramatically altered the narrative content of the appropriated imagery. Thus, in terms of the post-photography debates, these works also suggested the immaterial condition of the image; for these artists' use of appropriation demonstrated how an image might be excised from one material object and be relocated in another. However, where digital technology translated the image into invisible numerical codes, these works translated images qualitatively, that is through the effects of material expression. In this regard, the appropriated images that appear in these sculptures function as armatures designed to foreground the affective content of material expression, rather than the ideological content of framing that was so central to the Pictures Generation's work.

Jake and Dinos Chapman's 1994 *Great Deeds Against the Dead* is a case in point. This life-size sculpture grew out of *Disasters of War*, a series of eighty-three miniature dioramas, composed of plastic toy soldiers, that ape Goya's nineteenth-century print series of the same name. The ironic reference to greatness alluded to in Goya's title combines with his horrific subject matter to create a biting depiction of the inhumanity of war. In the Chapmans' hands, however, Goya's ghastly image reappears transformed into a cheesy Hollywood stage-set that is completely drained of pathos and bereft of social commentary.

Surprisingly enough, this dramatic transformation of Goya's content occurs even though the Chapmans have labored to maintain the figural details of Goya's image. In fact, both artworks depict three, nude, male corpses that have been brutally mutilated and appear hanging from a dead tree. In Goya's picture two figures wear a moustache, while the third appears clean-shaven; the Chapmans' is the same. Both works display a

Jake and Dinos Chapman,*Great Deeds Against the Dead,* 1994.
Mixed media (277 x 244 x 152.5 cm). Courtesy Jay Jopling, White Cube, London.
Photograph © the artists.

decapitated corpse whose severed arms hang just below the detached head. Even the gesture of these hands, presumably frozen with *rigor mortis*, is identical: one hand droops, while the other reaches upward as if grasping for its head. In Goya's etching this gesture is a heartbreaking sign of life's last breath; however, in the Chapmans' sculpture it becomes almost slapstick. If the composition of images is identical, then what accounts for these disparate affects?

On the one hand, the answer to this question is deceptively simple, for the Chapmans' sculpture follows a long tradition of visual parody, which engages imitation in order to articulate an ironic commentary on its source.[12] In this regard Duchamp's infamous precedent *L.H.O.O.Q.* offers insight.   Here ironic commentary occurs at two different levels. Duchamp's addition of facial hair alters the image of Leonardo's *Mona Lisa* and thus cues viewers to his second intervention: a new title that reframes the image in terms of a prurient pun. Numerous examples of this two-pronged approach to visual parody are evident throughout the later twentieth century: Rene Magritte's 1950 *Perspective II: Manet's Balcony*, Andy Warhol's 1963 *Thirty are Better than One*, Mel Ramos's 1973 *Plenti-Grand Odalisque*, John Baldessari's 1984 *White Shape* are just a few examples. The Chapmans' sculpture, however, revises this formula: for the image and title remain unaltered; instead, ironic commentary is orchestrated at the level of material expression.

The Chapmans have literally moved Goya's image into a new material presentation that generates entirely different affects. Goya's image, printed on a paper ground, suggests a powerfully atmospheric world that exists separately from the gallery space. Accordingly, viewing this dramatically reduced world becomes a somewhat private experience that viewers must enter via their imagination. When the Chapmans transform this image by recreating it as a life-size sculpture, the work's appeal to the imagination is replaced by a more physical encounter with the actual object. However, rather than invigorating this scene with a life-like quality, this dose of realism destroys the illusionary power of Goya's work, a condition that the Chapmans' materials expand upon. Ultimately, the hard and rigid surfaces of the Chapmans' fiberglass mannequins destroy the image's empathetic appeal to viewers' imaginations. Thus, where the ropes can be seen pinching into the once supple and vibrant flesh of Goya's figures, on the Chapmans' mannequins they become merely ornamental details on the hard surfaces. Situated in the stark white gallery, viewers recognize the Chapmans' diaorama for what it is: a stage-set featuring cast dummies whose seams are even visible. Quite effectively, the Chapmans' sculpture demonstrates how a dramatic shift in the material presentation of an image results in an equally dramatic shift in narrative tone.

While the Chapmans engage material expression in order to convey an ironic commentary on their source, many of their contemporaries take a more deadpan approach, a condition that aligns them with precedents in George Segal's *oeuvre*. For example, Segal's *The Dancers* (1971-73) engages Henri Matisse's 1909 painting *Dance* as its point of departure. To present Matisse's dancers as three-dimensional figures, Segal had to infuse Matisse's imagery with volume and anatomically correct his disproportionate figures.   The price of these changes is a more staid composition that actually focuses attention on the individual dancers rather than the movement passing through them.   This transformative outcome was further enhanced by Segal's process, for his dancers were cast from living models;   therefore,   the   sculpture   displays   individualized   portraits, indexically rendered through molds.[13]   Accordingly, where Matisse's unrealistic space and sketchy anonymous figures allow the sweeping energy of the dance to dominate the narrative content of his picture, Segal's sculpture suggests the slow and deliberate process of a group learning steps. Thus, while Segal's sculpture maintains a visually discernable relationship with Matisse's work that is further underscored by its similar title, it does not articulate a commentary on Matisse's work. Instead,   his   relationship   with   Matisse's   painting   is   translational,   it appropriates and reiterates the image but defines it in terms of a different material expression that transforms the narrative outcome. In both the Chapmans' and Segal's works the material expression translates imagery by producing interpretive effects that impact what an image conveys to viewers.

   When appropriation is understood as translation rather than copying, it becomes a serial process of moving imagery through different dimensions and material bodies that qualitatively transform the narrative content of imagery. Henri Bergson's concept of *duration* offers crucial insight here. For Bergson, duration is the continuous presence of the past gnawing into the future and swelling as it advances.[14] Accordingly, Bergson maintains that one moment does not merely replace another, rather the present prolongs the past, but not as it was; instead the past is in a constant state of transition. When the image is understood as an incorporeal temporal object that appropriation puts in motion, it too enters the present as the past transformed. According to Bergson physical matter alters the pace of the world's unfolding and in doing so it individuates "tendencies." [15] Restated in   terms   of   representation,   Bergson's   philosophy   thus   suggests   an understanding of the image as a temporal force that acquires qualities or individuation through its material expression.

Harold Edgerton, *Milk Drop Coronet*, 1957. Dye transfer print. ©Harold & Esther Edgerton Foundation, 2008, courtesy of Palm Press, Inc.

As noted at the outset, material expression happens in two different bodies: the body of the artwork and that of the viewer. Focusing on the former, Jennifer Bolande's 1987-88 sculpture *Milk Crown* uses appropriation to demonstrate how images specifically inherit individual tendencies or qualities from the physical materials that present them. These tendencies then transform the narrative content that the image conveys to viewers. Bolande's point of departure is Harold Edgerton's photograph *Milk Drop Coronet*. Inspired by the optical illusion of stillness that the bright flashes of a mercury-arc rectifier produces, Edgerton's photograph captures a milk drop suspended in mid-air.[16] As such, it makes visible what the human eye cannot apprehend. Thus, Edgerton's picture might be described as recording the impact of a force, namely gravity, on the material flesh of the milk. Indeed, as Edgerton's metaphoric title suggests, the pool of milk embodied the force of gravity and transformed it into the expression of a coronet form. When seen from this perspective, Edgerton's picture suggests the progression of a plot that moves from milk to drop to coronet.

Jennifer Bolande, *Milk Crown*, 1987. Cast porcelain (diameter: 5 x 18 cm), edition of 6. Courtesy of Alexander and Bonin, New York.

Bolande's sculpture collapses this plot into a single form: the coronet, but the physical body of this form conserves Edgerton's narrative through its material qualities. For when Bolande cast Edgerton's image in white porcelain, she actualized the expression of gravity in a solid three-dimensional object. Effectively, Bolande moved Edgerton's image into a new situation regulated by an entirely different set of physical laws. In fact, her porcelain material is no longer fluid like the milk. Also gone is Edgerton's mysterious red landscape and the illusion of weightlessness that his photograph conveyed to the milk droplets. Nevertheless, Bolande's material retains certain qualities of the source image, such as the reflective surface of the milk and its whiteness. More importantly, however, the extreme fragility of Bolande's porcelain captures and prolongs the temporal moment that Edgerton's photograph depicts. Ultimately, through her use of porcelain, Bolande re-presents the coronet as a solid but delicate object that has conserved the potentially destructive and temporal force of gravity within the qualities of its material body. In this regard Bolande's sculpture effectively demonstrates what Bergson described as the individuation of matter. For her physical matter allows what exists in Edgerton's picture as only a description to re-enter the world as an actual potential that is preserved in the material body of Bolande's *Milk Crown*. Quite simply, Bolande's sculpture holds and prolongs the past, both Edgerton's photograph and the first image that Edgerton's camera witnessed, namely gravity sculpting the pool of milk.

Significantly, Bolande's work in collaboration with Edgerton's demonstrates that qualities—such as whiteness, reflectivity or fragility—cannot appear in and of themselves, rather like an image, they require a material body for their expression and individuation. In fact, these qualities are not essentially tied to the physical matter that presents them, for as Bolande's work indicates whiteness and reflectivity can appear across a broad spectrum of different materials that include both milk and porcelain. Instead of being a sole function of material expression, qualities like temporal images are part of the world's potential that only becomes visibly palpable through their expression in a material body, which individuates and thus transforms them. In other words, materialization allows the image to encounter qualities, which transform its narrative content. Accordingly, material expression suggests another register of the image, one that appeals to viewers outside of abstract signification and in terms of physical sensibilities that viewers' bodies recognize as patterns.

Where physical matter provides the ground for an image to encounter temporal qualities that transform it, the viewer's body provides a ground for the expression of images to activate recognizable sensual patterns. As Kaja Silverman has argued our primary means of symbolization is located in the place,

> ...where memory meets external stimulus...Something must give itself to be seen, and a spectator must see within it the miraculous reincarnation of what-has-been.[17]

Silverman describes this act of "reincarnation" as a "visual condensation" that occurs "between a privileged unconscious memory and a perceptual stimulus in the present." [18] By way of explanation, she offers the example of a girl who recognizes the "sable coat of her beloved collie" in the jacket of a friend's father. According to Silverman, this recognition enacts a libidinal transfer that instills in the child a new appreciation for male musculature.[19] In this example a material affect—the quality of the coat—

triggers an embodied memory of what has been, which in turn expands the viewer's understanding of the present. According to Silverman, this transformation spreads backwards in time, not only expanding the viewer's perception of the present, but also altering her recollection of the past. Thus, the child's memory of the collie shifts even as it transforms her perception of the male figure. A similar effect can be seen operating in Zoe Leonard's (1992-97) sculpture *Strange Fruit (for David)*.

Drawing on the insights of the Pictures Generation, Leonard's title *Strange Fruit* invites viewers to examine her work from specific frames of reference, namely Billie Holiday's song about racial lynchings and a derogatory conception of homosexuals. These semiotic references are rendered literal in the material presentation of the work, for these are indeed *strange fruits* with their insides hollowed-out and their peels roughly stitched back together in a rather desperate attempt to recreate wholeness.

Zoe Leonard, *Strange Fruit (For David)*, 1992-97. Orange, banana, grapefruit, lemon, and avacado peels with thread, zippers, buttons, sinew, needles, plastic wire, stickers, fabric, and trim wax. (Dimensions variable.) Courtesy of Philadelphia Museum of Art. Photograph by Graydon Wood.

Leonard readily admits that this attempt at healing the skin is doomed, for her intention was to fail and thereby mourn the loss of a friend.[20] Leonard's parenthetical dedication "(for David)" directs us to her friend David Wojnarowicz, an outspoken gay artist who died of AIDS and whose portrait *Stitched* depicts him with his mouth sewn shut. For viewers, the recollected image of a mouth sewn shut intersects with Leonard's sewn fruit and vegetable skins to produce a symbolic understanding of Leonard's work in terms of another era when treatment for AIDS was essentially non-existent and attending the funerals of young friends became common.

Like the girl's recognition of her beloved dog's coat, the material presentation of Leonard's "strange fruit" also stirs the Wojnarowicz image of skin pierced by thread at another level. Through Leonard's work an embodied transaction occurs that calls the viewer's body to function as a witness that recognizes and recalls other decaying bodies steeped in the helpless aura of abject grief. At this level the viewer's body becomes a ground and the image generates patterns or aggregates of sensations that are recognizable and linked to other past experiences. Neurobiologist Francisco Varela has described this effect as "enactive cognition." [21] In this model, images point to referents through sensory links that are entirely dependent upon the individual perceiver's past experiences. Thus, the image performs significance by enacting aspects of the perceiver's embodied history; in Varela's words, meaning arises "from our capacity to project imaginatively from certain well-structured aspects of bodily and interactional experience to conceptual structures." [22] Accordingly, Leonard's work elicits grief from viewers by activating their bodies qualitatively: the incorporeal temporal image leaves the gallery and moves into the viewer's body, where it activates sensual qualities from the past that have been conserved there.

Ultimately, the power of Leonard's work rests entirely upon individual viewers' memories and perceptions. For viewers must not only recognize Leonard's reference to Wojnarowicz, but also experience the sensual qualities that Leonard's material expresses in terms of a lived experience of loss. In this regard, Leonard's work orchestrates an impact that recalls Barthes' description of the *punctum*. For as Barthes suggested about the punctum, the dematerialized image appears to "shoot" out of Leonard's artwork and wound the viewer.[23]

As Barthes has explained, the specific detail, which "punctuates" a picture, differs from person to person. Therefore, the activation of a *punctum* depends entirely upon an individual viewer's experience and recognition. To use Barthes words, "it is what I add to the photograph and what is nonetheless already there." [24] Effectively, the viewer's imagination grabs on to something that is *already* represented in the picture and develops it, literally re-imagining it and recognizing its presence in a new situation. Therefore, just as the girl re-imagined her connection to the beloved collie through the physical qualities of the father's jacket, the material expression of Leonard's work conjoins the affective content of the decaying fruit with an experience of other bodies decimated by disease. The reference to Wojnarowicz's mouth sewn shut then ties this experience to a particular historical moment.

Although Barthes maintains that the recognition of a *punctum* is entirely personal, Leonard's work demonstrates how a material sensibility might generate a recognizable pattern that speaks to a cultural history that a group of individuals might recognize. This is not to suggest that these individuals will all experience Leonard's work in the same manner or that their experiences of loss were the same. Quite the opposite, Leonard's work manages to trigger a sensual pattern that is recognizable to a group of people who witnessed the same historical moment but from different individual bodies.

As noted, the impact of Leonard's narrative relies upon an audience of witnesses whose bodies can testify to what has been. Needless to say, in time all of the people who witnessed the onset of AIDS will eventually pass away. Recognizing decay as a central component of the narrative of this work, Leonard and the Philadelphia Museum of Art, the custodians of this piece, have embraced this disappearance. Foregoing restoration efforts, the museum has agreed to Leonard's request that they continue to exhibit the piece until it has completely disintegrated.[25] However, until then, Leonard's work engages the viewer's body as a material substrate from which it solicits affective sensibilities that in turn stimulate and develop other images and narrative content. Moreover, as this essay has argued, this describes a new approach to representation, one that is defined by a dematerialized image whose narrative expressions are transformed by its passage through material bodies, both the flesh of human witnesses as well as the flesh of material objects.

Notes

[1] Douglas Crimp, "Pictures," exhibition catalogue (New York: Artists Space, 1977), unpaginated.

[2] Crimp, "Pictures," in Brian Wallis, ed. *Art After Modernism* (New York: The New Museum of Contemporary Art, 1984), 185.

[3] Hal Foster, *Recodings* (Port Townsend, WA: Bay Press, 1985), 166-179.

[4] Benjamin Buchloh, "Allegorical Procedures: Appropriation and Montage in Contemporary Art," *Artforum* 21 (September 1982): 43-56.

[5] Foster, *Recodings,* 100.

[6] See Martin Lister, *The Photographic Image in Digital Culture* (London: Routledge University Press, 1995).

[7] Mark B. N. Hansen, *New Philosophy for New Media* (Cambridge, MA: The MIT Press, 2004), 10.

[8] See Hubertus Amelunxen, ed. *Photography After Photography* (London: G+B Arts, 1996).

[9] See William J. T. Mitchell, *The Reconfigured Eye: Visual Truth in the Post-Photographic Era* (Cambridge, MA: The MIT Press, 2004).

[10] Roland Barthes, *Camera Lucida* (New York: Hill and Wang, 1980), 78.

[11] Timothy Druckrey, "From Dada to Digital," in *Metamorphoses: Photography in the Electronic Age* (New York: Aperture, 1994), 7.

[12] Linda Hutcheon, *A Theory of Parody* (Chicago: University of Illinois Press, 2000), 30-49.

[13] Jean Lipman and Richard Marshall, *Art About Art* (New York: E.P. Dutton, 1978), 109.

[14] Henri Bergson, "Creative Evolution," in S.E. Frost, ed. *Masterworks of Philosophy*, (New York: McGraw Hill, 1946), 151.

[15] Ibid, 169-71.

[16] Marta Braun, "The Expanded Present: Photographing Movement," in *Beauty of Another Order* (New Haven: Yale University Press, 1997), 183.

[17] Kaja Silverman, *World Spectators* (Stanford: Stanford University Press, 2000), 128-129.

[18] Ibid., 78.

[19] Ibid.

[20] Martha Buskirk, *The Contingent Object of Contemporary Art* (Cambridge, MA: The MIT Press, 2003), 145.

[21] Francisco Varela, "The Reenchantment of the Concrete," in *Incorporations,* ed. Jonathan Crary & Sanford Kwinter (New York: Zone, 1992), 329-334.

[22] Ibid.

[23] Barthes, *Camera Lucida,* 26-27.

[24] Ibid., 55.

[25] Buskirk, *The Contingent Object of Contemporary Art,* 145.

CHAPTER ELEVEN

CONNECTING THE UNCONNECTED

LISA STANSBIE

Nicholas Bourriaud suggests in *Postproduction* (2002) that:

> The artistic question is no longer: what can we make that is new? but how can we make do with what we have? In other words, how can we produce singularity and meaning from this chaotic mass of objects, names and references that constitutes our daily life? [1]

My practice *makes do with what we have*, but the chaotic mass of objects, names and references used are those that constitute the expanding contents of the internet, connecting information online that may never be connected otherwise. Using the internet as a research source for the creation of art work allows instant access to and collection of unedited information and images.

The process of curating and collecting using the world wide web is undertaken in order to create my own ever-expanding digital archive, which can function as a useable object. The intention is that the digital archive might potentially interrogate notions of appropriation and reinterpretation through constructing and connecting existing internet-based material. This *interactive archive* utilises a dialectical approach that intentionally searches for apparently random associations between information, images and objects. However, that which appears to be random, is always governed by myself as the author of the archive. In Georges Perec's novel, *Life a User's Manual* (1978), he explains that the art of making jigsaws,

> begins with wooden puzzles cut by hand, whose maker undertakes to ask himself all the questions the player will have to solve, and, instead of

allowing chance to cover his tracks, aims to replace it with cunning, trickery and subterfuge.[2]

The construction of the archive is made with the player/user/viewer in mind and deliberately creates paths of a labyrinth that sometimes end, overlap, repeat and occasionally finish where they began.

Using digital media has allowed the expanding connections to be created through the use of search engines as the *connectors* and the internet as its source (the internet itself being a mammoth archive). As a basis for creating knowledge, this largely unedited source could be said to undermine the traditional associations of *fixed knowledge*, often associated with the conventional material archive. However, with the continued expansion of the archive it has now developed into a tool to produce further work. Archive entries are used as points of departure to create further artworks in the form of satellite narrative film works.

The film works that have developed from the archive also have the potential to expand ideas located around site(s) for the work. Currently, the films exist simultaneously within and outside the digital archive in multiple sites and formats. Already in material art practice it is common to have different versions of a work. Using the digital, however, allows the work to be continually fluid by means of re-sampling/editing and allowing it to be shown in a variety of material and immaterial sites. In considering sites for the presentation of work, the development of the archive itself as a tool for research has enabled me to consider its presentation alongside the satellite works which have been generated from it. When displayed in material spaces it can be used by a viewer and seen in relation to the other works that have been derived and constructed from it.

Each narrative film work evolves from an archive entry and from this point onwards the methods used to create the film's narrative are similar to the rule-based constrained writing processes used by writers associated with the Oulipo group, such as Georges Perec. This is perhaps most ambitiously demonstrated in Perec's novel *A Void* (1962), written entirely without the use of the letter 'e'. This procedure of developing constraints within which the narrative is structured is used across all three film works to create their narrative. For example in *Apprehension* (2007) the starting point is the word Apprehension (in an archive entry) which was found through internet research. Apprehension's *breeding tree* was then also discovered from a stallion-breeding website and the names from the breeding tree are systematically used (in order) to hang the narrative around.

Lisa Stansbie, *The Emperor of The Moon*, 2006 (stills) DVD

The resulting stories, read in each case by voice-over artists, have narratives which are sometimes difficult to follow. This difficulty stems from the seemingly arbitrary nature of each narrative as it weaves a path directed by each name sequentially taken from the lists.

The Emperor of The Moon (2006)
Film 2 min 16 secs with digital narration

"The Emperor of The Moon" is the final sentence from the author Norman Mailer's best selling book *The Fight* (1975). Through search engines a list of Norman Mailer's best-selling books was discovered and a narrative is created by using the titles of these books in the order they appear in the list.

The Emperor of The Moon

The executioner's song was playing on the radio as we left. It was too stuffy to concentrate on the book and in my mind I replayed the fight scenes from the previous night. The men had all lain there breathless, chests steadily rising until no more, surrounded by the naked and the dead I decided it was time to leave.

Why are we at war? A feeling of hopelessness washed over me along with a sense of distance. My father had told me it was once referred to as an American dream. In the ancient evenings it was different. I remember times when Oswald's tale wagged so frantically that it shook his body and we would walk for hours through dimly lit streets in the meat-packing district.

This of course was before the unholy alliance of the two states. Things were never quiet after. One place was left untouched and it became a shrine to nostalgia. They called it the castle in the forest, yet it was no more than a stone house, decorated with greenery.

As a child I was told never to come to the castle as it was rumored there was a harlot's ghost that walked down the corridors past the spooky art that had been hung and forgotten. The castle now stood alone except for the company of the deer park.

I went back to the book 'The gospel according to the son' was the first section, but my heart was not in it. We began to pull away and as the tilting rocked me, I drifted off. I was awoken suddenly by a commotion. Passengers were looking around, straining to see from the small windows. The young girl next to me, with a concerned look, asked 'why are we in Vietnam?'

The Cloud Collector (2007)
Film 2 min 15 secs narrated by Gerard Fletcher

The Cloud Collector tells of an elderly man (The Cardinal) who since the 1950s has developed an obsession with taking photographs of the jet streams left in the sky by aeroplanes. *The Cloud Collector's* narrative is written to include the top ten best-selling novel titles from the 1950s in their 'list' order from 1 to 10. It stems from the archive entry '1950s'.

The Cloud Collector

Delivering the news to those who still required it in paper form, he rode his rusted BMX along Joy Street each morning. His route took him across the river and into the trees where the drone of the tarmac subsided into an uneasy silence, and then he would often see the colourless figure of the cardinal in the misty leaded window and feel slightly uncomfortable about his silhouette.

Since the 1950s the cardinal had been a collector. From his window, the wall opposite was etched with years of abuse and when he stared across, he would see fantastical arrangements within this urban monolith. His gaze was only broken intermittently by an expectant glance to the sky. Today he considered how the imprints on the horizon were reminiscent of the pattern on the pedestal his father had left him all those years ago, which now served as a plinth for his camera.

The flood tide from three years ago had damaged his best work, but the tattered ones were still included alongside the pristine books. The parasites that shared the books' wooden shelves crawled invisibly through the important images they contained, each one was religiously classified with sticky video numbers, like star money, that came, unintentionally, to enumerate the later years of his life.

Occasionally when he looked up to the traces in the sky they reminded him of a time when as a boy he had taken part in the jubilee trail and gained a trophy for his success as an adventurer. Thinking of these lost years often made him a disenchanted man.

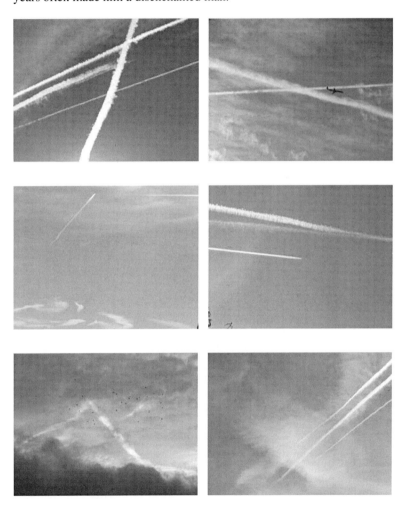

Lisa Stansbie, *The Cloud Collector*, 2007 (stills) DVD

Apprehension (2007)

Film 2 min 53 secs narrated by Mary Healy and music by Jeff Harbourne

Apprehension is a word within an archive entry and after research on the internet it was also found to be the name of a race horse. Following on from this *Apprehension's* 'breeding tree' was collected. Using the names of the horses a narrative was written to include each name in the order it appears in *Apprehension's* breeding tree.

In contrast to its source, the film's narrative is based around the delivery of a package, in a time when electricity and water have become scarce. However, the film's imagery references the structure of the narrative by showing horses which are edited from home movies from the 1950s.

Apprehension's Breeding Tree

In The Wings	GB	1986		First Kiss	GB	1983
Saddlers Wells	USA	1981		Kris	GB	1976
Northern Dancer	CAN	1961		Sharpen Up	GB	1969
Nearctic	USA	1954		Doubly Sure	GB	1971
Natalma	USA	1957		Atan	USA	1961
Fairy Bridge	USA	1975		Rocchetta	GB	1961
Bold Reason	USA	1968		Reliance	FR	1962
Special	USA	1969		Soft Angels	GB	1963
High Hawk	IRE	1980		Primatie	FR	1975
Shirley Heights	GB	1975		Lassie	GB	1956
Mill Reef	USA	1968		Vaguely Noble	GB	1965
Hardiemma	GB	1969		Vienna	GB	1957
Sunbitten	GB	1970		Pistol Packer	FR	1968
Sea Hawk	FR	1963		Gun Bow	USA	1960
Pantoufle	GB	1961		Georges Girl	USA	1959

Lisa Stansbie, *Apprehension*, 2007 (still image) DVD

Lisa Stansbie, *Apprehension*, 2007 (still image) DVD

Apprehension

It was with apprehension that we delivered the package to the man in The Wings. It was nearly six months since the last of the saddlers' wells had dried up and everyone, even the northern dancer, was forced to deal with the drought and periodic power cuts. The bars that lined the main street were now places of solace.

We had heard yesterday that Nearctic was now also without power and as we stood waiting nervously, Natalma the owner was already lighting candles in readiness around the semi-circle of the bar. This gave it the appearance of a fairy bridge, propped up with soulless creatures who, without a bold reason to consider leaving, remained in their special places.

The Wings was a dreary place, even with power. The grimy image hanging above the bar of a high hawk appeared to be circling over the customers, most of whom were out of work miners from Shirley Heights.

In whispered moments throughout the journey we had speculated about the contents of the package. It could contain the results of drilling from the Mill Reef, but Hardiemma didn't agree and explained that if drilling had taken place, the rest of the group would surely have appeared sun bitten or shown some signs of a tussle with the sea hawk.

The bartender offered us pantoufle with our drinks and we accepted, even though it was now triple the price. Placing one in my mouth and leaving it to melt I thought of the time I ate it in the orchard during a sticky summer after my first kiss with Kris. I must sharpen up I thought, Atan Rocchetta had entrusted us with this duty and we must be doubly sure to live up to his reliance on us.

The first thing that caught my eye was the Soft Angels' insignia on the back of his jacket. As we sat down he identified himself quietly as Primatie, and introduced us to Lassie, his companion. His vaguely noble air made me think he must have connections with the Vienna block. A man dressed like this, dignified and elegant didn't merge well with the pistol packers at the bar. I had begun to relax by studying him carefully but then, quite unexpectedly I felt a gun bow at my knee. Trying to steady my shaking voice as I spoke, I used my only escape route, 'I am George's girl'.

Notes

[1] Nicholas Bourriaud, *Postproduction* (New York: Lukas & Sternberg, 2002), 11.

[2] Georges Perec, *Life A User's Manual* (London: Vintage 2003), Preamble

CHAPTER TWELVE

TEXT: PROVISIONAL: PERFORMANCE

STUART BRISLEY

Text is provisional. It can be modified, cut, enlarged, chopped, battered, squashed and scattered. It is open to change and chance unless chained down and fixed as an intended impermeable object, as in a book, like a brick, or a stone. Beginning, middle and end. Dipping in and out of the text now chipped out, sometimes spattered, broken and scattered, it is held together by what goes on inside the head. The sense and space of mind does not exactly live in time, in the *mechanical tic toc* numbering each moment marking time. In contrast to linear time for example, there are alternative allusive modes which appear to break the mould.

To begin with, an interruption: I open my eyes and eventually get out of bed. It is the advent of the day, and the immersion in time passing after the unconsciousness of sleep. Later it is noon, then afternoon passes into evening, and night. Some fall into sleep as the day begins when the sun intervenes to mark the advent, a coming of days and nights, before human sentience and consciousness contrived to have each passing moment marked by the clock.

Taking a few steps aside, the text lies inert until read; then a reader shutters down the senses responsive to external stimuli to enter the mind`s space. Head space like radio, radio space where the imagination expands into a dimensionless arena to give it something specific. Is this what reading does? The text takes off from the surface some thirty to forty centimetres from the eyes. It doesn`t read exactly the same on subsequent readings. Children at a certain age desire to hear the same story again and again. It is never quite the same before fatigue sets in and it falls away, discarded. The degree to which it is consumed, eaten (a mean description of an understanding being nourished) means that it will have been killed or died as the reader marches inexorably onwards, like the caterpillar systematically consuming leaf food, (life depends on it), and afterwards is left with the remnants of skin and bone as memory, surface and structure. To read it again is to play with the phantom which doesn`t entirely come back to life, just as though the full-blown body has been consumed (it will not be completely absorbed in the first place). It hovers in the interstices, like the fantasies of those souls of the dead who can`t find peace. They can never be fully re-formed in life and be dead at the same time. This sense of narrative flows like a river, sprouts like a cauliflower in the head.

And in art/performance/live action, narratives are lurking, much like quiet breathing. To perform is to engage narrative as one of the performative functions as inexorably as day, as light used to follow night darkness when nature had its sway. Godlessness might be connected to the invention of electric light. There is too much light for a god to light up the world.

Take the body, essential to performance. The living, sweating, breathing, stinking, body. The body set to conform to social mores of appearance and behaviour. First then a clothed body, cleansed, washed, even polished, decorated and perfumed ready for the masquerade. This is a private affair, in a doubled privacy: in the living spaces, and then a further sanctum where the cleansing of the body takes place, where concentrations of waste material extruded from the body are disposed of through water.

Stepping out, the performer appears before a group of other, if not like-minded, persons shunting, shifting, moving or sitting down perhaps. Is this a theatre? No not likely, but it is not ruled out. Each individual is now part of a collective cellular-like body: an audience. The air warms to the complexity in the air: breath, carbon dioxide and methane.

The Broken Knee, R Y Sirb 2008

performance

Enter the performer who might be there already, or might step out from the collective body gathered for the event, as though one of its kind is going critical. Therein lies a tale, a story. A narrative has already emerged in the telling. It begins, but doesn`t continue, not on this page. A red herring like as not.

The body of the performer is alive and kicking, my body or another body. It moves. In fact it can`t stop moving even if some of the movements are more or less invisible. And it follows that the collective body which in this collective passive state is an audience (in its collective active state it could be a crowd or a mob) in movement as a collective, and also as a collection of individuals, each one breathing, fidgeting, moving. The human organism lives to move, the way gossip travels of its own volition driven through the social body. If not it hangs out to die.

These are all human bodies. (Some containing the parts of other mammals undergoing the digestive process as a sort of equivalence that is mammalian cannibalism). We sit ruminating above the engines of digestion occasioned by secret gaseous effusions expelled through clothing. The authorial voice is also the performer on the page. I am both the writer, the performer and later the first reader who is also an audience. As it is read by a reader so I fictitiously perform. I have a fictitious voice and make sounds resembling words, other sounds represent the written word and are understood in sound. Equivalent texts strung out in chains are the written interpretations of the sounds of words formed into necklaces—sentences. The audience are watching, suspicious, although they seem to be listening. Everything I thought I might do is no longer in my mind. It just isn`t there, as though it never was. Later it might return and disappoint me that I didn`t remember what I intended. I am not a parrot. But there is a gift in this. The immediacy of the situation begins to make its own narrative. Tell its own story, if only the audience will pay attention. They do in this case. I could interrupt the flow but do so at the risk of the event breaking down so that the audience would be unable to connect the shards and put them into semblances of narrative order.

I am a fictitious performer. There is more than one audience: the one inside the text. Readers in flesh and blood are another kind of participatory audience. They can read aloud to others and are thus able to produce yet other audiences and so on. Readers are free to engage or not. They might, for example, identify with those who have already left inside this text and put it down, or switched off the tape or stopped the disk.

I fall over something on the floor, a cable, some plastic rubbish, or a discarded book. It is a shaming experience in public. There is a damp gurgle of laughter. It hurts. My knee is crying in pain which spreads down to the foot. I manage to get up and try to walk, hobbling to alleviate the pain. This is going badly. I should swear and scream to draw attention

away from the pain but instead maintain a semblance of social decorum as
though it didn`t happen. Two more leave.

It is already swelling, filling out the trouser at the knee. Standing on
one leg, the other foot is now the recipient of a bowl of pain as it lightly
touches the floor to keep the body in balance. The words of Barbara
Suckfull are in my head. "Sunday Stop The Stop Twenty First
Stop"................... and then over here, and now standing on one foot to
give the other leg a rest, the knee and foot are writ large on a large banner
screaming pain in the mind`s space.

I try to remember what she wrote she said at the time in 1910.
I recall what she wrote as a drawing (*Inv recto* 1956) in the Archives of the
Prinzhorn Collection, Psychiatric Institute of University of Heidelberg
Germany. Her words are on my breath.

> "Sunday.The.21.August.1910.This.Bread.Was.Brought.To.The.Grille.By.
> Holzmeier.Of.Erbshaussen.The.Nurse.Eva.Katarina.
> Holzmaier.Of.Erbshaussen.The.Nurse.With.The.Red.Hair.Fine.And.She.
> Had.Sliced.It.Too.And.Pushed.It.Into.The.Grille.Too.
> And.In.My.Right.Hand.I.Had.The.Pen.Too.And.In.My.Left.
> HandThe.Pencil.Too.And.I.Had.To.Hold.This.Too.Close.Up.To.The.Grille.Hol
> d.Out.Too.AndOh.The.Red.Devil.Too.Reached.
> At.Once.For.The.Pencil.Too.And.The.PointWas.In.My.Hand.
> Too.She.Could.Not.Bear.To.Look.At.It." [1]

The text of this telling floats in time like stale bread, old and musty but
still active in its hardened shell. Her written words made a drawing in her
elegantly formed old Germanic script. Her fortunes as the farmer`s wife
must be imagined beyond the frame of performance routed back into the
asylum between 1910 and 1934. Like an iceberg, so much lying
underneath in subterranean solitude, it mimics the curvilinear enfolding of
the brain tucked up close against interior wall of the bony skull. She was
last heard of in the Werneck Asylum in 1934.

"Like an iceberg mimicking the enfolding of the brain." And again
hopping on one leg now silently mouthing: "The curvilinear enfolding of
the brain tucked up close against the interior surface of the wall of the
bony skull," like the drawing in the text.

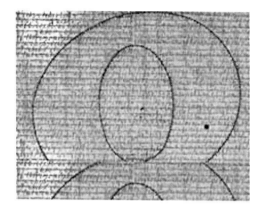

Barbara Suckfull, *Untitled*, 1910, pencil, pen, on
office paper 33 x 42 cm, Inv. 1956 verso

Hopping with the pain from her pencil stuck into my hand, and my left
knee throbbing to the tune of the heart. This injured knee, and the driven
bowl of liquid pain in the foot.

*Miniconjou Chief Big Foot dead after the Massacre
at Wounded Knee*. December 29 South Dakota, 1890.

Curiously the audience watch intently. They can probably sense that I am faking an injury. But not really. The body is centred, like a well balanced marionette. The limbs swing with a grace all of their own.

An audience has at heart the primitive senses of a primeval entity. How otherwise is it able to descend into mob violence? The shape of the audience is complete. My body is still, and silent in the room. We are not waiting. We are all listening. Now in silence and without conscious movement we listen in the silence. Later, without thinking I suddenly get up and limp out of the room. The body took itself out of there before the mind registered what was going on. So it isn`t over yet. It isn`t over and as I come back into the room I know the parts and broken bits in the memories of the audience will be processed into narratives, albeit not ones that I might have predetermined. It slowly breaks up. I sit on a chair. Some leave, smiling. Others shuffle away, out into the darker recesses of the mind. I can hear their voices slowly drift out of hearing. They might be calling up sequences to put together from seemingly disparate events, like a series of repaired fractures. The fictions treat that which was broken from the start. Or they may not have registered sufficient information for a story to emerge like gossip and are already somewhere else in their minds. I am fatigued by the effort. All that is left is the entry point of the pencil in my hand and the pages full of words.

RY Sirb

Notes

[1] All Barbara Suckfull's words quoted here are from the catalogue published by the Hayward Gallery on the occasion of the exhibition *Beyond Reason. Art and Psychosis: Works from the Prinzhorn Collection,* 5 December 1996 - 23 February 1997, organised by the Hayward Gallery.

CHAPTER THIRTEEN

BLOSSOM KEEPERS

ÅSA ANDERSSON

I look at the blossom keepers in Hiroshima. They prune, tidy, and trim. I try to learn, I dust, draw and write. I climb tiny mountains and the valley of the Milky Way.

Bridges take me over ponds and streams, while lines of shells, wisps of bamboo, trails of thoughts, exceed contours.

Shukkeien is a shrink scenery garden, and in this other world, landscape and miniature prevail. Behind the gaze, behind the garden walls, behind my own door, I search for an intimate space.

Rays of light merge in double-exposed emulsion, annexing fragments and distant locations. I borrow glimpses of landscape, and scenes on a tabletop. On the border of fragility, the image becomes a shelter.

Silver rice, ash and glitter, rest upon grass. An eyebath, a teardrop in a well. The lily of the valley, the city's old street lights. Also, the flower I picked as a child. I wore a referendum badge saying, "No to Nuclear Power," a smiling sun in its centre.

With its history of eradication and recovery, *Shukkeien* offers solace, it prospers and grows.

Nurture is a kind of washing, the garden is a tissue. Blossom keepers are pruning pine. Attention is kept on every needle.

©Åsa Andersson, From the series *Blossom keepers, Shukkeien, Hiroshima*,
2005-2009

CHAPTER FOURTEEN

NARRATIVES OF MASTERY IN THE *ZISHA* CERAMICS TRADITION OF CHINA

GEOFFREY GOWLLAND

Introduction

My interest in the process of making artefacts arises from research into the contemporary ceramics production of what is known as *zisha* (or Yixing) pottery, produced in the township of Dingshu, in the Jiangsu province of China.[1] Zisha teapots have been made since the 16th century in the area. Literally meaning *purple sand*, the craft derives its name from the hue of the local clay. In China, these teapots are reputed to be the best for brewing tea—the porous structure of the unglazed fired clay lets the tea *breathe* in the pot. Because of their connection with Chinese tea culture, these teapots have enjoyed the status of luxury items for centuries.

The craft was transformed into an *industry* by the socialist government, and production concentrated in a cooperative factory. However, following on the economic reforms of the late 1970s, artisans became once more able to set up private workshops. Many cater for an exclusive market of wealthy businessmen and politicians, for whom finely crafted zisha teapots are prestige items.

I conducted ethnographic fieldwork among the artisans of Dingshu, with the aim of understanding the modes of transmission of knowledge, acquisition of skills and development of expertise. An interest in the stories and narratives of these artisans was not initially to be part of the reflection; indeed, I was expecting to encounter a situation similar to that of other anthropologists working on craft, namely an environment where speech plays little role in the process of making artefacts—teaching is done through a process of joint attention [2] rather than through words, and artisans would be relatively ill at ease in verbalizing their experience.

In the case of zisha pottery, however, I was intrigued by the importance of verbal instructions in the learning of the craft, and by the fact that artisans, or at least some of them, would be keen to talk at length about their work.

Zisha teapot by Zhao Jianghua, 2006 (photograph by the author)

For instance, although at an initial stage apprentices are taught to take on awkward positions in an attempt to *shape their body* and position their hands, the teacher is soon able to direct the hands of the apprentice through speech: the apprentice internalises the endlessly repeated phrases of the teacher until able to complete all stages of the process without hesitation.

This importance of speech in the learning of the craft might also explain the words of one late master, whom I will call Gu Lao, who would use the analogy of speech to talk about his work: he claimed to have achieved such mastery over his craft as to be able to shape the clay with words alone. I will be returning to this rather interesting image.

But speech is also used in the narratives of the lives of individual artisans. I will be concerned in particular with the narratives artisans told about Master Gu Lao. These narratives, I want to suggest, play a role in the evaluation of the visual properties of pots, and serve to create a link between an object and its maker.

Faced with the omnipresence of speech in an environment that apparently did not require it, has led me to think about the role of speech in the making of artefacts. Indeed, I found myself unable, analytically, to *edit out* speech from my enquiry in the crafting process.

Anthropology, art and language

Yet from a theoretical point of view, there has been a recent trend in the anthropology of material culture and art to critique the use of metaphors and analogies of language in our thinking about objects. Arjun Appadurai, in his influential essay on regimes of value,[3] revealed the problems linked with thinking about objects as inert, and only put in circulation through words, correctly objecting against a tendency in the social sciences, and more broadly in Western thought, to regard the objects exchanged as gifts and commodities as the inert and mute media for the exchange of, ultimately, meaning, status, or symbols. Appadurai called for a "methodological fetishism" in the study of objects. Analysis, according to him, should be directed to things-in-motion, artefacts that traverse boundaries and change status, and through these trajectories acquire "biographies" of sorts. It is only by following these trajectories that objects come to throw light on their human and social context.

In line with this argument, and a decade later, Alfred Gell put forward an even more radical theory. In his monograph *Art and Agency,*[4] Gell argues that anthropology should consider artworks, understood in a broad sense as items that mediate social relationships, as agents in their own right. Gell borrows on the semiotics of Peirce, to consider how things can come to abduct the agency of persons. Objects come to represent persons, stand for persons, and achieve effects in the absenceof their creator. Importantly, his argument is one directed against those who insist on considering artworks in terms of meaning. Meaning, for Gell is not what anthropology should be looking at in things. To take an example he uses, a design reproduced on the shield of a warrior is not meant to convey any sort of meaning, it is not meant to be decoded, but rather to frighten the adversary. If the shield is efficient in this, it is carrying out the intentions of the person who carved it—in the absence of the latter.

I want to acknowledge the validity of some of these critiques, yet want to attempt to reintroduce language, speech acts and narratives in a context where clearly these are important elements for the actors involved. In such a context, how can one retain a sense of the materiality of things whilst taking seriously the narratives that surround them?

The work of the anthropologist Janet Hoskins is particularly pertinent here. Hoskins, mentions her frustration during her fieldwork in Indonesia whilst attempting to draw up the life histories of members of the community in which she was conducting research. She found that, although the people she interviewed did not seem to be interested in talking about their lives as a succession of events, they were willing to talk at length about certain objects in their possession.[5] Hoskins goes on to suggest that the biographies of things become in this sense a kind of substitute for the biographies of persons.

To explore the ideas of narratives and artefacts in zisha ceramics, I want to consider the figure of the master Gu Lao, who was said by many to have been the greatest master of the twentieth century. First, I will attempt to give meaning to his words to the effect that he could shape the clay through speech. At a deeper level of analysis, I will consider the very narratives that have constructed the master *as master*. Finally, I will look at the way narratives are involved in constructing an indissociable link between persons and the products attributed to them, in claims about authenticity. This will enable me to formulate a conclusion about the constitution of both persons and artefacts through narratives.

Speaking and listening to pots

I have mentioned the importance of speech for artisans. I come now to a rather intriguing manifestation of this importance, an instance where speech comes to be associated with the very shaping of the clay.

Zhang, who was one of the last students of Master Gu Lao, once told me that there is a saying in the local dialect, to the effect that some pots can *talk*. However, it only takes the greatest of masters to be able to make a pot that *talks* in such a way. Gu Lao was such a master. In fact he himself used that metaphor of speech to describe the way he worked. Towards the end of his life, he would tell his students that when he was making a pot, it would listen to him speak, "the pot listens to my words. " [6]

The idea is that if the master can *speak* correctly to the pot, the pot *listens*, and at a later stage will be able to *speak* when someone comes across it. To illustrate this point, Zhang told me an anecdote. Once, a scholar came across one of Gu's pots, and after observing it, said "this pot can talk." That it was a scholar who *heard* such things is important. Indeed, it is not given to ordinary people to *hear* a teapot! Anyone might recognise and remark on the beauty of the object, but only a few can really understand it; in the words of Zhang, this scholar could properly *see*.

There is an interesting blurring of registers in the story that Zhang told me. The scholar *sees*, and therefore *hears*? How should one understand this confusion of the senses? The pot might be able to speak, but not in the sense of telling a story; there is no message to decode, and it is not meaning that one derives from looking.

One might note that this description is a rather elegant instance of Gell's theory on the abduction of agency.[7] Gell talked about the capacity for objects to come to take on the agency of persons, so that they act as substitutes for certain persons, their maker for instance, in having certain effects on other people. Here, the agency of the pot in *talking* to others is its capacity for convincing others of the mastery of the artisan. This mastery, as I will explain later, is not to be understood only as high level of expertise, but as having attained a high level of culture.

But what is the master implying with the image of talking to the clay? I would put forward that what Gu seemed to suggest was a kind of sublimation of technical mastery. The image he used was one where thought and speech alone could produce a pot, where the skills and techniques mastered over Gu's career were somehow surpassed, and no longer needed. Another image he used to describe his work might make his ideas clearer. Gu used to say that when he made a pot, the clay was like a child: he would tell it what to do, "go left, go right," and the clay would obey his every command. The relation between master and clay here is then one of authority, the authority of a father over a child, and *speaking* to the pot implies ordering it about. In the image Gu used, it is these orders, this speech, that shapes the clay, rather than the hands or tools.

With this image, I suggest that the master was not only attempting to describe his experience, but also, through a self-narrative, was casting himself as a true master who could effortlessly translate his intentions into clay form. It seems that the master's words are implying that, in some sense, his works are the result of a kind of weaving of words and clay.

The words of the master were given to me as metaphors, yet I will take them literally in another context, in which the object becomes associated with a person. Before that however, I need to give you a sketch of the life of the master—or the narratives I have heard about him. These will explain some of the implications of these metaphors

Narrating the master

I did not hear the words of the master directly, as Gu Lao had died several years before I conducted my fieldwork. These were instead reported by some of his former students, with whom I had the chance to talk at length. I cannot vouch for how accurate the students were in reporting on the words of the master, but this is not what interests me here. Instead, I want to look for a moment at the way people have narrated the master. I will proceed now to a brief account of the story of the master as it was told to me by these students. Some moments of his life, highlighted by the narrators, come to have special signification, which I will interpret later.

One can say that Gu Lao's career was a rather atypical one. Born in the early years of the twentieth century, his career as an artisan starts in the 1930s, and reached its height in the 1980s and 90s. It encompassed the most tumultuous decades of Chinese contemporary history, and in that respect could only have been atypical.

It is unclear who his *real* master was, either his father's mother, or an artisan working for his father, an entrepreneur who had started a pottery business, though not a potter himself. Gu started at the age of eighteen, a relatively late age for starting an apprenticeship, though he was soon found to be particularly talented—talented enough to find work in Shanghai soon after the end of his three-year apprenticeship. There, he worked for a shop that was involved in the forgery of antique zisha pottery, to keep up with a high demand for that type of craft in the 1930s. This must certainly have been a unique opportunity for the future master to learn about classic designs— which were not easily available at the time, either in print or in museums—by having access to private collections and reproductions in books. Moreover, it seems that during the time Gu spent in Shanghai, he was also part of a circle of scholars, who would discuss art theory and Chinese culture.

After the Japanese war, Gu was forced to abandon his craft and to look for work in factories in Shanghai. In 1954, he was called to join a cooperative factory in the town of Dingshu, which became the only legitimate locus of production of the craft. There, as a teacher, he developed the core of his teaching and technical principles. Soon, the Cultural Revolution temporarily put an end to the production of high quality pottery, though activities resumed in the late 1970s, when the craft was *rediscovered* by a connoisseur from Hong Kong, who encouraged artisans to resume production of fine pots.

Gu Lao continued the practice of his art after he retired but in addition fervently took up the practice of calligraphy and read extensively about history and culture. In China, this is quite a common thing to do after retirement but, interestingly, in this case, his students refer to the high level of culture he had achieved, which enabled him to talk about his art with an unprecedented expertise. They also claim that it was only when he started practising calligraphy and reading about Chinese culture that he reached the height of his *genius*.

In this sketch of the master's life, there are a few points I want to take up. Important moments of Gu Lao's life were highlighted by the narrators from whom I heard these stories—in particular, his growing up amongst many talented artisans and his time in Shanghai as part of a circle of intellectuals who discussed art. Finally, I want to address his self-cultivation through the learning of culture and practice of calligraphy.

The anthropologist Yen Yuephing has identified the practice of calligraphy as an important element in the shaping of Chinese persons. She suggests that *wen* (literally writing) and *wenhua* (culture) are central components of personhood in China, and have come to be understood as a glossing over of the raw self by culture.[8]

One might recall the words of the scholar who imagined Gu Lao's pot talking to him about accomplishments. I believe it is to be taken as that quality that the master has developed, in his perfect comprehension of the principles of the craft, but crucially also in his engagement with Chinese culture, in particular through the practice of calligraphy and reading about

Chinese culture. These elements become apparent in the works of the master, and in that sense, there is another abduction of agency in operation, whereby artefacts come to acquire the qualities of the person as it is being shaped. In fact this is how Yen talks of calligraphy, the characters written in ink disclose the make-up of the person, in particular the person's morality.[9]

Hoskins has shown how certain objects can become intimately linked with persons, to the point where the narratives that surround these objects become alternative self-narratives. In the case of Gu Lao, the perfection of an object becomes not so much a token of the expertise of the master as much as the manifestation of the latter's self-cultivation and moral character, which in Chinese culture are developed through the reading of classics and the practice of calligraphy.

I now want to briefly turn to an instance in which this link between person and object comes to be made a little more concrete. There is an important problem of forgery in the Yixing art world. Each object is stamped with the name seal of its creator, but even that seal is easily forged. The only solution for collectors of the craft who wish to determine the authenticity of items in their collections is to seek the assistance of those artisans who were familiar with the maker. In the case of Gu Lao, it was his former students who carried out this task, the same persons who recounted to me the narratives of his life.

Authenticating the master's work

I heard of one such instance from the artisan Zhang who, together with two other former students of the master, were asked to determine whether a pot had indeed been made by the master. Looking at the pot, the students did not simply decide on its authenticity, but pointed out certain features of the work that proved their point: these were perfection in craftsmanship, perfect balance of proportions, a sense of harmony. In sum, these amounted to perfect adherence of the technical and aesthetic principles of the craft and a perfect rendition of them in clay form.

Narratives play a crucial role here. As the artisans single out the characteristics of the pot, these are referred back to the achievements of the master and his self-cultivation through calligraphy and learning of culture and history. The surface of the pot becomes the rendition of the figure of the master and the object comes to be indissociably linked with its maker for the very fact of corresponding to the image of the master formed through narrative.

What intrigues me in these expressions of a link between master and work is that they appear during sessions of authentication. Hypothetically, the authenticator could be wrong, a good forgery might be passed off as authentic, and vice versa. But the words of the former students of the master are authoritative. Through these sessions of authentication, a link is created between an object and a person that might not have existed before.

The object comes to provoke speech in the person who is evaluating it, and it is through speech, and by referring to the idealised life of the master, that the authentication is validated.

Conclusion

I want to suggest that through words, stories and narratives, in reference to the life of Gu Lao, the authenticator is creating an image of the master, and submitting the object to the test, comparing it to the figure of the master. Yet it is also true that the object is fully agent in inspiring these words, in establishing itself as authentic.

There is an interesting process of exclusion, through selection, of objects that come to best correspond to the figure of the master. In fact narratives are performing this function of exclusion. Only those objects that are deemed to correspond to the level of excellency that the master is said to have achieved during his life-time come to be evaluated as authentic.

I mentioned Appadurai's caution that things are not set in motion with words, and one might point out that this is what I am claiming here. However, my position is different: I would suggest that there is, instead, a dialectic in operation, whereby words and narratives create artefacts, but also artefacts in-themselves inspire and sustain these words and narratives.

Notes

[1] This article is based on doctoral research and fieldwork conducted in the Jiangsu Province, China, in 2003-4, with a return visit in 2006. Doctoral research was made possible by the Sutasoma Award (Royal Anthropological Institute), the Anthony Wilkin Fund (Faculty of Archaeology and Anthropology, University of Cambridge), the Ling Roth Fund and Richards Fund (Department of Social Anthropology, University of Cambridge). This article was written when holding a postdoctoral research fellowship at the London School of Economics, funded by the Economic and Social Research Council. The names of informants that appear in this article are pseudonyms.
[2] See for instance Jean Lave and Etienne Wenger, *Situated Learning: Legitimate Peripheral Participation* (Cambridge: Cambridge University Press, 1991), 47-52.
[3] Arjun Appadurai, "Introduction: Commodities and the Politics of Value," in *The Social Life of Things: Commodities in Cultural Perspective*, ed. Arjun Appadurai (Cambridge: Cambridge University Press, 1986).
[4] Alfred Gell, *Art and Agency: An Anthropological Theory* (Oxford: Clarendon Press, 1998).
[5] Janet Hoskins, *Biographical Objects: How Things Tell the Stories of Peoples' Lives* (London: Routledge, 1998), 1-4.
[6] Interview 30 September 2004.
[7] Alfred Gell, ibid.
[8] Yuehping Yen, *Calligraphy and Power in Contemporary Chinese Society* (London: Routledge, 2005), 46
[9] Ibid., 65-7.

CHAPTER FIFTEEN

UNPACKING MY FATHER'S LIBRARY

POLLY GOULD

Funny things, books, as Walter Benjamin remarked in his essay *Unpacking My Library* of 1931, they are not always kept for reading, neither they all used up in the reading of them, but the fact of them as objects persists also, and insists on recognition. Books are also dumb things, things with different stories to tell from those stories printed on their pages. Something so supremely readable as a book might also be an un-interpretable object.

Books, when gathered into a collection like a library, acquire the special quality of a collected object, which has been selected and chosen for some *disinterested* reason. The effect of this is to save them from *use*. Collections are a renewal of the past in the present. As I unpack my father's library I have Benjamin's words in mind:

> Inheritance is the soundest way of acquiring a collection. For a collector's attitude toward his possessions, stems from an owner's feeling of responsibility toward his property. Thus it is, in the highest sense, the attitude of an heir, and the most distinguished trait of a collection is its transmissibility (.......) But one thing should be noted: the phenomenon of collecting loses its meaning as it loses its personal owner. [1]

Although I have acquired a library by the *soundest* means, I am left with the problem of how to inherit the past. Each book can be read once more, open for new interpretation, but the meaning of them to my father, to their personal owner is obscure. The *phenomenon of collecting* has lost the organising principle of the *personal owner,* whose perspective ordered each book into some position in a constellation. It is hard for me to tell which book, which passage may have been of significance. I read them askance.

Pin board made up of photos, newspaper articles, old letters, Polaroids, tape cassettes and drawings, used by the author in the performance *Landscape and Libraries – or what is it that I have lost?* Author's photo.

My opinion, by no means original, is that time does not quite move in straight lines. My history does not function with clear cause and effect, along a line of succession; but on the contrary my memories get re-fashioned with the perspective of new experience. A parallax effect is experienced. This is the effect one gets when closing one eye and pointing at an object. Then opening that eye and closing the other eye to find that one is now pointing at something different. This different view is available by virtue of the distance between your two eyes, a gap of only ten centimetres or so. The parallax effect makes our human visual perception of depth possible. It is also makes it possible for astronomers to measure the constellations of the stars, and the size of the moon.

Gaps of time create this parallax effect also. But for me, with the rope of a linear causality unanchored, memories float free like flotsam and jetsam, the chaotic remains of a shipwreck. I need to pin them down once more, to fix them even, into a temporary constellation to get some sense out of them: that is, to make them readable.

The pin-board in my studio works as a holding place for this; it is a place of montage for fragments, a space to make a constellation of the evidence and remains of pieces of things that I have collected. It is a repository for memories. Different episodes and moments from my life coincide there on the flat plane of a makeshift notice board. Making a photo of it forces it into a composite whole when really it is a mess of pieces that can be reshuffled. Conceiving of it as a *painting* gives the incidental and contingent collection of fragments a cohesion into a totality. A similar manoeuvre is found in the hindsight of biography exemplified in the tidiness of an obituary. Biographies smooth the fragmented experience of a life into a coherent narrative. In both cases it is the technique or technology of reproduction that turns disparate events and assorted objects into the appearance of a whole.

Detail of pin board. Author's photo.

At the centre of my notice board is this announcement from the newspaper. I had cut it out and stuck it into my diary. It reads 'Malcolm Gedge from East Sussex has a divine message for whoever may be listening, "TIME IS A FALLACY AND AN ILLUSION, THEREFORE THERE IS NO FUTURE TIME OR PASTIME."'

The philosopher Agnes Heller in *The Theory of Modernity*, says that to modernists the past is seen as an unchangeable necessity and the future as total freedom.

> In the modernist view, the present is like a railway station where we denizens of the modern world need to catch one of the fast trains that run through, or stop in this location only for a few moments. Those trains will carry us to the future. Settling in the railway station would have meant stagnation – for them.[2]

For them, this is the impossible-to-inhabit place, the present moment of the railway station where the "businessman" that Benjamin speaks of would buy a book to "while away" the time of the journey. But he is not a true collector of books in the vein that Benjamin describes, and is perhaps a victim of this wrong-headed way of understanding the past also. Benjamin's idea, that history should be seen through the metaphor of a constellation, that the past should be viewed by a person, in the present, as a spatial relation of events, counters this. When history becomes geography, the past is no longer unchangeable, and although the future is not necessarily free, the present has the chance to be made habitable once more.

Five years ago, I inherited my father's books. They were mainly about medicine and public health, but there were some significant exceptions, like *Artists and Writers Year Book 1919*—the year of his birth—*The Fens Its Ancient Past and Uncertain Future*, and *The Longacre Book of Trains*. He used to keep a model railway engine on his desk, a toy from his childhood. I have taken over the library from his study where he used to work. I have been sorting through his filing cabinets, his knick-knacks and boxes of old tape cassette recordings. He would dictate on to tape or over the phone, articulating all the punctuation.

Some of the books used props in author's performance *Landscape and Libraries—or what is it that I have lost?* Author's photo.

AUDIO TAPE (father): "Quote up hyphen 2 hyphen date stop um paragraph. What is needed brackets and it is something that the latest British report signally fails close brackets is a recognition that teaching people how to learn is a special skill in its own right stop I wish—capital and italics—competence to practice had spelt that out—stop."

He would dictate his articles onto a small tape cassette machine in his study, surrounded by this library of books on public health and medicine. As a child it was one of the things that I liked to play with best in his office, going over his dictations with my stories.

Detail of pin board. Author's photo.

AUDIO TAPE (father's voice): "And now I am standing in exactly the same position the same distance form the microphone and I am talking in the same kind of tone of voice not projecting not talking in the sort of voice that I would myself use in front of a microphone in a studio even though my face was only two feet or eighteen inches from it but In the sort of voice that some rather dull bugger might use at a boardroom table or a lecture dais—dais and now on my 57th birthday on the 26th January 1976 which is a bleeding miserable day all bloody round, I give you a toast of the future."(child's voice) "Once upon a time there was a little girl."

At around the same time that I was sorting through my father's books, I was struck with a profound yearning for the landscape of my childhood: that is, open fenlands, flat fields and the widest skies. I used to go walking with my father in the Fens where I grew up. We would walk and talk. It reminded me of a photo on my pin board that I took while gazing out of the window of a train fifteen years ago. It looks like the Fens but is actually an alien place to me. I was on my way somewhere I had never been before, far away from home. I had felt an excruciating joy while in this in between place, neither one thing nor the other, dislocated, free, neither here nor there, and of no consequence. Now, a little wiser perhaps, I can see that I may have been riding Heller's modernist train to the free future. The landscape was endless, open and totally lacking in middle distance.

And now I am standing in exactly the same position the same distance from the microphone and I am talking in the same kind of tone of voice. At some point I realised that there was a visual resemblance between my pin-board and the letter rack or *quod libet trompe-l'œil* paintings of sixteenth century artists. It contained photos, letters, pieces of writing, scraps of newspaper, drawings and objects. Take note, for a *trompe-l'œil* to succeed it requires either a very limited depth of field; the things represented should be nearly flat, or alternatively it should employ an illusion of a *window* onto another space, exploiting Albertian perspectives. Successful *trompe-l'œil* must avoid depicting objects in intermediate space, as this is where the parallax factor comes into play most strongly. I love *trompe-l'œil*. Windows onto landscape, like television, slippery images that close pictures within pictures. They fascinate and grip me. Papers in a *trompe-l'œil* painting still seem to intrude into the space of the

Detail of pin board. Author's photo.

viewer, even thought they are flattened. They disrupt the distinction between the picture plane and the viewer's reality. They seem to jump across a limit. They exact a similar kind of shock as that moment when the past interrupts the present, or when one finds a quotation out of context.

I have been sorting though my father's books, his old papers, letters, and things like a biscuit tin of stuff for train sets, and boxes of dusty tape-cassettes I have been going through his old recordings, his interviews, listening and transcribing. The recorded sound is like a trick of the ear, a *trompe-l'oreille*, but in this case it is not space that is overcome, but time. Voices from the past are heard in the here and now, collapsing the distance of intermittent years, into a shocking immediacy—like the flattened plane of a *trompe-l'œil painting*. These paintings work best with dead things and flat things as their subject matter. The hanging game bird is preferred to a caged songbird. We don't expect the former to move, so find its stillness unsurprising. Neither do we expect the dead to speak.

Model railway pieces used a prop in author's performance *Landscape and Libraries—or what is it that I have lost?* Author's photo.

AUDIO TAPE – (father): "The book is published by ES Livingstone, of Tebbitt Place, Edinburgh. It's priced at twenty shillings and postage under our old system of currency was ten pence. That then is all for this time. As before the abstracts are repeated on both tracks of the tape to reduce time wasted in re-winding. (REWIND)…to reduce time wasted in re-winding."

And now I am standing in exactly the same position the same distance from the microphone and I am talking in the same kind of tone of voice at a lecture dais. A lectern is meant as a support for giving lectures, isn't it? But in my father's study he used a lectern as a place of reference. My father would take me to this dictionary that rested there to refer me to points of spelling or meaning He would sometimes leave me little notes in answer to my queries as to the meaning of some word or the proper context for its use.

Detail of pin board showing audio tape cassette. Author's photo.

In her introduction to *Illuminations,* Hannah Arendt writes of the collector's persona as both preserver and destroyer,

> The collector destroys the context in which his object was once only part
> of a greater, living entity. [3]

Arendt speaks of how the time in which he lived had disobliged Benjamin
of inhabiting both modes.

> History itself – that is the break in tradition which took place at the
> beginning of (the twentieth) century – had already relieved him of the task
> of destruction as he only needed to bend down, as it were, to select his
> precious fragments from the pile of debris. [4]

And equally, Benjamin's writing style was concerned with a re-
articulation of fragments, most often achieved through the use of his little
black books, repository of his other major collection, that of quotations.

> The main work consisted in tearing fragments out of their context and
> arranging them in such a way that they illustrated one another and were
> able to prove their raison d'être in a free-flowing state, as it were. [5]

Detail of pin board. Author's photo.

I prefer Walter Benjamin's understanding of historical thinking as a constellation: events perceived through the situated historical perspective of a subject inhabiting his or her own story—once upon a time there was a little girl—as a child I would tell stories on my father's cassette machine, the one he used for dictating articles in his study, going over his dictations with my voice.

Benjamin presents history as a montage not as a narrative: as visual and spatial, as a constellation of events. And in amongst this constellation, *things* speak to us. Collections that have been preserved are imputed with the power to connect us with the past. They connect us because of their capacity for transmissibility. The right balance between preservation and renewal must be maintained. Inheritors must also be interpreters of the things that become theirs. We must be able to re-collect them, to organise them into constellations of our own in order to take care of these dead things, to attend to the peculiar way in which dead things are capable of speaking to us in the present, and in order to be able to take these belongings with us, into the future.

In the negotiation between tradition and newness, some care should be taken. And interpretation should not be overdone. Sontag, in her seminal essay, *Against Interpretation,* makes a plea for dwelling with the "appearance" of works of art rather than "excavating" them out of existence in a search for meaning.[6] Equally, perhaps collecting offers a model for the preservation and transmission of things from the past to the future in a process of recollection and renewal. Towards the end of his essay, Benjamin writes:

> I am not exaggerating when I say that to a true collector the acquisition of an old book is its rebirth. This is the childlike element, which in a collector mingles with the element of old age.[7]

Benjamin shares this sentiment in his regard for children of whom he writes "For children can accomplish the renewal of existence in a hundred unfailing ways. Among children, collecting is only one process of renewal."[8] We find this principle of birth, as that which allows for the renewal of culture, also in Hannah Arendt's idea of *natality*. This is the capacity, as she describes in *The Human Condition*, to insert oneself into the world and "begin a story of ones own."[9]

I have been struck with a profound yearning for the landscape of my childhood. When I was there in the Fens the other weekend I noticed what

I have noticed before: sound is different there. You can hear things over a great distance: there is nothing to interrupt it. Sound collapses, and your gaze just shoots off into the distance with nothing to catch it, the lines of hedgerows, ploughed earth or ditches just carry your eyes faster and further. A train at the edge of as far as you can see, sounds as if it is very close, as close as the rustle of wind on the hedgerow at your feet, or the caw of the black crow at the farther edge of the field.

Model train belonging to author's father as a child and used as prop in author's performance *Landscape and Libraries—or what is it that I have lost?* Author's photo.

On the train last week, I listened in on a conversation between a little girl and her father; she was about six years old and he was in his late fifties, like me, and my father, thirty years ago. It was just the two of them together on the train. She was writing and asking him, "How do you spell ALIEN?" And she asks how to spell flower, and sock, and she asks again and again, one disjointed word after another, and she demands for him to spell *train* and *bird* and again and again he responds. "Is moon M-O-O-N?" "Yes," he says, "It is."

AUDIO TAPE: (train tannoy announcement): "Good morning Ladies and Gentleman we will shortly be arriving at London, Kings Cross where this train will terminate. I would like to remind passengers now leaving the train to make sure you take all your belongings with you."

The sound of a train whistle fading.

Notes

[1] Walter Benjamin, *Illuminations* (Pimlico, London, 1999), 68.

[2] Agnes Heller, *A Theory of Modernity* (Oxford and Massachusetts: Blackwells, 1999), 7.

[3] Hannah Arendt in Benjamin, *Illuminations*, 49.

[4] Ibid.

[5] Ibid., 51.

[6] Susan Sontag, *Against Interpretation* (London: Vintage, 1994).

[7] Benjamin, *Illuminations*, 63.

[8] Ibid., 69.

[9] Hannah Arendt, *The Human Condition* (University of Chicago Press, 1958), 176.

PART III

THE CINEMATIC ESSAY

INTRODUCTION: THE CINEMATIC ESSAY

JANE TORMEY

… a film with its own logic, its own correspondences within itself, its own echoes and rhymes and comparisons. Margaret Tait[1]

Telling Stories considers how art practices relate ideas using their own "logic." This section provides a focused application of the issues and ideas that reoccur throughout *Telling Stories* in the specific context of the *Cinematic Essay*. Sixty years ago the French critic and film director, Alexandre Astruc outlined his vision for a cinematic language in "The Birth of a New Avant-Garde: La Camera-Stylo" (1948). He predicted that cinema would free itself "from the immediate and concrete demands of narrative, to become a means of writing just as flexible and subtle as written language." [2] The cinematic essay is a form that attempts to meet this challenge, incorporating documentary practices, dramatised elements and experimental approaches. It can include poems, photographs, narration and text and is one of the most inventive, challenging, self-reflexive and polysemic forms in current cinema. Characteristically, it emphasises theme over plot and the discovery of narrative through a reflexive and self-critical approach to moving image production.

Astruc's call for a "freestyle of film-making" that enables diverse ideas and a range of expressions solicits tensions in the direction of cinematic form. Later in life, he warns that allowing directors a free rein "would make films that were too artistic, too literary or too esoteric." However, it is these ingredients, borne of contradiction, which set the cinematic essay apart. The essay form is typical of aesthetic practice that is multi-faceted, interdisciplinary and not confined to conventional forms—in this instance, the cinematic narrative. The cinematic essay is difficult to classify within the traditional genres of fiction, drama, documentary and experimental cinema. Genres and styles are fused and collaged: Margaret Tait's personal recollections with a poetic visual delight (*A Portrait of Ga*, 1952), Chris Marker's travelogue with personal diary (*Sans Soleil*, 1983), Patrick Keiller's fiction with political, psycho-geography (*Robinson in Space*, 1996), Alexander Sokurov's photographic focus with philosophical speculation (*Elegy of a Voyage,* 2001), Guy Maddin's documentary with autobiography (*My Winnipeg,* 2007). What links them all, is a disregard for conventional expectations of meaning, of narrative or of unified compositional style. Instead, ideas are pursued through various investigative means, presenting *reality* via multiple expression rather than unitary effect. They each present forms of realism that deny translation into narrative clarity and which allow the factual, the fictional, the autobiographical, the political, the social and the global, to collide.

Astruc's analogy of film with writing is repeated often: in descriptions of Marker, as an essayist "who writes in images" [3] or in Agnès Varda's concern (1961) that "cinema had got lost in cinematographic fiction and it didn't approach … the problems which the novel did." [4] And as with a novel, Varda's descriptive passages run beside dialogue, and discussion of abstract ideas beside descriptive anecdote (Varda, *Les Glaneurs et la Glaneuse,* 2000). But the analogy does not account for the visual expressions that result from the many collisions of style that occur in the essay form. More fundamental, is Siegried Kracauer's insistence that the enabling potential of film, beyond the restrictions of conventional cinematic form and narrative, can "redeem us" from our dormant relation to the physical and cultural world, photographically, and assist us in "discovering the material world with its psychophysical correspondences." [5] The essay form, maintaining what Connolly describes as a "continuous tension" between stylistic approaches, continues to test Kracauer's belief in the possibilities of film as a medium to provoke the viewer. The "logic" of the essay film confronts the seductive nature of film, the manner in which its artifice transforms reality and its potential for social impact. The balance of tensions between the intimate and the political, the visually poetic and the social, distance and abstraction gives the essay form its dynamic.

Interestingly, the film essay increasingly appears as an art form in gallery exhibition (for example, Matthew Buckingham's *Muhheakantuck—Everything has a Name*, 2003, Alfredo Jaar's *The Sound of Silence,* 2007). In contrast, as Don Boyd points out, 2008 saw a number of films on general release that do not follow predictably mainstream narrative structures—Terence Davies, *Of Time and the City*, Steve McQueen, *Hunger* and Alex Gibney, *Gonzo: The Life and Work of Dr. Hunter S. Thompson.* He suggests that digital technologies and internet dissemination release small budget productions from the controlling power of the mainstream film industry and facilitate what he calls the "cinema of ideas."[6]

The *Cinematic Essay* section explores the grammar of the essay film and its relevance to filmmakers and theorists working in contemporary film-making. It examines the manner and structure of narrative and counter-narrative, authorial presence, style, language, rhetoric and ideas with reference to works by, for example, Chris Marker, Agnès Varda, Jean-Luc Godard and Alexander Sokurov. It brings together contributions from writers and film-makers, which discuss the background and contemporary themes of the cinematic essay form; social, political and poetic. The *Cinematic Essay* papers provoke consideration of two aspects in particular that repeatedly reverberate across the different perspectives. The first is the manner of depiction (Tait's "logic" or poetry), the potency of the image and its particular form of resonance that provokes associative chains of memory and reference in the structural form of the film, in Agnes Varda's terms, "gleanings." The other is the nature of authorship in the way our relationship to the author is challenged by the insertion of subjectivity; the film-maker's subjective position in the particular manner of discourse demands an active viewing. Dialogic encounters confuse our conventional relationship with the film as the process communicates on different levels and in different ways: author to himself (Davies), speaking through others (Marker), speaking as commentator (Varda), speaking of recall (Maddin). Both themes, of "logic" and authorship, address the condition of spectator, enunciator, narrator. They demand a procedure in the viewing that does not preclude an ending as in narrative forms. What is perhaps common to these two perspectives, between poem and discourse, is the self reflexivity and the authorial voice—the questioning nature of the authorial voice—and of questioning the position of the authorial voice.

Notes

[1] Margaret Tait, speaking about *Where I Am is Here* (1964) in *Subjects and Sequences: A Margaret Tait Reader,* eds. Peter Todd and Benjamin Cook (London: Lux, 2004), 161.
[2] Roy Armes quotes extracts from this essay in *French Cinema since 1946, Volume Two: The Personal Style* (London: Zwemmer Ltd. 1985), 137-144.
[3] Armes, *French Cinema,* 134
[4] Cited in Alison Smith. *Agnes Varda* (Manchester University Press, 1998), 6.

[5] Dagmar Barnouw citing Kracauer's *Theory of Film: the redemption of physical reality* (1960) in *Critical Realism: History, Photography and the Work of Siegried Kracauer* (Baltimore; London: John Hopkins University Press, 1994), 56.

[6] Don Boyd. "Certificate: Thoughtful," *The Guardian*, 12th November, 2008, 24.

CHAPTER SIXTEEN

THE MELANCHOLY IMAGE:
CHRIS MARKER'S CINE-ESSAYS AND THE
ONTOLOGY OF THE PHOTOGRAPHIC IMAGE

JON KEAR

It was André Bazin who first used the term cine-essay to refer to Chris Marker's films, borrowing the phrase from Jean Vigo's description of his own film *Ã propos de Nice*, he wrote that Marker's *Lettre de Siberié* (1957) was "a documentary film essay at once historical and political but written from the point of view of a poet." [1] This succinctly encapsulates what for Bazin represented the "special case" of Marker's filmmaking, its "unconstruable synthesis" that combines the autobiographical and the impersonal, the political and the poetical, the historical with the fictional, the global with the most quotidian, discreet and intimate. These oppositions have remained the core principles of the dialectics of Marker's cinema. *Lettre de Siberié,* his first major cine-essay, is a case in point, a travelogue presented in the form of a personal letter that charts Marker's impressions of the technological and economic modernization of Siberia in the aftermath of Stalin's death. Though funded by the periodical *France-USSR* and the Foreign Ministry of the Soviet Union it explicitly rejects the documentary style of Soviet socialist realism in which all images of the State had to be, in Marker's own words, "above suspicion" and "positive until infinity." [2] While the film makes no mention of the Gulags to which Stalin sent countless political dissidents to their death, it maintains a wry and somewhat ironical view of the process of renewal and renovation and is sensitive to all in the landscape that jars against conventional wisdom about the region, to everything that fails to conform to official dictat and common cliché. *Lettre de Sibérie* is a hybrid essay that reflects not only on the reconstruction of Siberia as a modern Soviet state but on the Siberian landscape, the conjunction of old and new, the persistence of nature and the onset of modernity that co-exist together. [3] The film's travelogue is as much a journey into the possibilities of cinema itself as an experimental medium, the montage is a sundry collage that intermixes black and white with sepia and colour footage alongside the often rapid editing together of newsreel footage, still photographs, pixilated animation and animated cartoons and even a fake 1950s style American advertisement marketing that ultimate Siberian luxury commodity, the reindeer. The innumerable *mots d'auteur*, playful references, digressions, intermixing of genres, guileful word play and self-conscious impressionism point the way toward the idiosyncrasies that would typify Marker's mature style. The film crystallised what were to become the abiding characteristics of Marker's future cine-essays, with their experiments with montage and subversion of normative cinematic conventions and likewise, through such operations, announced Marker's intention to de-mythologise objective documentary filmmaking by way of forms of self-reflexive commentary upon the film's own modes of construction. This self-reflexivity has become an ever more conspicuous aspect of his filmmaking over the past twenty years and his later major films are as much an inquiry into the history of cinema as a cultural form as they are the form of the history of our culture.

Writing of Proust, Walter Benjamin remarked "all great works of literature found a genre or dissolve one." [4] The same might be said of Marker's films particularly the later so called docufictions like *Sans Soleil* (1982) and *Level 5* (1996), which freely unpick the conventions of the documentary genre and open onto other vistas, such as post-cinema; the CD-ROM *Immemory* and *Level 5's* filmic memory archive, as Raymond Bellour has remarked, might be said to be premature works that anticipate future technological media that have yet to fully arrive.[5] In Marker's hands the cine-essay has been a consciously contrived alternative to the documentary film, a term he has himself continually eschewed believing it to have no relevance to his work. Marker has seen the cine-essay as a mode of engagement with the representation of past and present events that almost systematically finds a place for everything that traditional rationalised histories regard as a surplus and seek to exclude from their mode of discourse: the idiosyncratic, heterogenous, self-reflexive, aphoristic and digressional. His cine-essays have employed a mode of operating that is questioning rather than conclusive, that destabilizes many of the conventions we habitually associate with the discourse of documentary and which serve to domesticate it. Marker's cine-essays therefore concern themselves with representing the past and present events in the form of a historical discourse that is at once archaeological, investigative, demythologising, but which eschews the authority and objectivity of traditional historical representation, and which, like the micro-histories of Michel Foucault or Michel de Certeau, ultimately calls into question the production of truth and the status of the their own discourse.

Despite Marker's notorious aloofness, the absence of Marker's own presence from the majority of his films, these cine-essays are intensely personal in tone and in the manner in which they allusively interweave private and public memory, often setting in train references that evidently have a personal set of associations, as in *Dimanche à Pekin* (1955) where impressions of picturesque China are coloured by allusions to his childhood memories of Jules Verne and watching popular Hollywood movies. This personal tone, owes much to the frequent use of the form of the travelogue and the epistolary mode of address so often present in Marker's most important films, genres that one can trace back to antiquity (the conjunction of old forms and new has been a characteristic of his work, which has been janus faced, looking both to the future and back to the past).[6] An inveterate traveler, Marker's films catalogue his visits to different parts of Europe, Asia, Latin America and Africa, exploring the political and cultural histories of these landscapes. These essays, a record of impressions of travels back and forth between the pre-industrialised landscapes of Africa and Latin America and the post-industrialised economies of Japan and the west, offer a searching examination not only the disparities between different continents, the difficult transitions and uncertain circumstances that have faced post-colonial countries experiencing modernity in quite distinctive ways, but also the persistence, despite westernisation of alterity, of other recalcitrant modes of understanding; the residual store of myths, fables, past historical events and ideas whose traces still inhabit everyday language and cultural rituals. This journey across continents has never simply been a search for contrasts but an encounter with indigenous forms of thinking and cultural expression that western civilisation has gradually forgotten or marginalized. It is also by way of this *worldliness*, through articulating the invisible ties that bind the history of continent to continent, that Marker has tacitly remained one of the most interesting commentators on not only the history of these other continents but on his own.[7]

Marker's travelogues with few notable exceptions come in the form of letters, sometimes to named addressees, as in his letters to Alexandre Medvedkine in *Le Tombeau de Medvedkine*, though mostly to unnamed addressees that make the spectator into a confidant.[8] These letters span the five continents and equally the boundaries of time; the addresses to and from Marker's interlocutors come from the present and the past and sometimes, as in *Level 5*, from beyond time. However, these letters mostly issue from Marker's own always unseen presence, invariably refracted through the voice of others, both male and female, that provide the spoken commentaries to his essays. *Lettre de Siberié,* famously begins "I am writing to you from a faraway country" and later restates "I am writing to you from the end of the world." [9] *Sans Soleil* echoes these words some twenty-five years later.

This epistolary tone imposes a certain style, an *indefinite consistency*, to borrow Merleau-Ponty's useful phrase, on an otherwise diverse oeuvre made up of timely meditations on hot topics, such as his *Loin de Vietnam*, his shorts on the Allende government in Chile in the 1970s, or his more recent work on the Balkans, and more long term projects such as his many essays on post-war Japan, which began with *Le Mystere Koumiko* (1965) and which at intervals he has continued to return to, as well as his reflections on the fate of revolutionary political struggles and the convoluted histories of post-colonialism, first touched upon in his early collaboration with Alain Resnais, *Les Statues meurent aussi* (1953).

The preference for the epistolary essay alludes back to the literary basis of his early work as a poet, writer and journalist. The aforementioned opening sentence of *Lettre de Siberié*, "I am writing to you from the end of the world" ("Je le vous écris du bout du monde") is a quotation from the poet Henri Michaux's *Plume précédeé lointain intérieur* (1938), whose oeuvre has been immensely influential on Marker.[10] This literary basis remains a key departure point for understanding the form of his cine-essays. For all the force of Marker's imagery, as Bazin has written, the prevalent relation in Marker's films is that from ear to eye: "The primordial element is the sonorous beauty (of the enunciation) and it is from there that the mind must leap to the image." [11] The recognition of this "lateral editing," as Bazin refers to it, is not of course to see the word or soundtrack as constituting a discursive element that serves to check or contain the figural plenitude of the image, nor to see the image as a mere supplement to the voice, the visual imagery of Marker's films, particularly in his later cine-essays, asserts its force at every juncture, often establishing an independent, ironizing relation to the text. The image is neither reducible nor subordinate to the word, nor is the word itself devoid of its own figural and even disfiguring qualities—the aphoristic and poetical linguistic frame of Marker's commentaries combined with the fluid and often highly experimental editing of the montage of images, exploits the full potentialities of verbal and visual language. Rather, it is to recognize that the soundtrack plays a crucial structural role in framing, commenting upon and opening channels through which the polysemy of the image resonates. Words comment upon or glide across images, on occasion ponderously, alternately at a pace that is hard to keep track with, but always in a way that questions the relation between sight and sound, the visual and the verbal, As Yvette Biro has remarked, Marker's dynamic editing in *Sans Soleil* (1982), and the complex interaction of word and image in the film, sets up a tension between the film as a fragile warehouse of memory and the mind's struggle to combat the destructiveness of time.[12] The relation between commentary and image, is one that poses questions for viewers about what we see, what it is in the image that touches us and what it is in the image that eludes us. In so doing Marker's films are drawn into a metacritical perspective that reflects back upon the ontological status of the image and its hermeneutics, in short the status we give to the image and the problems it poses of interpretation.

In his earlier work the focus of his attention in this respect is the way words can frame the image. *Lettre de Siberié* sets up ironical juxtapositions between the soundtrack, image and narration, as in the famous sequence where the same footage of the city of Yakutsk is accompanied by three different styles of commentary that frame the footage in distinctly contrasting ways. Here as in *Si j'avais quatre dromadaires* (1966), in which a cameraman and two friends meditate on a series of images, the photograph is treated relatively unproblematically, as an empirical document. It is its translation into words, into a hermeneutical framework, that is the subject of scrutiny. But this question of the captioning of photographic imagery, the semantic relation of image and text in creating meaning, has later been supplanted by a preoccupation with the role of film in mediating reality and constructing public memory. In later films the issue of photographic truth becomes questioned and its potential to generate myth comes to the fore of Marker's attention. This tendency reflects a broader shift in Marker's films onto the role of images in historical discourse and the image's potentiality as a trigger of subjective memory. To put this another way, it is the examination of the way in which the image forms a matrix for the complex interrelation of past and present in the image that becomes the pre-eminent concern of his more recent work. This amendment has coincided with a significant change in mood and tone in Marker's films.

Despite the undimmed future mindedness of Marker's filmmaking, his continued concerns with the political and ethical possibilities of cinematic and post-cinematic forms of representation, Marker's filmmaking has nevertheless undergone a significant change in emphasis, a shift from a focus on the present's relation to the future, to the relation of the present to the past. His most political films of the 1960s, under the influence of the experimental vanguard of Soviet filmmakers, were broadly intended as consciousness raising contributions to the ideological struggles to the post-second world war, but his most important films from the mid-1970s on have sought to re-examine the failure of the revolutionary ideals of this era to achieve its ideological ends and the reverberations of this for the present intellectual and political climate. In his most ambitious recent films, which might be seen as tone poems or concept films dominated by a particular prevailing idea or mood, he is persistently drawn back to melancholic reflections upon this past, and its violent ideological clashes. In these films footage from the political struggles of the 1960s and 1970s (including images of guerrilla warfare in Africa and Latin America, social conflicts and struggles for independence and liberty from colonialism in these continents, but also of course the revolutionary struggles against hegemonic capitalism in Europe and America) is frequently intercut with images from the present to highlight the discontinuities between the political landscape then and now, probing how the burden of the political fall out of this era continues to leave its imprint on the present in a myriad of ways.

Le Fond de l'air est rouge (1977) and *Sans Soleil,* made five years later, are poignant essays on the diminishing expectations for leftist intellectuals and the loss of a clear sighted Marxist vision of the future. The fragments of the past that make up the histories of these films, the references to time and place preserved in the imagery of revolutionary struggles, are permeated by embittered and melancholy reflections. The film focuses on the failure of the libertarian politics that informed the aspirations of Marker's generation to change the world in the form anticipated. Given the prominent role Marxism occupied in French intellectual life in the post-Second-World War period, the failure of the ideals that spurred the *événements* of '68, have perhaps been felt more acutely by the left in France than anywhere else in the west. The history that emerges from Marker's later films is, accordingly, an often dark and disturbing one, invoked in the symbol of Clio, the muse of history and geography, as an intransigent muse of chaos. Regardless of Marker's reflections in his films on the possibility of new media, such as the internet, in establishing new modes of freedom, interactivity and political association, his films present the viewer with the grim and bloody carnage of the twentieth century; a fragile and fraught relationship exists between Marker's reflections about the possibility of future political reconstruction with the dispiriting legacy of the political violence that has marked the recent historical past.

The histories contained in these films provide a vivid and kaleidoscopic perspective on the 1960s, showing the ways the political struggles of this era fundamentally changed the world but failed ultimately to realise its broader utopian aims. In attending to the particular struggles that characterised this epoch, Marker continually reflects upon the limits of historical representation, the attendant blindness and misrecognition that accompanies attempts to understand the present in the full complexity of its continual becoming. Eschewing History's transparent gaze, his films are attentive to the exclusions and omissions of more traditional forms of historical account, continually drawing our attention to the tropes that frame and mediate our perception and image of events and the vexed questions that attend our attempts to understand the unfolding of the past, present and future. In this way his film's attempt to provide alternative interventions into historical discourse that open spaces of reflection and questioning rather than provide definitive accounts of events.

It is tempting to see these recent films as expressions of mourning and melancholy; the theme of mourning is indeed made explicit in his later film, *Level 5*, a free replay of Resnais's *Hiroshima mon amour*, which combines the mourning of the protagonist Laura for her deceased lover with an examination of the attritional battle of Okinawa, which almost entirely wiped out the Okinawan race and led to the bombing of Hirsoshima, while *Sans Soleil* is named after Mussorgsky's melancholic song cycle of love and loss.[13] The two films can in this respect be seen as companion pieces, sharing many of the same themes, subject matter and preoccupations. In his essay *Mourning and Melancholia,* Freud writes that while mourning is the conscious acknowledgment of the loss of a love object and the gradual withdrawal from this object, melancholy results from an individual's inability to break the narcissistic identification that formed the basis of the original attachment to the lost object.[14] The lost object in question is in one respect the lost ideal of the left depicted in these films and with it a certain form of history, but the melancholy of these films also expresses itself in an attachment to the image fragment of the past as both a source of plenitude and loss. The melancholy of

Marker's later films, turns on this tension in Marker's treatment of the image segment or fragment of the past that preserves an aspect of the past itself, and a recognition of the constructedness of the photograph as an image that disfigures the past, that indelibly marks it (that is to say it neither presents an image of the past as it was nor leaves the historical record of the past intact). This conflict as Patrick ffrench has recently remarked expresses itself in an attachment to image on the plane of immanence and as a conduit to the recovery of a deeper set of historical meanings.[15] While attentive to what the photographic image can preserve of the past, at the same time Marker harbors a radical scepticism about the limits of historical representation, the blindness and misrecognition that accompanies our attempts to understand the past through the interpretation of the images that derive from it. His films are in one sense an archive of historical footage that draws us into reflecting on events that have been marginalised or forgotten in official histories, while the attendant commentaries that are brought to bear on the image point to the restricted access these images provide of the past and myths that they have served to generate about it. Hence Marker is simultaneously drawn to the idea of the photograph as something that can preserve historical fragments of the past, while also acutely recognising the limits of the image as not so much a preserved fragment of time, but something that has been abstracted from or displaced in time.

The idea of the photograph as a surviving fragment of time has most famously been associated with André Bazin's essay "Ontologie de l'image photographique," where it has commonly been connected with a defence of photographic realism.[16]   Yet, rather than seeing the photograph as a natural image, a simple reflection or presentation of reality, Bazin attempts more subtly to provide a phenomenological account of photographic sign that explains how the photograph presents itself and is experienced through consciousness and, in some respects more importantly, the underlying psychological responsiveness it provokes in its viewers rather than its claims to truth and reality. At the heart of Bazin's account is a distinction between two forms of realism between a pseudo-realism, a concern with illusion or mere appearance, and a deeper realism, which he equates with a desire to give significant expression to the world. Bazin sees photography not as a true likeness, but as satisfying a deep-seated desire for identity substitutes that can resist the ultimately inexorable march of time. Photography's "realism" serves a subconscious desire to have "the last word in the argument with death by means of the form that endures."[17]   It is for this reason that Bazin begins his account of the evolution of the arts with the embalming of the dead, a practice he describes as responding to a fundamental psychological need to defend the body against the passage of time, against death: "To artificially preserve the bodily appearance is to snatch it from the flow of time. The first Egyptian statue, then, was a mummy tanned and petrified in sodium …Thus is revealed, in the origins of sculpture its primordial function: to preserve being by means of its representation." [18] The invention of photography and cinema thus fulfils a deeply ingrained psychological desire to preserve the world and to carry forth the past into the present.

But the question of what is preserved of the past in the photographic image and how we are to reconcile the psychological desire for restoration of the past with the photographic image itself poses a complex question. The issue of what kind of testimony the image provides of the past pervades non-fiction or documentary filmmaking, where the role of the image as primary source material, a kind of witnesses to events, is accorded a central role. The image as a surviving primary source document invariably serves as testimony to the real, as evidence of the events represented. In this respect the image performs a key role in valorising interpretations of the past, asserting the reliability and authority of the narrative that is relayed of those past events. Yet such documents are mediated in several different respects, both in terms of their immediate conditions and context of production and in the history of their reception, in which such documents are transformed and translated, inflected by the historical discourses and debates of the context in which they are later interpreted.

The fact that the photographic image possesses the capacity to outlive the actual event it depicts complicates our ability to discriminate between what occurred and our representations of it. The photographic image as the trace of an event substitutes its presence for the contingency of the absent moment it depicts, replaces the event itself with the image of an event, creating, in Marker's own phrase, a legend for it. It is in Marker's critical reflection on the image as testimony, that we can understand his strong disavowal of the term documentary to describe his films. *Le Tombeau de Medvedkine* (1993) is prefaced by a quotation from George Steiner: "It is not the literal past that rules us; it is the images of the past." The film is a probing inquiry into the meanings of this quotation through an examination of the uses to which cinema was put in the Stalin era. In the course of the film Marker charts how *Kino Pravda*, the revolutionary cinematography of early Soviet vanguard filmmakers, was gradually stifled and snuffed out as film was increasingly utilised to assert the authoritarian presence of Stalin and promote his own official version of events. Marker's survey of this "kingdom of the shadows" as he refers to it, draws our awareness to the complex interface between reality and celluloid. Examples range from the carefully choreographed 'show-trials' filmed in strict conformity with the conventions of socialist realism, to the passing off of reconstructed Second World War battle scenes for the actual events. Eisenstein's *Bronenosets Potyomkin* (*Battleship Ptomekin*) (1925), so transformed the Ptomekin legend that statues made to commemorate the events were modeled on actors who took part in the film, and, as a consequence of the absence of actual film footage of the events of the October uprising, a film of Adrianov's theatrical restaging of the revolution has since widely been reproduced by publishing houses as the real thing.

This exploration of visual testimony is continued in *Level 5* in relation to archival photographic imagery that has acquired an iconic status as visual documents that bear witness to the battle of Okinawa. Here the selection and manipulation of film footage to fit narrative ends is the focus of Marker's scrutiny. In one passage the protagonist Laura shows footage of a man, subsequently known as Gustave, fleeing with his body on fire after a bombing raid in Borneo. This footage is initially shown as it was in newsreels at the time, ending with the man collapsing and apparently expiring on the ground. The commentary reflects on the power of this image as a haunting symbol of the brutality and inhumanity of war, indeed this footage has been used as visual evidence in different wars around the world (including Okinawa, the Philippines and Vietnam), but goes on to point out how the sequence was edited in such a way to suggest the victim's death. The restored footage, screened immediately afterwards, offers a different conclusion, showing Gustave scrambling to his feet and surviving the ordeal.

At stake here is more than simply a question of the status of the image as visual evidence.[19] In each instance, the examination of the iconicity of the image is not merely a reflection on its meanings in relation to the event in question, but on its later historical reverberations. Hence the image of Gustave burning is associated with later imagery of napalm victims in the Vietnam war, in particular the famous photograph by Kim Phuk of a young Vietnamese girl, naked and suffering from severe napalm burns, running along a road in South Vietnam (a photograph that became such a potent image for the protest movement against the Vietnam war).[20]

Marker's conception of the photograph is thus not one that regards the image as a transparent window onto the events it depicts, but as an *enigmatic message*, that has the power of the image to haunt the imagination even when it has been decoded, understood to be framed, staged or constructed. The examination of these images thus becomes an investigation of the *imaginary* of such images and their complex and shifting histories, revealing the way they connect to other images and events, inflecting them and being inflected by them in turn.[21] Detached from the midst of the original moment in time in which they occur these surviving images from history, far from reconstituting the past, become the raw material from through which the image of the past is continually re-imagined.[22]

As these examples suggest, any attempt to preserve a simple division between events and the images that represent them has to take into account the presence of technologies such as film or photography at those events, and its shaping force on them, either in the form of staging a spectacle in which the photographic representation becomes self-valorising or by inflecting how an event is remembered. Just as in Stendahl's autobiographical *La Vie de Henri Brulard*, where the narrator recalling the scene of a battle he was once engaged in becomes aware that what he is describing is not the battle, but his recollection of an engraving made of it, in Marker's films we are constantly made conscious of the imbricated relationship of representation and history, as well as the gaps between lived histories and their reflected images.[23] In *Sans Soleil* the fictional protagonist is quoted in his letters as stating:

> I remembered that month of January in Tokyo or rather I remember the images I filmed of the month of January in Tokyo. They have substituted themselves for my memory. They are my memory.[24]

Marker's foregrounding of the editorial operations, the frequent discussions in his films of the juxtaposition of particular images, the semantic questions he asks about the act of filming or interpreting film footage, the way we are drawn into the decision making process of composing his films, all need to be seen as a mode of self-reflection that contests the illusion of film as a transitive instrument of reality and the characteristic mode of concealment of its framing operations. Yet, while these strategies of estrangement speak to Marker's critical attitude to the photograph as a fragment of reality, the above quotation speaks of the allure it nevertheless holds for the viewer, an allure given such powerful analysis in Bazin's *Ontologie de l'image photographique*. Marker's enterprise thus becomes a melancholic and elegiac one, lured by this fragment of time that the image re-presents and the recognition that ultimately it points to a void which can never be filled, the absence of the original moment. The photograph's form is the marker of a sense of loss as well as the illusion of something preserved. It signifies the absence of the thing and is thus implicated in its loss.[25] In this way Marker's own position seems to parallel the protagonist of his film *La Jetée* (1962) who is both possessed by the image and by his own loss of the past from which it derived.

Notes

[1] "Un essai documenté par le film...a la fois historique et politique, encore qu'écrit par un poéte." André Bazin, "Chris Marker, Lettre de Sibérie," in *Le Cinema français de la Libération à la Nouvelle Vague* (Paris: Cahiers du cinéma, 1983), 179-181. See Raymond Bellour's discussion of this in Raymond Bellour, "Le Livre, aller, retour," in *Qu'est-ce qu'une Madeleine? A Propos du CD-ROM Immemory de Chris Marker*, Yves Gevaert ed. (Paris: Centre Georges Pompidou, 1997), 66.

[2] Chris Marker, *Commentaires* (Paris: Editions du Seuil, 1961), 43.

[3] Nora M. Alter, *Chris Marker* (Urbana and Chicago: University of Illinois Press, 2006), 27.

[4] Walter Benjamin, "The Image of Proust," in *Illuminations*, trans. Harry Zorn (London: Pimlico Press, 1999), 197.

[5] Bellour, "Le Livre," 124-126.

[6] Alter, *Chris Marker*, 26.

[7] A clear correspondence exists between the films Marker was making at this point his series of journalistic publications known *Petit Planète*, notable for their experimental typography and layout. Each volume described a particular country with photographs and personal impressions intermixed with facts and statistics. This has yet to receive the attention it deserves.

[8] Alter, *Chris Marker*, 26.

[9] Chris Marker, *Lettre de Siberié* (1957).

[10] Henri Michaux, "Plume précédeé lointain intérieur" in *Biographies N.R.F*, ed. Jean-Pierre Martin (Paris: Gallimard, 2003) 193.

[11] Bazin, "Chris Marker, Lettre de Sibérie," 180.

[12] Yvette Biro, "In the Spiral of Time," *Millenium Film Journal*, (Autumn/Winter 1984/85): 174.

[13] To regard the two films as companion films is not to occlude their differences. *Level 5* is about the difficulty of mourning, while the earlier *Sans Soleil*, isn't really a meditation on melancholy, it is melancholy, a filmic expression of a particular state of mind. For *Level 5*, see Jon Kear, "A Game That Must Be Lost,"

in *The Image and the Witness*, eds. Frances Guerin and Roger Hallas (London: Wallflower Press, 2007): 129-142. For *Sans Soleil*, see Jon Kear, *Sunless,* (Wiltshire: Flicks Books, 1999).

[14] Sigmund Freud, "Mourning and Melancholia," in *General Psychological Theory*, ed. Philip Rieff (New York: Collier, 1963), 170.

[15] Patrick ffrench, "The Immanent Ethnography of Chris Marker, Reader of Proust," *Film Studies* 6, (Summer 2005): 87.

[16] André Bazin, *Qu'est-ce que le cinéma?* (Paris: Les Editions du Cerf, 1994), Hugh Gray ed. and trans., *What is Cinema? Vol. 1* (Berkley and Los Angeles: University of California, 1967), 9-16,

[17] Bazin, *What is Cinema?* 9-10.

[18] Ibid.

[19] The connections between Marker's work and Roland Barthes's writings have remained largely unexplored in the literature on Marker (Bellour alludes fleetingly to it) but provide a productive area of comparison. In many ways the development of their ideas follows a comparable trajectory and their work shares similar reference points. Barthes *Mythologies* and *La Chambre Claire* remain key texts for understanding Marker's own approach to the photographic image. Roland Barthes, *Mythologies* (Paris: Seuil, 1957) and *La Chambre Claire; note sur la Photographie*, (Paris: Editions du Seuil, 1980).

[20] Maureen Turim, "Virtual Discourses of History: Collage, Narrative or Documents in Chris Marker's Level 5," *Sites* 4, no. 2 (Fall 2000): 370.

[21] On this aspect of Marker's use of images, see Yvonne Spielmann, "Visual Forms of Representation and Simulation. A Study of Chris Marker's 'Level 5'," *Convergences* 6, 2, Summer 2000: 31-40 and Raymond Bellour, "Le Livre, aller, retour," 65-109

[22] Sigmund Freud, *Beyond the Pleasure Principle* (1920) in trans. and ed. James Strachey, *The Standard Edition of the Complete Works of Sigmund Freud*, vol. XVIII (London: Hogarth Press, 1955), 13-17.

[23] Stendahl, *La Vie de Henri Brulard*, trans. John Sturrock (London: Penguin, 1995), 15.

[24] Chris Marker, *Sans Soleil* (1982)

[25] See Richard Stamelman, *Lost Beyond Telling: Representations of Death and Absence in Modern French Poetry* (Ithaca, New York: Cornell University Press, 1985), 20.

CHAPTER SEVENTEEN

PLAYING WITH DEATH.
THE AESTHETICS OF GLEANING IN AGNÈS
VARDA'S *LES GLANEURS ET LA GLANEUSE*

JAKOB HESLER

1. Reading the World. The Poetics of the Essay Film

"One cannot produce something that bears witness as coldly as one would make a sausage," the young Agnès Varda said in a 1961 group interview with Georges Sadoul.[1] The sentence alluded to King Vidor's famous comparison of the studio system to a sausage factory; it also challenged Sadoul's tentative definition earlier in the interview of documentary as *potato film*, in terms of use value, as opposed to the sublimely useless flowers of fictional film.[2] But most importantly, Varda's phrase described her own approach to documentary filmmaking. Pure objectivity is not what the documentarist could or should strive for: bearing witness always implies the subject. This approach has remained central in Varda's non-fiction oeuvre ever since. These films, however diverse thematically and formally, all combine objective observation and personal perspectives.[3] This double strategy is also one reason why many of them can be called essayistic. The recent DVD edition of Varda's mostly non-fictional short films has made this aesthetics more easily accessible.[4] Yet in this context, her feature-length *Les glaneurs et la glaneuse* (*The Gleaners and I*, 2000) is of particular interest. Like the shorts, it is both objective and subjective: thematic enquiries into socio-economical and artistic practices of gleaning, that is picking up leftovers after harvest, alternate with footnotes on art history and intimate self-portraits of the artist as ageing woman. But more than that, the film also autoreflexively complements essayistic practice with a dense theory of the essayistic, centred in the conceptual image of gleaning, which I shall explore in the following. The theme of gleaning refracts essential aspects of Varda's entire oeuvre, to which I shall return only briefly in the concluding section. The main thrust will be the exploration of gleaning as economical, ethical and aesthetical practice in *The Gleaners*. I suggest an interpretation along the lines of Theodor W. Adorno's poetics of the literary essay ("The Essay as Form," 1958).[5] With Adorno the essay film's irritating oscillation between subjective and objective filmic modes, between art and argument, can be analysed as its core strategy. While not producing autonomous art proper, the film essayist frees herself from rigid conventions of objectivity so as to gain insights that escape the mainstream discourse of sobriety. Thus, the perspective from Adorno reveals profound connections between the seemingly irreconcilable personal and observational strands of *The Gleaners*. The author subject's presence in the frame is neither pure autobiographical expression nor an indication of vanity, as the voluntary literacy teacher Alain F. suspects in the sequel *Les Glaneurs et la glaneuse... deux ans après* (2002). Subjectivity has an epistemic function. Gleaning then emerges as a "methodically unmethodical" (Adorno) approach to the world, a non-linear enquiry into the marginal, in a process of "luck and play," whose subjectivity and finitude render it all the more perceptive and precise.[6]

In his essay about the essay, Adorno is not so much concerned with the form's literary history. In a critique of Descartes' *Discours de la Méthode*, he rather sketches a programmatic poetics of philosophical writing. The essay takes into account the crisis of rationality in post-enlightenment modernity. Instead of using its object merely as an example for already established concepts, neatly separating form and content in a positivist manner, the essay configures its material in a non-hierachical textual process. Thereby it opens itself up to aspects that escape the mathematical ideal of truth in Cartesian science, an ideal similarly present in the evidentiary rhetoric of documentary. Adorno's poetics of writing is at the same time one of reading, a theory of interpretation not only directed at cultural artefacts, but at human experience in general. Transposed to *The Gleaners*, Adorno's concept of essayistic reading reveals an important dimension of gleaning. Ever since Alexandre Astruc's caméra-stylo, the essay film has been analysed in terms of filmic writing: the film essayist uses the camera (in *The Gleaner*'s case: a handheld consumer Digicam) with the same stylistic freedom and logical precision as the novelist uses the pen. Varda herself has for decades advocated a related concept, her famous cinécriture, cine-writing.[7] Yet whereas these notions of filmic writing refer to the production side, the concept of gleaning expands the model towards filmic reception and adds to cine-writing the dimension of cinematic reading. Not only do viewers read film, film itself is engaged in reading. The two aspects actually converge: film's aesthetic organisation, the writing, embodies the reading. Just as Adorno sees the literary essay as an endeavour in reading an object, gleaning can then be read as a form of cinematically reading the text of the world. Gleaning is understanding.[8] It sets out with the immediacy of visual appearance but then tries to break through "what masks itself as objectivity"—for example potato size standards.[9]

2. Taking Potatoes, Taking Pictures. Ethics and Aesthetics

Varda does not make documentaries like one produces sausages. She rather makes them like one picks up potatoes on a field after the main harvest. At least this is what emerges from *The Gleaners*, with which Varda has made a *potato film* after all, if not quite in Sadoul's sense. Here, the potato, and the hand that is reaching for it, filmed with the other hand, star as metapoetical Leitmotive that pertain to all dimensions of gleaning. Early in the film, one sees a heap of abandoned potatoes on a plantation somewhere in the French province. For the farmers, they are useless rejects: they do not meet the measurement standards expected from a marketable potato. For the many individuals just arriving on the site in the scene, they are free food. These people are gleaners in the literal sense of the word, searching rural fields or urban bins for edible leftovers. In the wake of industrial farming, gleaning now focuses on the leftovers of consumerism, things incompatible with the system of exchange. Many people glean out of poverty, and it is to them to whom Varda dedicates much of her film in tactful empathy. However, she is not making a socio-political reportage. The unemployed man who offers gleaned objects to his neighbours, the two star chef who gleans wild herbs—neither is reducible to their economical condition. Gleaning implies an awareness of the dignity of matter that corresponds to Adorno's idea of the essay's non-violent relation to the object. In gleaning, like in the essay, ethical motives coincide with an epistemic approach beyond traditional knowledge. Gleaning is "working without knowing," and thus comparable to psychoanalysis, as winemaker and Lacanian psychoanalyst Jean Laplanche puts it in *Les glaneurs et la glaneuse... deux ans après*. The analyst picks up the patient's unconscious discourse leftovers, what transcends the system of ego rationality; the gleaner picks up what transcends economical rationality. In a tableau vivant in the film's first few minutes, Varda imitates a painting of a gleaner by Jules Breton and then exchanges the wheat for the camera. She is a gleaner as well, in fact a gleaner of gleaning, as she reveals when she points her little camera at the camera that is actually filming. The ethos of gleaning leads her to dismiss the pseudo-objective standards of journalism.[10] These tend to dissolve the marginal into pre-established structures of signification, in order to maintain the status quo.[11] Varda's film is far from a conventional victim documentary and its conceptual victimisation, which repeats the violence it pretends to elucidate. Instead, Varda opts for a very intimate interview style.

Gleaning is a mode of experience, a mode of aisthesis in the literal Greek sense of perception. Sensitive to what Adorno calls the non-identical, to what exceeds the logic of identity, it refrains from reducing experience to the already known. This differential aesthetics is also symbolised in the potato sequence. When Varda comes across a potato in the shape of a heart, she is intrigued: a potato can be more than a potato – it can be a sign. Here, not only does the heart as the icon of misericordia signify the ethical use of refuse, which is put into practice in a meal program that Varda inititates in a later sequence under the name *Good Heart Charity Meals*, but also, the poetical reading of the potato points to an aesthetic dimension in the modern sense of art practice. Varda pursues this theme further in numerous portraits of gleaning artists. The artist, transfiguring matter by profession, can redefine agricultural waste or disused consumer products as raw material and thereby undermine the ruling semantic of things. The point of this is not to reintegrate semiotic waste in the cycle of consumption, as Varda seems to suspect in the case of an exhibition of highly priced works by the artist Sze at the Fondation Cartier in Paris.[12] Gleaning rather exposes uselessness itself. This points back to the tradition of the ready-made, and also to Walter Benjamin's description, in his Arcades Project, of the rag-picker / flaneur / poet who strolls through society's rubble gathering semiotic building blocks for his allegories of modernity.[13] In Varda, the ethical aesthetic of gleaning as a rebellion against the terror of total usefulness had a precursor in *Sans toit ni Loi* (*Vagabond*, 1985). This film about the young homeless woman Mona respects the dignity of the protagonist by not spelling out reasons for her incomprehensible behaviour and for her negation of society's rules. Varda has called this Mona's "great No." [14] The vagabond Mona, with her roaming and straying, also anticipates another aspect of gleaning: its particular style of movement.

3. Cine-Hand. The Subject of Play

The gleaner is a gatherer, not a hunter. Whereas Cartesian science and journalism follow a methodos, that is a systematic unidirectional path to truth, gleaning moves in a style that defies ideals of methodical orderliness. *The Gleaners* is not structured according to an argument, but as an informal travel diary, including several motorway sequences: not as a linear expedition but as a flânerie, reminiscent of Varda's earliest documentaries, the comissioned travelogues *Du côté de la côte* and *O saisons, ô châteaux* (both 1958) with their serene strolling and profound contemplation. What appears to be arbitrarily subjective is in fact methodically unmethodical: the aimlessly strolling gleaner is open to unexpected finds that in turn lead to clues for further strolling, such as an eclectic painting found by Varda in a flea market, which combines the motifs of two famous paintings of gleaners. Strolling and finding correspond to the literary essay's trial-and-error character, the approach of "luck and play" that is encapsulated in the word *essay, to try* itself.[15] This notion of play is central for Varda, who is almost addicted to the play with words, as many of her film titles show, and also to the play with images. Varda devotes a striking autoreflexive sequence to the play in *The Gleaners*. In one of the motorway scenes, she sits in the car and pretends to grab passing trucks, forming a frame with her fingers. Her hand *takes pictures* and seemingly crushes the trucks in the process. Varda comments: "Again one hand filming the other hand, and more trucks. I'd like to capture them. To retain things passing? No, just to play." The playing subject, detached from everyday rules, is free to try out new concepts on objects, for example to see a heartening symbol in heart-shaped foodstuff. The play is a virtually infinite process of de- and re-contextualisation, Kant's play of imagination in the aesthetic judgement. In *The Gleaners*, there are many examples of such playfulness. When Varda compares mould on the ceiling of her flat to abstract paintings, she frames it, like she did with the trucks, but this time with a special effect. Other instances of playfulness include the scene with the accidentally recorded bouncing lens cap or the recurring staging of scenes and paintings. Varda, who had done similar art historical travesties before, appears to enjoy them greatly.[16] This highlights another aspect of "luck and play," or rather "Glück und Spiel," as the German original has it. German Glück means both luck *and* happiness: play and pleasure are related intrinsically. For the Marxist Adorno they point to a utopian future.

The agent of the playful taking of pictures is exposed in both the motorway and the potato sequence: the hand. Like the potato, it opens up a spectrum of metapoetical aspects.[17] The author's hand entering the frame is a figure of self-reflexivity. In a related sequence of unsparing close-ups of her wrinkled hand, Varda calls this "(her) project: to film with one hand my other hand. To enter into the horror of it." Yet she does not seek to overcome the horror, to stabilise the self. Remarkably, her self-portrait, while using the classical narcissistic device of a mirror, gives it a disturbing twist: the mirror featured in the sequence does not show the expected face of Varda, but, surprisingly, an enigmatic drawing of a face. When Varda films souvenirs she brought from Japan, she says: "For forgetful me, it's what I've gleaned that tells where I've been." But what is a self that does not know where it has been? The biographical details of *The Gleaners* do not form a coherent autobiographical narrative. They are rather, like the hand, elements of the auto-reflexive discourse. Varda's hands imply both the receptive (cine-reading) and productive aspect (cine-writing) of taking and making pictures. The brand new handheld Digicam that Varda uses for most of the film is in fact the ultimate incarnation of the caméra-stylo, a perfect cine-pen fitting in the author's palm, enabling unprecedented intimacy.[18] Furthermore, the hand is the body's most outward extremity, an authorial proxy between subject and object. It is a metonym of greeting and touching, hinting at Varda's empathic interview style. This tactile approach suggests a cinema beyond the dogma of evidentiary visibility.[19] The cine-hand supersedes the cine-eye. It does not clench into a cine-fist but attempts a non-violent style of taking. At the same time it belongs to a concrete person, to an ageing woman facing death.[20] With Varda's hand, the author's mortality and fallibility literally enter the picture. This radically subverts the documentary code of handheld sequences, in which the author usually functions as guarantor of authenticity. It also points to the fundamental importance of temporality in gleaning.

4. Capturing Passing. The Temporality of Gleaning

Yvette Biró has suggested that time is a main protagonist of Varda's films.[21] This can easily be extended to *The Gleaners*. Many gleaned objects in the film show the mark of time. The motorway sequence reveals Varda's epistemological reaction. She would like to "capture" the trucks, she says, but not "to retain things passing." To retain would imply to appropriate the object and so to halt its temporality. Yet that seems exactly to be what Varda usually does with her gleanings, e.g. when she creates a veritable collection of heart-shaped potatoes. But Varda ironically admits the metaphysical urge to stop time when she comes across a clock without hands. "This is my kind of thing. You don't see time passing." In the next sequence, she shows what appears to be a cropped photograph of her face moving laterally behind the clock: a dialectical image of the collision of stillness and passing in capturing. Varda goes on to say: "I like filming rot, leftovers, waste, mould and trash." One day, she returns home and finds her potato collection in an advanced stage of decay. These images show the return of repressed temporality: the potato, extracted from its context by the collector to save it from death, dies nevertheless.[22] But there is more to these images: the strange beauty of the bizarre rot formations. The gleaner turns the tables, plays with figurations of death, and transforms passing into an aesthetic experience. Retaining objects is to some extent inevitable in capturing. Yet in its temporal playfulness, gleaning respects the object's intrinsic temporality. This may sound exaggerated when applied to potatoes, but it is of the utmost importance with human objects, objects that are actually subjects – like Varda herself.

Again, in Varda's "project" of filming herself, temporality, "the horror of it," is central. Like Mona, and like Cléo in *Cléo de 5 à 7*, Varda is going to die, but she turns this fate into an epistemic adventure. She approaches death in the process of dying, which from an existential point of view converges with the process of living, as Martin Heidegger famously suggested in *Being and Time*. The gleaner's peculiar temporal communion with the object resembles Heidegger's approach to existential temporality. He argues that the temporality of human self-experience differs from scientific notions of time, since the human subject is mortal and temporal. Self-understanding is only possible if one tunes in to this temporality of finitude. And that is precisely what happens in *The Gleaners*, on the levels of autobiographical and social time, but also on the level of cinematic time: the film itself is a playful edit of gleanings whose temporal structure, in connection with the sequel, would deserve an analysis of its own. However, whereas Heidegger advocates full self-comprehension, Varda is aware of its horrifying limits, as she goes on to say: "I feel like an animal. Worse: I am an animal I don't know." In this lucid self-detachment, Varda's cinécriture suggests an aspect of cine-writing that goes beyond Astruc's author-centred caméra-stylo: the incising temporal effect of écriture in the poststructuralist sense. It is not possible to pursue these implications further here. However, for the purposes of non-fiction theory, it must be noted that in films dealing with human experience, reflected subjectivity is in a way more objective than timeless objectivity, different from what proponents of a scientific concept of truth in documentary studies contend.[23] In the essay film's "intellectual experience," truth indeed proves to have, as Adorno puts it, a "temporal core."[24]

5. Collected Works. Gleaning Varda's Oeuvre

Expositions of concepts always run a risk of exaggerating their importance. Yet in the case of gleaning, it is difficult to resist its analytical appeal for Varda's oeuvre on the whole. In this remaining paragraph, I can merely point to some aspects. I have already mentioned gleaning as a style of movement that could be explored in more detail in the early tourist shorts' travelogue-style strolling, or in Cléo's and Mona's existential straying.

The art collector is a stroller as well - subject of *Ydessa, les ours et etc.* (2004) about Ydessa Hendeles, the American artist-cum-curator-cum-collector of teddybears. Varda turns into a collector of images herself in films such as *Daguerréotypes* (1976), a string of portraits of people who live in her street, or *Les dites cariatides* (1984), where she reads a series of shots of female statues and deconstructs late nineteenth century architectural language. Documentary as a collection of shots was already a theme of *Salut les Cubains* (1963, entirely composed of still images). Still another form of gleaning is the compilation film, which gathers and reads pre-existing footage, like Varda's *L'Univers de Jacques Demy* (1995) with extracts from Demy's work.[25] A less known project of image reading is Varda's *Une minute pour une image* (1983), a collection of TV shorts each dwelling on one particular photograph.[26] However, perhaps the most attractive aspect would be the aesthetics of self-gleaning. In *Ulysse* (1982), Varda engages in a complex close-reading of an old photograph she took in the 50s, including an interview with the model 30 years later.[27] *The Gleaners* similarly points back to Varda's very beginnings, to her first independently produced non-fiction film, the post-surrealist collage *L'Opéra-Mouffe* (1958). Both films are marked by subjective perspectives: the meditation on death in *The Gleaners* answers that on pregnancy in

L'Opéra-Mouffe. The film begins with a self-portrait of the pregnant Varda and then combines everyday life views of the poor Paris market road Rue Mouffetard, interspersed with fictional episodes, erotic and dreamlike, and surreal tabletop arrangements involving disconcertingly cruel imagery of gestation. If *L'Opéra-Mouffe* engages in gleaning the psyche's internal stream of images from a pregant woman's point of view, *The Gleaners* directs the look outward and, by the very act of dwelling on the mortality of the author-subject, transcends it so as to gain new perspectives on the world.[28]

Notes

[1] Georges Sadoul, "Rendez-vous aux amis. Deux heures autour d'un micro avec Agnès Varda, Henri Colpi, Armand Gatti et Alain Resnais," in Georges Sadoul, *Chronique du cinéma français 1939-1967. Ecrits (1)* (Paris: Union générale d'éditions, 1979), 226-246; 245. In this interview, Sadoul gathered (with the exception of Chris Marker) the informal circle of filmmaking friends that was later labelled the Left Bank Group and that can be seen as the cinematic essay's historical origin.

[2] Vidor is quoted in Steven J. Ross, *Working-class Hollywood. Silent Film and the Shaping of Class in America* (Princeton: Princeton University Press, 1998), 121.

[3] This approach has often been noted (cf. Jean-Yves Bloch, "Cléo de 5 à 7. 'Le violon et le métronome'," in: *études cinématographiques* 179-186 (1991): 119-139; 127. Varda herself refers to her non-fiction work as *subjective documentary*. (cf. Agnès Varda, "Ich filme gerne echte Menschen." In Astrid Ofner, ed., *Jacques Demy / Agnès Varda* (Vienna: Viennale, 2006), 94-96; 96).

[4] *Tous Courts*, 2007, Ciné-Tamaris. On DVD 1, Varda lists the film *7 P., cuis., s. de b.* (1984) explicitly as an "essai." The film, an imaginary exploration of an empty house, combines documentary and narrative strategies. However, it does not involve the discursive dimension that will be essential in my approach.

[5] Theodor W. Adorno "The Essay as Form," trans. Robert Hullot-Kentor and Frederic Will, *New German Critique* 32 (1984): 151-171. I quote the reprint in *The Adorno Reader,* ed. Brian O'Connor (Oxford: Blackwell, 2000), 92-111.

[6] Adorno, 93. In a partly similar argument, Anne Rutherford has detected a poetics of mimetic experience in *The Gleaners*. She insists on the importance of subjectivity and affectivity, but underestimates the role of discursive thought. Cf. Anne Rutherford, "The Poetics of a Potato Documentary that Gets Under the Skin," *Metro* 137 (2003): 126-131.

[7] For her definition of cinécriture, cf. Agnès Varda, VARDA par AGNES (Paris: Cahiers du cinéma, 1994), 14. Varda's concept appears to be directed at auteurist readings of Astruc exaggerating the significance of the actual screenwriting.

[8] Martin Heidegger points to this when he analyses the ancient Greek concept of Logos as reading, gathering and laying, based on the etymology of Greek legein, Latin legere and German lesen. Reading (legere) implies taking and gathering (colligere), understanding (intellegere) and selecting (eligere). Cf. Martin Heidegger, "Logos (Heraclitus Fragment B50)," in *Early Greek Thinking*, (New York: Harper & Row, 1975), 59-79.

[9] Adorno, 93.

[10] In a late episode about a legal quarrel between punks and a supermarket manager in a provincial town.

[11] Cf. Adorno, 103.

[12] Ironically, the same gallery recently hosted Varda's photography exhibition *L'Île et Elle* (2007).

[13] Varda has always been fond of found objects, cf. the surrealist scenes in *L'Opéra-Mouffe*. It is relevant that Varda had started her career as a photographer: the surrealist aspect of Varda's work fits, at least historically, to Susan Sontag's thesis about photography's essentially surrealist sensitivity: collecting and quoting images can be seen as a surrealist activity.

[14] Agnès Varda, *VARDA par AGNES*, 168.

[15] Adorno, 93.

[16] Compare Varda's photograph *Autoportrait à Venise* after Bellini in Agnès Varda, *VARDA par AGNES*, p. 4-5. Also cf. Frank Curot, "Références picturales et style filmique dans *Jane B. par Agnès V.*" In *études cinématographiques* 179-186 (2003): 155-171.

[17] For a discussion of hand sequences in two other eminent film essayists, cf. Volker Pantenburg, *Film als Theorie: Bildforschung bei Harun Farocki und Jean-Luc Godard* (Bielefeld: Transscript, 2006): 235-274. Pantenburg himself does not use the term *essay film*, which he criticises as either too narrow, if defined in a genre sense, or too wide, if defined as a filmic mode. However, these definitions are not mutually exclusive. Adopting *both* of them amounts to a useful delineation of the essayistic in cinema.

[18] Bruno Cornellier has argued that after the lightweight innovations of the 1960s, Varda's DV technique marks a new stage in the technology of documentary. Cf. Bruno Cornellier, "La glaneuse et sa caméra. Ou la réinscription de la subjectivité par le numérique,"
http://www.cadrage.net/films/glaneursetglaneuse/glaneursetlaglaneuse.html

[19] Jake Wilson has called the camera style in *The Gleaners* tactile because it is more concerned with texture than with large three-dimensional canvasses. Cf. Jake Wilson, "Trash and Treasure. The Gleaners and I,"
http://www.sensesofcinema.com/contents/02/23/gleaners.html#1

[20] The sequence recalls Varda's farewell to her husband Jacques Demy, *Jacquot de Nantes* (1991), with its close-ups of Demy's wrinkled hands, and also the opening sequence of *Cléo de 5 à 7*, where hands deal out threatening Tarot cards. The theme recurs in Anne Huet's interview film *Du coq à l'âne (des mains et des objets)*, which focuses exclusively on the hands of the interviewers and of Varda.

[21] Cf. Yvette Biró, "Les caryatides du temps. Ou le traitement du temps dans l'oeuvre d'Agnès Varda" *études cinématographiques* 179-186 (1991): 41-55; 41.

[22] Conversely, Varda's visit at the Marey museum in *The Gleaners* could be seen as an attempt to heal photographic capture. Varda shows the chronophotographies as film clips, not as individual shots, in a sense undoing the violence of Marey's chronophotographic rifle.

[23] Cf. Noël Carroll, "Nonfiction Film and Postmodernist Skepticism," in *Post-theory. Reconstructing Film Studies,* eds. David Bordwell and Noël Carroll (Madison: University of Wisconsin Press, 1996). It is no coincidence that Carroll chooses the example of an ahistorical marine biology film in his facile apology of scientific truth standards in documentary.

[24] Adorno 99.

[25] It is remarkable that the compilation film was created and advanced by women, Esfir Shub and later Left Bank intellectual Nicole Védrès, whose *Paris 1900* (1947) was an important inspiration for Resnais and Marker, and probably also for Varda. A feminist reading of gleaning would be very desirable but cannot be pursued here.

[26] Interestingly, the first of the 14 shorts included in *Tous Courts* is devoted to the pictures of Algerian women by Marc Garanger that were also a subject of Harun Farocki's later essay film *Bilder der Welt und Inschrift des Krieges* (*Images of the World and the Inscription of War,* 1989).

[27] The three shorts *Salut les Cubains*, *Ulysse* and *Ydessa* were combined for theatrical release as *Cinévardaphoto* (2004) and are included on *Tous Courts*.

[28] I would like to thank Michael Patrick Weedy for proofreading my manuscript.

CHAPTER EIGHTEEN

RETRO-MODULAR CINEMATIC NARRATIVE:
JEAN-LUC GODARD'S *MASCULIN FÉMININ*
IN THE DIGITAL AGE

ALEX MUNT

This is where the trouble begins. Is the cinema catalogued as a whole or a
part?
—Jean-Luc Godard[1]

Fig. 1 New Wave theme for
publicity of Flickerfest Film
Festival 2009
(Sydney, Australia).
© Flickerfest

The French New Wave is officially middle-aged. The 50th anniversary of
this momentous film movement is being celebrated with a slate of film
retrospectives, exhibitions, books, DVD media together with a general
enthusiasm for New Wave imagery. To cite three recent examples: the
retrospective screened at the Australian Cinémathèque *Breathless: French
New Wave Turns 50*[2]; Richard Brody's new book *Everything is Cinema:
The Working Life of Jean-Luc Godard*[3]; and the "Catch the next new
wave" theme adopted by 2009 *Flickerfest* Film Festival[4] for its
promotional trailers and publicity. In each case, Jean-Luc Godard is cast as
a key figure in the revival. These phenomena are part of a wider 1960s

revival in contemporary culture, think: the reappearance of the mini, the shift-dress, geometric fabrics and retro make-up design of dark eyeliner and long lashes. In Australia, upcoming young actor Gracie Otto has appeared as Jean Seberg in Godard's *Breathless* (1959) inspired *Flickerfest* trailers and as 60s fashion icon Twiggy in a *Cosmopolitan* magazine feature on "retro-glam makeovers." [5]

The 1960s are also in vogue for the cinema. And it is in this spirit, that this essay proceeds via a *jump cut* that splices together two distinct moments of the cinema separated by half a century: where the *Nouvelle Vague* collides with an emerging wave of international low budget, digital cinema. The UK has the *microbudget* feature filmmaking scheme *Microwave* (Film London) and *Warp X*, a new digital film studio based in Sheffield. *Warp X Australia* will be in action in 2010. And in the US, it is the *Mumblecore* D.I.Y. digital film movement that provides the momentum. There is a certain retro tone to the description of 'new' low budget cinema, one that connects with the New Wave and its counterpart film movements. *Warp X* call for a "re-tox" of British cinema by way of "an injection of adventure" and an "antidote to the prevailing diet of blandness and repeated formulas." [6] The twenty-something Mumblecore filmmakers have been dubbed "slackavetes" —to describe their part 1990s Indie slacker and part 1960s John Cassavetes inspired cinema.[7] The momentum of contemporary low budget cinema is being driven by the allure of digital filmmaking and its potential to reinvigorate narrative cinema in the spirit of its celluloid predecessors.

In the digital age, media theorist Lev Manovich is quick to point out that low budget, digital filmmaking is linked to the allied *cinéma verite* style movements of the late 1950s to 1960s. He provides the label *DV Realism* to situate the formal and aesthetic dimension of this *new* cinema, exemplified by the *Dogme* film movement of the mid 1990s.

> Like today's DV realists, the 1960s 'direct cinema' proponents avoided tight staging and scripting, preferring to let events unfold naturally. Both then and now, the filmmakers used new filmmaking technology to revolt against the existing cinema conventions that were perceived as being too artificial. Both then and now, the key word of this revolt was the same: 'immediacy'.[8]

Manovich is correct in this appraisal. However, the annexation of digital cinema to "immediacy" alone restricts the capacity to forge new symmetries between these two fertile periods of the cinema. There are two particular areas of neglect. Firstly, a reconsideration of the role of the script, and alternative scriptwriting discourse, and secondly, the focus on feature film form, or cinematic form. Within this space, this essay seeks to bring together, and indeed collide, the French New Wave with opportunities for emerging (post-Dogme) low budget, digital cinema. To this end, it exploits Jean-Luc Godard's *Masculin féminin* (1966) as a salient case study. The essay seeks to reveal the co-presence of immediacy *and* bold alternative scriptwriting, as fundamental to innovative and rigorous cinematic form. The evolution, and indeed mutation, of Godard's distinctive 1960s cinematic form, exhibited in *Masculin féminin*, will be promoted as a case for *retro-modular narrative* today, within the context of the wider contemporary digital media culture.

Masculin féminin: 15 faits précis (1966)

Aesthetically, *Masculin féminin* can easily seem like one of Godard's more casual efforts: a collection of fragments, notes, improvisations. Looked at closely, it coheres into a tight pattern ... [9]

Masculin féminin: 15 faits précis can be situated as part of an unofficial trilogy that includes *Vivre sa Vie: a film in 12 tableaux* (1962) and *Une femme mariée: Fragments of a film shot in 1964* (1964). The films are united by their commitment to a specific mode of cinematic form, where the parts challenge the whole. The subtitles to each film title provide the hint. *Vivre sa Vie* is Brechtian in design. For Godard, this was a cinematic exercise in *theatre verite*, that is, a narrative feature film assembled from a "series of blocks ... which can't be touched."[10] For Susan Sontag, *Vivre sa Vie* embodied a new language for the cinema, one where "the ordinary causal sequence of narrative is broken ... by the extremely arbitrary decomposition of the story into twelve episodes."[11] In *Masculin féminin* Godard reworks the idea of a *block*, or tableaux based cinematic form. As the last film in his (unofficial) trilogy *Masculin féminin* reveals the splintering of the feature form itself. Just one year later, Godard would announce his own *fin du cinéma* with *Week End* (1967).

This essay locates the discreet charm of *Masculin féminin* within its very instability: a film precariously balanced at the threshold of narrative cinema and Godard's more essayistic cinematic collages to follow. Godard's *15 precise acts* of *Masculin féminin* are identified with intertitles that take the form of big white (supergraphic) numerals over black. The numerals are introduced with gun shot sound effects. The precision of the acts has been debated. Louis Gianetti remarks "Godard deliberately assigns arbitrary numbers to the episodes, and sometimes even skips the numbering of two or three scenes in a row" then "introducing a scene with 4/A."[12] Likewise, Ken Dancyger and Jeff Rush note an "erratic" progression of numerals within a "self-conscious structure."[13] However, emphasis on the *imprecision* of the acts detracts from the most interesting object, which is the modular cinematic form itself.

Modular Narrative

Allan Cameron uses the term *modular narrative* to describe a trend in contemporary cinematic form identified in Independent, Hollywood and international narrative cinema. His focus is toward those films that function as radically achronological narratives, such as *21 Grams* (2003) and *Irréversible* (2002).[14] For Cameron, modular narrative is present when:

> Contingency asserts itself both as diegetic force and as structural principle: modular narratives mimic contingency itself by leaping between narrative segments in apparently arbitrary or unpredictable ways.[15]

Using this broad definition of modular narrative—this also presents as a model that can be retroactively applied to cinema of the past. With this logic, *Masculin féminin* can be situated as a retro-modular narrative: Godard's *15 precise acts* of 1966 time-shifted to 2009.

Godard describes *Masculin féminin* as "the story of a boy who's in love with a girl, and things don't go well because this girl is in love with another girl."[16] The boy is Paul (Jean-Pierre Léaud) and the girls are Madeleine (Chantal Goya) and Elisabeth (Marlène Jobert). The plot is informed by two Guy de Maupassant short stories: *Le Signe* (The Signal) and *La femme de Paul* (Paul's Mistress). However, *Masculin féminin* is a bare literary adaptation given Godard's ascetic approach to his source material. This view is supported by the fact that Maupassant's publishers confirmed that the rights were not required to proceed with distribution.[17]

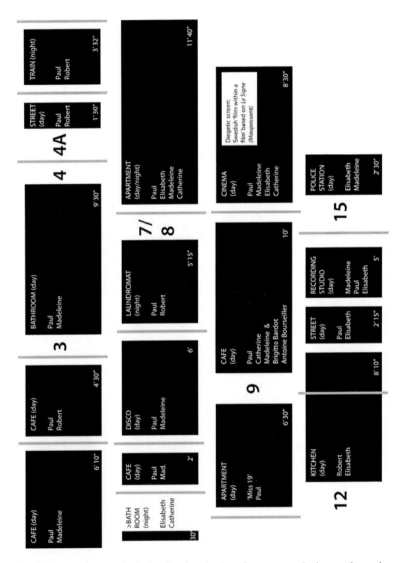

Fig. 2 Feature Form. A distinctive low-budget form accrued via an alternating pattern of cinematic *Blocks* (black rectangles) and *Shards* (grey vertical lines). The *Blocks* (duration 5-10 mins.) function as elongated scenes set within generic city spaces. The *Shards* (30 sec.-2 mins.) are street montage elements (with voiceover narration) inserted between. Godard's numerical intertiles (as *Hot-Spots*) are included here in the order.

In *Masculin féminin* Godard works with a modular narrative via a deft manipulation of narrative units. In his DVD commentary, on the *Criterion* DVD disc, Adrian Martin notes the fact that a disproportionate amount of narrative information is actually absent, since it occurs *between* the acts.[18] For example, the lesbian relationship between Madeleine and Elisabeth, central to *La femme de Paul*, is given subtle treatment on screen. For Maupassant, the relationship leads Paul to his death. For Godard, Paul's death remains ambiguous—noted in a bureaucratic exchange between Madeleine and the police officer filing the report. Here, in Godard's act #15, Dancyger and Rush locate in the film "an explicit, overt, narrating structure" where "the script acknowledges its artificiality, freeing it from hiding the coincidences that determine all narrative structure." [19] In other words, by #15, the narrative must necessarily resolve and Godard does so expediently, in less than three minutes. This represents Godard's commitment to predetermined modular form, over traditional expectations of narrative trajectory.

Godard's *trame*

The modular form of *Masculin féminin* is related to Godard's idiosyncratic approach to scriptwriting. He has been quoted "making a film involves superimposing three operations: thinking, shooting, editing."[20] The marginalisation of a writing phase, in this description, is deceptive given the materialisation of a script.

> I don't really like telling a story, I prefer to use a kind of tapestry, a background on which I can embroider my own ideas ... I just write out the strong moments of the film, and that gives me a *trame*.[21]

Godard likens his scripts to a *trame*, a wire scaffold used for tapestry and textile weave. A rare insight into Godard's *trame* was gained by Philippe Labro on his visit to the set of *Masculin féminin*:

> A sort of work plan ... a thin notebook of a dozen pages or so, divided into what they call 'work sequences' (there are thirteen of them), but when the real shooting starts, Godard gets out his sketchbook (an eight-by-twelve-inch spiral notebook with a blue cover). The dialogue and the scene directions are recorded in it in his handwriting (dark blue ink, lines close together, without too many thing crossed out).[22]

Labro notes a script of thirteen parts, or *work sequences*—a modular script. The *trame* predetermines the feature as an accumulation, or assemblage, of narrative parts. It also represents the minimisation of cinematic units which is in sharp contrast to the narrative patterns promoted in mainstream screenwriting discourse that advise "the average length of a feature film scene is around two minutes, so 50-60 scenes give you the skeleton of a feature script." [23] In contrast, Godard's *trame* (be it 12, 13 or 15 parts) functions as scaffolding for a rich cinematic architecture to be executed during his "thinking, shooting, editing" phases.[24] Furthermore, in the screenwriting manuals: a *scene* occurs "when there is a shift in time and location" and a *sequence* functions as "a thematically-linked series of scenes." [25] Godard distorts these notions of chronological scale. In *Masculin féminin* his *15 precise acts* actually function (in typical terms) as elongated *scenes* of screen duration more akin to *sequences*. Thus, for Godard, the cinematic form is a kind of *grand sequence*, that is, an assemblage of fifteen *thematically-linked* long scenes. This alternative mode of cinematic form, argued here as *retro-modular narrative*, is one entirely appropriate for today's wave of low budget film production. The use of a minimal number of (elongated) scenes offers a viable alternative to the wildly fragmented, and costly, narrative patterns promoted in contemporary screenwriting discourse. It is important to note here that *Masculin féminin* was indeed a low budget feature of its time, produced for a meagre $150,000.[26]

Database Narrative

In her book *New Digital Cinema*, Holly Willis describes the database form as one "eminently suited to digital filmmaking and a digital aesthetic." [27] She tracks theorists Lev Manovich and Marsha Kinder in their analysis of "database narrative" in pre-digital cinema. Manovich posits Dziga Vertov as the "major database filmmaker of the twentieth century" with reference to *Man with a Movie Camera* (1929).[28] Kinder locates this mode of narrative in international art cinema via the films of Luis Buñuel.[29] She offers a valuable definition:

> Database narratives refers to narratives whose structure exposes or thematizes the dual processes of selection and combination that lie at the heart of all stories and that are crucial to language: the selection of particular data (characters, images, sounds, events) from a series of databases or paradigms, which are then combined to generate specific tales.[30]

The aim of these theorists, in their reconsideration of a century of cinema, is to expand the possibilities for new, interactive digital media.

However, this thinking is equally prescient for new narrative cinema in the digital age. In this next section, Kinder's concepts of *hot spots* and *narrative fields* are (re)located within Godard's *Masculin féminin*. In addition, a host of other spatial narrative patterns are identified in the film: *shards*, *zones* and *layers*. It is argued that these forms provide the capacity to fuel retro-modular narrative today.

/Hot Spots. Kinder notes the numerous incongruous objects that surface in the films of Luis Buñuel, such as the cow on the bed in *L'Age d'or* (1930). She describes these as *hot spots* (akin to the graphic hyperlinks of today's digital media) that permit "story, camera, character, or spectator to move from one scene or narrative realm to another." [31] In Godard's *Masculin féminin* two alternative kinds of narrative hot spots exist. The primary hot spots are the fifteen numerical intertitles that (like Buñuel's objects) tolerate narrative leaps within the feature form. Godard's numerals are graphic *links* that chain together, often disparate, narrative modules. The second hot spots, in *Masculin féminin,* are the series of brief urban montage sequences spliced between the block-based narrative modules.

Shards: Narrative *Hot-Spots.*
Masculin Féminin, by Jean-Luc Godard © 1966 Argos Films

They are assembled from arbitrary Parisian street shots and are often accompanied by Paul's (off-screen) voiceover. This combination of moving image and sound, in the form of cinematic *shards*, accord with Godard's own description of his film as a "chronicle," or report, on French youth.[32] As narrative hot spots the shards, like the intertitles, permit shifts both between, and within, narrative modules. Both brands of Godardian hot spots supply the narrative feature film with that "illusion of narrative cohesion even when the film has little or no plot"—like Buñuel's objects.[33]

/Fields. Louis Gianetti notes of *Masculin féminin* that "although a great deal takes place in the movie, the events seem random and detached."[34] This observation works with Kinder's concept of *narrative field* as a database of cinematic ideas (executed as moving pictures and sounds) that reveal "the arbitrariness of the particular choices made, and the possibility of making other combinations which would create alternative stories."[35] In *Masculin féminin,* Godard (like Vertov and Buñuel) works with a database- like form that precedes Lev Manovich's *new media* methods of selection, combination, variation and repetition.[36] In this sense, Godard *remixes* his five fictional characters, in alternate configurations: Paul & Madeleine; Paul & Robert; Madeleine & Catherine-Isabelle; Robert &

Fields: Rotation & repetition of characters
Masculin Féminin, by Jean-Luc Godard © 1966 Argos Films

Elisabeth; Paul & Madeleine & Elisabeth. Using isolated pairs and triples, mixed within a modular form, Godard is able to illustrate the central theme of the film of alienated youth. Gianetti highlights the level of repetition and variation in the film:

> Godard has been condemned for his habit of 'dragging in' gratuitous episodes. Many of his scenes are set in public places ... and at times he seems to let the camera wander off randomly. But a closer analysis usually reveals that these 'gratuitous' scenes are actually variations or parallels to his major theme.[37]

Zones: Discrete city spaces
Masculin Féminin, by Jean-Luc Godard © 1966 Argos Films

Adrian Martin offers the term "permutation" to describe the series of "rotating duets" in the film.[38] Now the structure of *Masculin féminin* is evident: a feature film accrued by a reiteration of narrative parts/units/modules linked via numerical and montage hotspots. This provides an alternative narrative pattern beyond the typical act-structure discourse masquerading as screenwriting advice. To zoom in, Godard's narrative modules also defy the conservative wisdom that each cinematic unit must be structured with a beginning, middle and an end.[39] In contrast, his cinematic units are all *middle*, mostly presented as informal inquisitions or Q&A style interviews. Here, *Masculin féminin* is fractal in form—the structure of the parts mirrors that of the whole.

/Zones. The database form of *Masculin féminin* also works as a catalogue of urban spaces. Godard oscillates generic Parisian spaces, both public and private, to accumulate a feature: from the bedrooms, bathrooms and kitchens of non-descript Parisian apartments to the street cafes, restaurants, laundromats, discos and theatres of the city. The narrative shifts abruptly: day to night, light to dark, day to week, week to month, with scant regard to the expectations of classical narration—in preference for a cinematic form that favours spatial over chronological montage. Furthermore, Godard maps these spaces intensively *within* each cinematic module. Adrian Martin notes this in Godard's dissection of an everyday café (in Act #1) where "Godard explored every aspect of filmic form—revealing the space little by little." [40] To take a further example (in Act #11) Godard exploits the space of a cinema theatre: in one module he shifts Paul from the cinema seats, to a bathroom cubicle, into the projection booth itself and then to the street outside. And in new digital cinema a reconsideration of filmic space is underway. Ganz and Khatib posit that a key transformation in this domain is towards an extension of the *filmic zone*. That is, the reconfiguration of the space, behind and in front of the camera, with new digital cinematography. [41] So, for low-budget digital cinema today, the fusion of these two ideas makes for an exciting proposition—a Godardian mapping of space combined with an expansion of the filmic zone.

/Layers. Godard has described *Masculin féminin* as "an antishow ... a film between one reflection and another." [42] Two layers can be read in the film. The *show* narrative layer is occupied by the Maupassant inspired character drama, whilst the *antishow* layer contains a documentary like cinematic essay. The antishow contains Godard's chronicle of places, fashions, music, media and political slogans of the day. In this regard, Dancyger and Rush highlight *Masculin féminin* as a "perfect illustration" of *mixed mode* narrative, a "paradox between the artificial and the documentary." [43] Godard's dual layers are revealed when the antishow punctuates, and erupts, into the show layer. For example, in the opening scene (Act #1) a random shooting takes place outside the café where Paul and Madeleine meet. From a sound perspective, it is the brutal gunshot sound effects that explode with each numerical intertitle that signal the intrusion of the antishow. Here, the film functions within Kinder's wider notion of database narrative where "possibilities seem limitless, where randomness, repetition, and interruptions are rampant." [44]

In *Masculin féminin* the alternate layers overlap via narrative *superimposition* where Godard creates composite characters by a superimposition of their real world identities with those of the fictional narrative. This idea is articulated by Nicole Brenez who describes the film as a "Godardian confrontation between fictional, documentary, and reflexive images" and highlights the fact that the portraits are simultaneously fictional characters (Paul/Madeleine) and the actors themselves: Léaud as a symbol of the New Wave and Goya, a successful *Yé-yé* pop singer of the time.[45] This is heightened by a series of cameos injected into the narrative, most famously that of Brigitte Bardot with Antoine Bourseiller.

Layers: Paul/Madeleine vs. Jean-Pierre Léaud/Chantal Goya
Masculin Féminin, by Jean-Luc Godard © 1966 Argos Films

Masculin féminin is an explosive film formed with competitive, oppositional and superimposed layers. The poster for Godard's next following feature *Made in USA* (1966) presents a striking image to illustrate the precarious condition of the narrative feature: it is a graphic collage of the characters pasted on a primary yellow background that has been peppered with machine gun perforations. Today, new digital cinema has been identified as a "site for the collision, layering, interpretation and general orchestration of disparate elements" in relation to the trend towards multi-screen narrative in the work of Mike Figgis and Peter

Greenaway.[46] In contrast, this case study of *Masculin féminin* serves to reinforce the idea that the presence of multiple layers *within* the singular cinematic frame itself may still represent a far more radical excursion for the cinema.

Conclusion

The ambition of this essay has been to expand the possibilities for emerging, low budget cinema today via a close reading of Jean-Luc Godard's *Masculin féminin*. Retro-modular narrative has been proposed as a cinematic form ripe for engagement in the digital age. This calls for a renewed, and intensive, focus on the cinematic part within an overall modular cinematic form, within the boundaries of feature narrative cinema. The scriptwriting process of Jean-Luc Godard, as a series of work sequences (or *trame*) has been isolated as the architecture of his distinctive mid 1960s film form. In addition, this essay has highlighted an array of narrative forms, located in international art cinema, at the disposal for filmmakers today. These include database, module, zone, field, shard and layer. These reflections on the cinema of Jean-Luc Godard, some fifty years later, provide an explosive catalyst for emerging low budget cinema today.

Notes

[1] Tom Milne, trans., "La Femme Mariée," in *Godard on Godard*, eds. Jean Narboni and Tom Milne (London: Secker & Warburg, 1968), 208.

[2] Australian Cinémathèque, "Breathless: French New Wave Turns 50," Queensland Art Gallery: Gallery of Modern Art, http://qag.qld.gov.au/cinematheque/past_programs/2007/breathless_french_new_w ave_turns_50.

[3] Richard Brody, http://www.amazon.com/Everything-Cinema-Working-Jean-Luc-Godard/dp/0805068864/ref=sr_1_1?ie=UTF8&s=books&qid=1220240225&sr=8-1*Everything Is Cinema: The Working Life of Jean-Luc Godard* (New York: Metropolitan Books, 2008).

[4] Flickerfest, 18th International Short Film Festival, "Catch the next new wave," http://www.flickerfest.com.au.

[5] *Cosmopolitan*, September 2008, ACP Magazines, 88-90.

[6] WarpX, "Low Budget Feature Film Scheme," UK Film Council and Film 4, http://www.warpx.co.uk.

[7] Alicia Van Couvering, "What I Meant to Say," *FilmMaker* (Spring 2007) http://www.filmmakermagazine.com/spring2007/features/mumblecore.php.

[8] Lev Manovich, "Old Media as New Media: Cinema," in *The New Media Book,* ed. Dan Harries, 209-218. (London: British Film Institute, 2002), 212.

[9] Adrian Martin, "The Young Man for All Times," *Essay for Criterion Collection,* (2005),
http://www.criterion.com/asp/release.asp?id=308&eid=434&section=essay.

[10] Tom Milne, trans., "Interview with Jean-Luc Godard," in *Godard on Godard,* eds. Jean Narboni and Tom Milne (London: Secker & Warburg, 1968), 185.

[11] Susan Sontag, *Against Interpretation, and other essays* (New York: Picador, 2001), 199.

[12] Louis Gianetti, *Godard and Others: Essays on Film Form* (London: Tantivy Press, 1975), 45.

[13] Ken Dancyger and Jeff Rush, *Alternative Scriptwriting: Successfully Breaking the Rules. Third Edition* (Oxford: Focal Press, 2002), 47.

[14] Allan Cameron, "Contingency, Order, and the Modular Narrative: 21 Grams and Irreversible," *The Velvet Light Trap,* 58 (Fall 2006): 65-78.

[15] Cameron, *The Velvet Light Trap,* 66.

[16] Pierre Daix, "An interview with Jean-Luc Godard," in *Masculine Féminine a film by Jean-Luc Godard,* ed. Robert Hughes and Pierre Billard (New York: Grove Press, Inc, 1969), 236.

[17] Robert Hughes and Pierre Billard, ed., *Masculine Féminine a film by Jean-Luc Godard* (New York: Grove Press, Inc, 1969).

[18] Adrian Martin, "Commentary" *Masculine Féminine,* DVD. Directed by Jean-Luc Godard. Melbourne Australia: Madman Entertainment, 2006.
http://www.criterion.com/asp/release.asp?id=308&eid=434&section=essay.

[19] Dancyger and Rush, *Alternative Scriptwriting,* 47.

[20] Milne, *Godard on Godard,* 185.

[21] Richard Roud, *Jean-Luc Godard* (Bloomington/London: Indiana University Press, 1967), 49.

[22] Philippe Labro, "One Evening in a Small Café," in *Masculine Féminine a film by Jean-Luc Godard,* ed. Robert Hughes and Pierre Billard (New York: Grove Press, Inc, 1969), 226-230.

[23] John Costello, *Writing a Screenplay* (Herts: Pocket Essentials, 2006), 121.

[24] Milne, *Godard on Godard,* 185.

[25] Costello, *Writing a Screenplay,* 157.

[26] Winston Wheeler Dixon, "Twenty-Five Reasons Why It's All Over," in *The End of Cinema As We Know It: American Film in the Nineties,* ed. John Lewis (New York: New York University Press, 2001), 356.

[27] Holly Willis, *New Digital Cinema: Reinventing the Moving Image* (London: Wallflower Press, 2005), 41.

[28] Lev Manovich, *The Language of New Media.* (Cambridge, MA: The MIT Press, 2001), 9.

[29] Marsha Kinder, "Hot Spots, Avatars, and Narrative Fields Forever. Bunuel's Legacy for Digital New Media and Interactive Database Narrative," *Film Quarterly,* 55 (2002): 2-15.

[30] Kinder, *Film Quarterly,* 6.

[31] Kinder, *Film Quarterly,* 8.

[32] Robert Hughes and Pierre Billard, ed., *Masculine Féminine a film by Jean-Luc Godard* (New York: Grove Press, Inc, 1969), 222.

[33] Kinder, *Film Quarterly,* 10.

[34] Louis Gianetti, *Godard and Others: Essays on Film Form* (London: Tantivy Press, 1975), 30.

[35] Kinder, *Film Quarterly,* 6.

[36] Manovich, *The New Media Book,* 209-218.

[37] Gianetti, *Godard and Others,* 33-34.

[38] Martin, *Essay for Criterion Collection*

[39] Elliot Grove, *Raindance Writer's Lab: Write & Sell the Hot Screenplay* (Oxford: Focal Press, 2001), 65.

[40] Martin, *Essay for Criterion Collection*

[41] Adam Ganz and Lina Khatib, "Digital Cinema: The transformation of film practice and aesthetics," *New Cinemas* 4 no. 1, (2006): 21-36.

[42] Richard Roud, *Jean-Luc Godard. (*Bloomington/London: Indiana University Press, 1967), 93.

[43] Dancyger and Rush, *Alternative Scriptwriting,* 47.

[44] Kinder, *Film Quarterly,* 8.

[45] Nicole Brenez, "The Forms of the Question" in *For Ever Godard*, ed. Michael Temple, James S Williams and Michael Witt (London: Blackdog Publishing, 2004), 173.

[46] Holly Willis, *New Digital Cinema: Reinventing the Moving Image* (London: Wallflower Press, 2005), 38.

CHAPTER NINETEEN

TRANSCRIPT

STEPHEN CONNOLLY

I began working in film because some things were too complicated to say. In other words, I felt that I could not address the complexity of a situation through any other visual, aural or written enunciation. Constructing a film—images and sound, temporally placed in continuous tension—moves towards addressing the intricacy of things. Film enables both the creation of a *sense* of the chosen topics or themes at hand, and a reflexive relationship with their portrayal. The cinematic essay is a film that engages with the world from a number of different directions. The pattern of these engagements, within the work, is as important as the approaches themselves.

How might a cinematic essay acquire content and form? My initial approach starts with a dogmatic question or assertion, always already recognised as an unworkable speculation, but useful as a focus and an organising armature. Work begins with research, in an attempt to support the speculation. The assertion is never approached directly—it lies beneath the surface of the research. Material is found by proceeding intuitively and laterally and with the understanding that this process may feature in the finished work. This, of course, is an approach taken by other types of artists. However, it is comparatively rare in film that the process be shown, and sets apart the cinematic essay from other approaches to the medium.

As the research material is placed in a framework, the original assertion melts away so that something more interesting and complex can emerge. That is, an essay film emerges from the collected images and sounds as the initial argument of the film disappears.

*'Enhanced transcript' of a Q & A session at the BFI in December 2008 after a screening of **The Whale** (2003), **Great American Desert** (2007) and **Más Se Perdió** (2008). These short essay films are part of an ongoing*

*series of works called **Afflicted States**. Thanks to Sacha Craddock (facilitator), Adam Clitheroe, Sandra Gillespie, Sally Stafford and Neil Stewart.*

Can you tell us about *Afflicted States*?

Afflicted States is a series of works begun in late 2001, when exploring the relationship between the individual and state seemed to take on a new urgency. These short films relate the present to the past, through an exploration of political experience within consumer society, and react to a perceived historical amnesia and erasure of the preceding decade.

A title crops up in your new work *Más Se Perdió*: 'Reality is materially conditioned' - and this resonates with your approach to image and particularly sound. Can you talk about this?

If the starting point is the material process of making the work—most times the films are shot without a traditional film crew. As the films are personal and solo efforts, in practical terms, it is tricky to shoot picture and record sound at the same time. So recording sync sound—captured at the same moment as image—is a problem of practice, but I've tried to turn this difficulty into an expressive advantage.

If the sound for a film is conceptually split from image, the sound track can be treated as a composition in its own right and subject to its own independent rules, patterns of generation, and development through the temporal run of the work. The sound track can be thought of as a soundscape. This also means that, within the process of making, although the content of the picture may set off a journey to find analogous sounds, the distance between the suggestion of sound from an image, and the actual sound acquired and used, creates critical possibilities. Expressively, this distance can contribute to generating a degree of tension in the soundscape.

For example, the sounds of a stadium in *Great American Desert*, which accompany the archive images of the Los Angeles Coliseum, were sourced in a football stadium of a similar size—120,000 seats—in Ann Arbor, Michigan. The stadium of the acquired sound is empty—in this sense the opposite of the full stadium in the archive images. A palpable sense of presence arises from the sounds of people exercising, by running up and down

the aisles, and the sounds of rope hitting flagpoles in the empty stadium. Given the themes of patriotism and nationalism running through the film, these sonic signifiers of stadium—while at the same time coupled with their implied intimate space and scale—become extremely resonant.

Working with sound is not limited to sounds that are particular however, even the sound of wind in trees, in the background of a image for instance, can be pulled to the foreground, mixed and treated to create new expressive possibilities.

In terms of sync and the spoken word, is it necessary to see the act of speaking to authenticate the words as belonging to a person (or an image)? This 'ascription' can be made problematic. Spoken word may also generate a different mode of listening within an audience. Skepticism regarding the truth-value of spoken content for instance, can be heightened when the image of the speaker is absent and the evident affirmation of the face is denied. The "voice of god" assumptions invoked for voiceover are sensitive to context and content, and can be easily broken and played with.

Up until recently, the film soundscapes don't generally include music, so the classical music sounds in *Más Se Perdió* mark a new departure. During the shoot, I became conscious of how classical music in a Cuban context took on a certain rhetorical quality—a classical band accompanied the May 1st parade in Havana for instance—and I wanted to work with this. There are historical links between classical music and nationalism—the soundscape of the film makes the suggestion these links are present in the discourse of the *apparat* in Cuba.

The music-like sounds in *Más Se Perdió* are extracts from a ballet— Sleeping Beauty—in keeping with the visual exploration of a ballet school building. This sound was sourced from LPs "played" by hand, thus de-naturing their musical qualities and rendering it as "sound."

In the post-production process of my work, the picture generally gets edited very quickly—reaching a rough cut in a week is average—while the sound may take up to a year to source, edit and mix. This long gestation time allows testing and experimenting with relationships between sounds and sound and image.

Do you use a strategy of withholding information in the work? If so, how, and why does this work?

The work presents the world in fragments, and there may appear to be linking information missing. These lacunas are intended—they are holes designed to arrest and draw in the curiosity of the audience. For example, *Great American Desert* presents two perspectives on nuclear destruction— an account of interviewing the aircrews that dropped the bomb on Hiroshima, which opens the film, and newspaper coverage of the autumn 1945 re-staging of this bombing, as light and sound entertainment, in a victory pageant at the Los Angeles Coliseum.

Although it is not stated, a connection between the early atomic era and this contemporary desert landscape, littered with recreational vehicles, lies in the planning ideas pursued in the face of the threat of the Soviet nuclear bomb. The prevailing wisdom of the 1950s, was that the maximum survival of the population in the event of an attack, was to be achieved by dispersal and mobility of the population. These general ideas have had considerable impact on trends in the development of the American urban landscape in the last 50 years.

The appearance of Ulrike Meinhof in *The Whale*, addresses a lacuna in popular memory. The film shows Meinhof speaking on a talk show, raising the question of the efficacy of peaceful protest. We may care to remember she later became a member of the Red Army Faction (aka the "gang" which bears her name), responsible for attacking US military installations in a campaign of violence lasting a number of years. However, her social origins in the middle class (like many in the RAF) and her successful media career previous to her participation in terrorism, are less often acknowledged.

Más Se Perdió explores the ruin of a ballet school, the design and construction of which, in the face of widespread shortages just two years after the revolution, was specifically sanctioned by Casto and Guevara. The camera explores the plastic, expressive form and unique materials of the ruined school, and we learn by inter-title the building was declared complete in 1965, more or less in the state in which we see it now.

By the time of the school's completion, the "materialist turn" of the left had begun, as also evidenced in the Sovietisation of the Cuban *apparat* and the buildings faced official neglect. The internal tensions within this conceptual move are signposted in the film by an inter-title, dated 1968:

> *Hypotheses for the future are converted into utopia, into fiction. Reality is materially conditioned.*

The author is Roberto Segre, a Cuban Architecture critic; the quote sums up his views on the building.

Do you use conceptual rules when shooting or choosing images?

I don't generally use conceptual rules that govern the way images are created or what they depict—I think addressing the provenance of images and exploring formal pictorial issues is the terrain of a previous generation of experimental filmmakers such as John Smith and William Raban. Instead, general guidelines are generated, before and during the shooting of the film. The guidelines are expressive in intention and effect, and very much govern how places and things are presented.

For example—*The Whale* was shot only in afternoons after mornings of rain—this generated the distinctive blueish/green cast to the park images in the film. In context, this lush and watery English landscape as distinct from the parched and dry look of the City of the Dead in Cairo, is pertinent. In my work, establishing difference is an important tactic in expressing meaning.

Shooting *Great American Desert,* I asked my partner to drive slowly, following the points of the compass, away from, and back into the small town of Quartzsite, the film's location. On their own these images would make the most boring road movie of all time, and this was intended: the images reveal the unrelenting, spread out, strip of commercial property and settlement that is the town.

It is a landscape of mass consumerism and mass experience of "nature." The film images document the commercial, the constructed, the multiple, the banal; in a place that is celebrated in popular culture as the frontier of the lone individual, the South West US.

Just two lenses were used for most of the shots in *Great American Desert*, standardising how place looks to us. Finally, the tonal warmth and colours which we associate with the area—red, orange and yellow—were graded out of the film.

Colour and tone are also used expressively in *Más Se Perdió.* In the images of the ruined ballet school that form the major spatial world of the film, inside is shot in black and white, colour is used outside. This simple system is deployed to put in suspension, to put on hold, ideas of past and present that we may apply to the depiction of a ruin. Naturally, a ruin invokes the place of the past in the present. The use of two systems of depiction, with their temporal *colour auras*, cancel each other out.

Colour aura is also foregrounded in the repeated sequences of workers building a road in *Más Se Perdió*. These images have a punchy super 8 home movie feel—a *colour aura* that date-stamps them as from the past. However, each of these sequences is prefaced by an inter-title, announcing the date and time of the shot (12.35am, 16 February 2008)—the temporal location of the film is the same as it's production—in contradiction to the *colour aura* the images possess. This mis-match of *colour aura* to image document suggests clues as to the *fitness*, or relevance of the representation, to the time of production of the work.

Tell me something about using text in your work.

A significant part of the research time for the work is spent in the Library. Texts are a significant part of the environment in which the work is made. Central to the meaning-making method of the work is allegory—the work superimposes texts and reads them through each other. Texts as titles also operate in film to break the "spell" of a work—the audiences' experience of being in the images and soundscape is to a degree interrupted by the appearance of text. In general the work seeks out these interruptions, as it presupposes an active viewer.

You repeat the inter-titles itemising the date and time of shots in *Más Se Perdió*—why?

One function of dates and times itemised by inter-titles in *Más Se Perdió* has been mentioned above: operating in combination with the "colour aura" of the worker sequences to perform a self-reflexive critique of these images. Another function of these inter-titles is to contextualise the central visual depiction in the work, the exploration of the ruined ballet school in a suburb of Havana, Cuba.

The city of Havana has many architectural ruins. Much of the fabric of the city dates to the pre-revolutionary period (pre 1959), and a lack of capital investment since then has led to decay and dilapidation. It follows, that albeit the filming of colonial or pre-revolutionary Havana may document an aspect of the city, the depiction of decay brings with it a political charge. In a Cuban context, without qualifying material, creating the conditions for an empathic relationship in an audience with the undoubted

aesthetic qualities of these ruins, may amount to equating the last 50 years
of the life of the city, in the revolution, as decay. This is not the project of
this film.

Thus *Más Se Perdió* very particularly documents a modern ruin, and a ruin
of the current political regime: the Ballet School, part completed 1965, is
an authentic ruin of the revolution. The question of why the school was not
completed by the revolution is unanswered, and as discussed above, a
central lacuna in the work.

The date and time inter-titles identify a temporal location for the work—in
this case the same as the time of the production of the film. Thus the inter-
titles suggest the shots are authentic documents of quotidian activity, and
function, by foregrounding the time of production, to reinforce the
connections between the historical dimension of the ballet school and the
temporal ascription of the film. Finally, the inter-title repeats are also a
rhetorical tactic, and mirror the blocking of image sequences into groups
of three through the work.

**I see in your work a movement towards defining a sense of community
and a sense of hope through people being connected. There is a sense
of the work being a human response to these big things—politics, the
social and so on—although the work is quite modest. The work gives
me a feeling that things will be ok despite everything!**

It is interesting you say this. Before working in film, I was employed by
Social Services caring for homeless people. These are some of the most
excluded and marginalised people you can find. If you adopt their
perspective, the social: 'Society'—can appear like a huge structure, an
edifice, hanging over and above, a structure which also excludes them.
That vision is about power. And the experience of being with them gave
me an appreciation of the operation of power—political, economic—as a
system of relationships, woven into the fabric of the social sphere.

I'd suggest for me, making meaning in film is centrally concerned with
setting up relationships—between images, sounds, time, space, the real,
the depicted, the omitted, artifice, and so on—there is a natural fit between
this content—political relationships—and the moving image medium. In
other words, to my mind, film is an ideal medium to explore political
power in the social sphere. So most of my work explores a dialectic
between the individual and social. These relationships are explored in

(corner of)
calle Oficios &
calle Santa Clara
Havana old town
16 february 2008
12.35 hrs

(corner of)
avenue de los
Presidentes
Havana
02 may 2008
18.13 hrs

National School of Ballet
Cubanacán, Havana

06 may 2008

design and construction
begun by order of
Fidel Castro & Che Guevara
january 1961

National School of Ballet
officially declared complete:

26 july 1965

opening of school of ballet
on this site:

postponed indefinitely

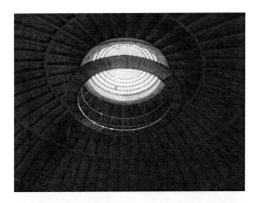

different contexts through the temporal journey of each film.

And I think—to try to answer your question more directly—once these things are given form, are revealed as palpable, are revealed as possibly even having aesthetic possibilities, they then take on human dimensions and scale. The fact that the work tries to address them, means also that the work is not disinterested. I hope there is a human concern with value, which maybe seeps across to an audience. It's not just about the narrative, the visual, or the 'spell' cast by the moving image.

CHAPTER TWENTY

WHO IN THE WORLD:
ESSAY FILM, TRANSCULTURE
AND GLOBALITY

CATHERINE LUPTON

An international conference on essay film took place at Lüneberg University, Germany, at the end of 2007.[1] Sven Kramer, one of the conference organisers, commented in his introductory speech that essay films eschew nationalistic concerns and address themselves directly to the arena of the global. Now you could reasonably dispute this assertion, by pointing to examples of essay film that are deeply involved with issues and questions pertaining to the nation—for example, the works of Alexander Kluge or Patrick Keiller. Yet for me Kramer's passing observation remains intriguing, because it seems to intuit and crystallise an important facet of contemporary essay filmmaking that has not been widely attended to. In what follows I propose to explore this claim that essay films proffer a specific form of address to the global, by examining the interconnections between essay film, transculture and globality. I take the perhaps unfamiliar term *globality* from Darren O'Byrne's work on global citizenship. He prefers it to the contested term globalization because it permits focus on the subjective stance that for him forms the basis upon which people may identify themselves and act as global citizens. Although this stance and experience are certainly complex, O'Byrne defines globality concisely as "an awareness of, and an ability to relate directly to, the globe." [2] I will suggest that the forms and approaches characteristic of essay film can broach this type of global awareness, by their projection of, and reflection upon, subject positions that seek in various ways to confront the world as a whole.

Before coming to focus on those essay films that engage directly with globality, I want to offer a working definition of essay film, and at the same time examine how essay films dovetail with the forms and preoccupations associated with transcultural and transnational cinema. It is indeed striking how many prominent practitioners of essay film emerge and operate from positions of transcultural identification: Chris Marker, Agnès Varda, Harun Farocki, Trinh T. Minh-ha, Johan van der Keuken, Joram ten Brink, Peter Mettler and Hito Steyerl among them. Moving towards a definition of essay film that rests upon the classic delineations of the literary essay offered by Adorno and Lukács,[3] there is a remarkable congruence between the qualities commonly associated with essays, and those that Hamid Naficy in particular has identified within what he calls the accented cinemas of exilic, diasporic and postcolonial experience.[4] The essay is seen as process-oriented, provisional, fragmentary, elliptical, self-aware, self-effacing, anti-authoritative and generically hybrid or undecidable. Naficy's accented cinemas are liminal, intersticial, again generically hybrid or unstable, and created by filmmakers whose subjectivity is variously characterised as "partial, fragmented and multiple .... hybridized, syncretic, performed or virtual." [5]

The essay, written or filmed, can be defined as a site for enacting the process of thought and reflection upon and around a given topic, which is always at the same time a process of enquiry into the self who thinks: one of Montaigne's foundational pronouncements for his *Essays* is the deceptively simple "I myself am the subject of my book." [6] For me, the experience of essay film is that of being as if inside a reflective consciousness in the very process of thinking, with all that that entails in the way of digression, revision, provisionality, uncertainty, free association, free lapse into memory; as well as the constant reflexive instability of a subjectivity that knows itself to be perpetually altered by the act of thinking. In Adorno's formulation:

> The thinker does not think, but rather transforms himself into an arena of intellectual experience, without simplifying it. While even traditional thought draws its impulses from such experience, such thought by its form eliminates the remembrance of those impulses. The essay, on the other hand, takes them as its model, without simply imitating them as reflected form; it mediates then through its own conceptual organization; it proceeds, so to speak, methodically unmethodically. [7]

Adorno's discussion of the essay places a strong emphasis upon its politically and ideologically oppositional character, its work of formal and conceptual subversion against fixed dogmas and rigid, received categories of knowledge—those hegemonic forms of understanding that typically

efface their own provisionality by repressing the historical processes that
have gone into their creation. Although Naficy recognises that accented
cinemas are not always stridently oppositional, they are nonetheless in his
estimation steeped in politics and critical of dominant cinematic forms and
institutions, because they speak as it were in accents from and between
their margins: juxtaposing, hybridising and destabilising their modes,
genres and styles.[8]

Contemporary lived experiences and creative negotiations of
transcultural and transnational identities are evidently intertwined with the
processes of globalization, and with the questions, issues and conceptual
frameworks that have emerged from the now very substantial study of this
phenomenon. Notably, the deterritorialized imaginative spaces of the
transnational serve to highlight the limitations and inadequacies of the
modern nation-state as a frame of reference and analysis. At the same
time, many of the most visible examples of transnational cinema remain
complexly anchored to one or more specific sources of cultural or national
identity; and as a corollary of this, so do many critical studies of
transnational cinemas.[9] In Trinh T. Minh-Ha's *Surname Viet Given Name
Nam* (1989) and Atom Egoyan's *Calendar* (1993), for example, characters
and social actors (often one and the same) oscillate between Vietnam and
the USA in the first film, and Armenia and Canada in the second, as
distinctive, deeply contested, sites of (non-)identity and (non-)belonging.[10]
In neither example do the complexities of transnational experience, and the
symptomatic presence of globalization within them, lead directly or
automatically to an awareness of globality.

There does however exist an intriguing cluster of essay films which in
my opinion do unfold from and towards a position of global
consciousness, one which significantly transcends both the transnational
allegiances of the filmmaker, and whatever subjects she or he has chosen
to film. The works I have in mind are Chris Marker's *If I Had Four
Camels* (1966) and *Sunless* (1982), Trinh T. Minh-Ha's *Reassemblage*
(1982) and *Naked Spaces – Living Is Round* (1985), Bill Viola's *I Do Not
Know What It Is I Am Like* (1986), Joram Ten Brink's *The Man Who
Couldn't Feel and Other Tales* (1997), Johan van der Keuken's *Face
Value* (1991) and *Amsterdam Global Village* (1996), and Peter Mettler's
Gambling, Gods and LSD (2002). These works are admittedly few in
number, diverse in approach and intention, and extremely scattered in their
historical and geographical provenance. Some also put pressure on my
working definition of essay film, particularly *Amsterdam Global Village*,

which is an extended observational and interview-based documentary that does not overtly adopt the devices used by the other films to posit the workings of reflective consciousness. In most of the named examples it is the voice over commentary which enacts the process of thought, although both *I Do Not Know What It Is I Am Like* and *Face Value* find visual analogies for this in, respectively, Viola writing quietly in an enclosed room (until disrupted by an elephant), and the various subjects of *Face Value* framed closely and subjecting the camera to intense scrutiny.

What my sample of films do have in common is, firstly, some movement of travel, or transcultural encounter, that combines with the presence of a subjective agency that displays an open-minded respect for the alterity of the subjects being filmed. Secondly, these are films that open beyond signifying primarily whatever specific, local, cultures or places they include, such that their most privileged signified (or at least a very important one to come to terms with) is the world as a whole—a world, moreover, comprising textured diversity and complexity. Taken together, these various elements foster both a consciousness of globality, and an indispensable acceptance of and commitment to the diversity and complexity of the world. Such acceptance and commitment is not only, as O'Byrne asserts, a vital prerequisite for contemporary global citizenship, but also a foundation of what Thomas Harrison sees as the broader ethics of essayism: the way that the essay remains provisional, unstable, aleatory and unfixed in subjectivity, precisely because the thinking self remains open to being constantly reformulated by engaging with the complexity of the world.[11]

It is worth anchoring these abstract claims through closer reference to some of my examples. In Trinh's *Reassemblage* and *Naked Spaces*, the Vietnamese-American filmmaker stages voices that speak, in her beautifully suggestive phrase, "next to" images of traditional West African lifeways. In doing so her films open up critical questions of how one encounters and frames cultural and gendered Otherness, questions which deliberately challenge and destabilise many of the dominant institutionalised assumptions of western anthropology. This challenge has a global resonance that is not adequately explained by recourse to either Trinh's transnational identity as a Vietnamese-American, or the specific West African cultures she has filmed, or indeed to the common legacy of French colonial occupation that they share. To put it very simply, Trinh could have included footage from a different geographical location (say, the

Amazon rainforest), or from multiple locations around the world, and still arrived at the same eloquent set of reflections and challenges.

Chris Marker's *Sunless*, which in many respects is the touchstone for the global essay film tendency I'm concerned with here, likewise points unconvincingly towards what we may know or surmise of Marker's Russian / American / Hungarian origins and French native citizenship (recalling his fondness for simultaneously multiplying fictional alter-egos and effacing or dissimulating his physical and biographical presence); and far more towards a general condition of global circumnavigation that prompts reflection on how one goes about gathering and processing images—processing in a technical sense, as well as making sense of—in an increasingly globalised and time-space compressed world.

The premise of *Sunless* is that a fictional, globetrotting cameraman named Sandor Krasna, who touches down compulsively in Japan, Iceland, Guinea Bissau, Cape Verde, San Francisco, the Ile de France and a few other places, sends letters to an anonymous woman who reads and comments on them. As well as Krasna's footage (which is of course Marker's), the film includes archive material drawn from works by other directors and Marker's own back catalogue. A number of sequences in the film can serve to highlight Krasna's position as a global subject. Quite early on, Krasna returns to Tokyo to rediscover familiar locations in a city in which he, as someone who has no allegiance to family or homeland, professes himself at home among twelve million anonymous inhabitants.[12] His self-positioning within the classic stance of the carefree nomad-flâneur, however, is subtly undermined by the detachment of the woman's commentary at this point: she is not quoting Krasna but speaking about him, opening a space in which the viewer may, for instance, become conscious of the position of privilege from which Krasna travels the world (that of the white European male).[13] It is also revealing that, if at the beginning of the sequence Krasna (via his letters) is able confidently to identify and label the sites which appear visually—the Ginza owl, the Shimbashi locomotive, and the temple of the fox atop the Mitsukoshi department store – as his foray through Tokyo progresses, the voice lapses into silence, leaving a complex weave of sounds, and a flow of images that seem both ordinary and increasingly elusive. The subject dissolves without resistance under pressure from the world.

In a slightly later passage of the film, Krasna spends an extended period in his Tokyo hotel room watching and filming the television.

Sunless here proffers a remarkable staging of the condition of the global subject, located somewhere on earth but confronted with a flow of mediated images and sounds that compress the space of the world and the time of history right in front of them, compelling new habits of sense-making and action. Indeed, the very excess of speech in parts of this sequence, as Krasna compulsively seeks to make sense of and philosophise about his encounter with Japanese TV, foregrounds the complex semantic labours that the negotiation of rapid globalised media flows entails. As O'Byrne argues, the difference between contemporary global citizenship and older models or professions of world citizenship, which date back at least to the Western classical world, rests substantially on the way that modern mass media and communications technologies have transformed public consciousness of the globe and global events.[14] It is now virtually impossible for the global citizen to imagine acting on a pure and homogenous abstract "world," derived from limited awareness of and encounters with the complex interconnectedness and fearful intractability of world events, as well as the immense diversity of world cultures and experiences.

Peter Mettler's *Gambling, Gods and LSD* unfolds a rambling, open-ended and immensely ambitious enquiry into common global experiences of transcendence, which voyages through Canada, the Southwestern United States, Switzerland and Southern India. As with *Sunless*, Mettler's own transnational status as a Swiss-Canadian goes only a very limited way towards explaining the trajectory and ambitions of his film, and the mode of subjectivity that operates within it. Mettler claims that his operating principle for *Gambling, Gods and LSD* was the possibility of not looking for something while he was filming, but just looking.[15] Although it is tempting to pounce on this kind of statement for being wildly naïve, or dissimulating the filmmaker's own agenda; it remains worthwhile trying to keep faith with it, for what it conveys about the ethics of essayism. Mettler's stated intention is convincingly borne out in the aesthetic approach of *Gambling, Gods and LSD*: the insistently mobile first person camera; extended, contemplative observational sequences (the film runs to three hours in length); judicious editing choices that emphasise the mechanics of the journey and the abrupt unfolding of unexpected new encounters; and an intricate soundtrack that interweaves ambient music, direct and reworked/recontextualised diegetic sounds (including the voices of interviewees), and sporadically the essayistic voice of Mettler, reflecting on where and how the film is going. The net effect of these techniques is that the archetypal western spiritual seeker's journey from

West / North to East / South, unfolds as a global trajectory in which distinctions between self and Other, the exotic and the everyday, break down and become blurred. In *Sunless*, we learn that Sandor Krasna has travelled around the world four times and is now interested only in banality. One way of interpreting this comment is that enough routine exposure to other places and cultures will force the recognition that one person's frozen spectacle of the exotic is just the ebb and flow of another person's everyday life. As Catherine Russell comments, Mettler's quest for global knowledge and transcendent experience exists in uncomfortable tension with the materiality of the humdrum ordinary lives that his subjects are desperately trying to escape from.[16] Yet crucially, under the gaze of his camera, religious festivities in Mumbai seem just as bizarre, and just as unremarkable, as the devotions of the Toronto Airport Christian Fellowship church, and the candid recollections of a German-Swiss couple interviewed about their former heroin addiction.

How to respect the alterity of different global cultures, without distorting or reducing them to the shorthand of the exotic or the fundamentally same, while at the same time acknowledging and elaborating the ways in which, in a globalized world, they unfold as interconnected and interdependent? This remains a central question for both contemporary global citizenship and approaches to global representation. I have suggested that a number of significant contemporary essay films approach and open up this question in productive ways, by positing subjective states that transcend specific national or cultural allegiances, and seek somehow to confront the world as a whole. These works might be claimed as direct acts or records of global citizenship, or might simply offer a point of reflection upon and around what the subject positions of globality could be.

Notes

[1] "Der Essayfilm: Ästhetik und Actualität," Lüneburg University, Germany, 29 November-2 December 2007.
[2] Darren O'Byrne, *The Dimensions of Global Citizenship* (Portland, OR: Frank Cass & Co. Ltd., 2003), 90.
[3] Theodor Adorno "The Essay as Form." in *The Adorno Reader*, ed. Brian O'Connor (Oxford: Blackwell, 2000), 91-111; Georg Lukács, "On the Nature and Form of the Essay," in *Soul and Form* (London: Merlin Press, 1974), 1-18.

[4] His central work on the subject is *An Accented Cinema: Exilic and Diasporic Filmmaking* (Princeton: Princeton University Press, 2001). Although the term essay film is not one Naficy himself employs, his book nonetheless refers at some length to filmmakers like Chris Marker, Trinh T. Minh-ha and Jonas Mekas who in other contexts are readily embraced as film-essayists.

[5] Ibid, 13

[6] Michel de Montaigne, *The Essays: A Selection* (Harmondsworth: Penguin, 1993), 3.

[7] Adorno, "The Essay as Form," 101.

[8] Naficy, *An Accented Cinema*, 26.

[9] Consider many of the essays and extracts found in collections like *Global Local: Cultural Production and the Transnational Imaginary*, ed. Rob Wilson and Wimal Dissanayake (Durham NC: Duke University Press, 1996); *Multiculturalism, Postcoloniality and Transnational Media*, ed. Ella Shohat and Robert Stam (New Brunswick, NJ: Rutgers University Press, 2003), *Transnational Cinema: The Film Reader*, ed. Elizabeth Ezra and Terry Rowden (London and New York: Routledge, 2006).

[10] It is significant that in both films the distinction between fictional characters and social actors is provocatively blurred. *In Surname Viet Given Name Nam*, Vietnamese-American women are recruited to play the roles of actual Vietnamese women who lived through the aftermath of the war, with the resonances of their characters' experiences within their own everyday lives in the USA being foregrounded at the end of the film. In *Calendar*, the central characters, an Armenian-Canadian photographer and his wife, are played by director Egoyan and his wife Arsinée Khanjian.

[11] O'Byrne, *The Dimensions of Global Citizenship*, 90-92; Thomas Harrison, *Essayism: Conrad, Musil and Pirandello* (Baltimore and London: John Hopkins University Press, 1992).

[12] This passage alludes to Marker's first discovery of Tokyo in the film *The Koumiko Mystery* (1964).

[13] Here I draw on Stella Bruzzi's perceptive discussion of the complexities of the female narrative voice in *Sunless*, in her *New Documentary: A Critical Introduction* (London and New York: Routledge, 2000), 57-65.

[14] O'Byrne, *The Dimensions of Global Citizenship*, 92.

[15] "Transmitting the Invisible," interview with Peter Mettler, *Dox: Documentary Film Quarterly* 42 (2002): 14-15.

[16] Catherine Russell, "Cinephilia and the travel film: *Gambling, Gods and LSD*," in *Jump Cut* 48 (Winter 2006)
http://www.ejumpcut.org/archive/jc48.2006/GodsLSD/index.html

CHAPTER TWENTY ONE

ON FOG AND SNOW: THOUGHT AS MOVEMENT, OR THE JOURNEY OF THE ESSAY FILM

LAURA RASCAROLI

I was afraid of falling… then movement started.
—Sokurov, *Elegy of a Voyage*

While suggesting the impression of a musical or poetic composition that is melancholy in tone, the title of Alexander Sokurov's video *Elegy of a Voyage* (*Elegiya dorogi*, France/Russia/Netherlands, 2001) simultaneously conveys the idea of a (pensive) musing—a musing about travelling, or perhaps even of musing *as* travelling. A dual impression is, indeed, conveyed by the film: that there is a movement, a direction, a progression that belongs to thought; and that thought itself is movement—and that it travels by its own accord, almost independently of the subject.

Sokurov conjures such notions by thinking aloud while he travels, and by letting the thinking be triggered by the travelling, thus associating the two activities; as well as by problematising and undermining his own agency as both traveller and filmmaker. He does it, for example, by portraying his self as sunk in a disconcerting reverie; by describing the origin and motivations of his trip as beyond his grasp; by representing himself as possessed by motion, and at the same time as someone who is passively carried by vehicles (a boat, a car); by misrecognising places, or being only vaguely familiar with them; and by inscribing a split consciousness in the film—Sokurov is here simultaneously a silent *rückenfigur* and a disembodied voiceover.

I will return to these strategies later in my discussion, where I examine their motivations and effects in greater detail; first, however, I will contend that *Elegy of a Voyage* may be described as an essay film—or better, as a film in-between essay and travelogue. While developing my argument, I will explore the rhetorical strategies and textual commitments of essay films and of cognate forms that belong to the domain of the essayistic.

Of the essay, *Elegy of a Voyage* has a number of features, and firstly that it is a heretical text, in that it does not obey the laws of any genre and, indeed, resists classification—as in Adorno's contention that "the essay's innermost formal law is heresy." [1] Other critics have repeated the same concept in different words: the essay "does not obey any rules";[2] therefore, it is "*not* a genre, as it strives to be beyond formal, conceptual, and social constraint";[3] or, even more radically, it is a "nongenre." [4] However, no text exists in a void; the essay film owes to a number of traditions, and is indeed fruitfully described as "a meeting ground for documentary, avant-garde, and art film impulses." [5] This definition undoubtedly suits *Elegy of a Voyage*, which is all three things at once. Shot in Betacam SP, the 48-minute *Elegy of a Voyage* was born as an installation commissioned by the Boijmans Van Beuningen Museum, Rotterdam. Subsequently, reframed as non-fiction, it was nominated for Best Documentary at the 2001 European Film Awards, and screened at a number of film festivals. It was then digitally distributed by Facets, a company that specialises in art film, in its series devoted to the oeuvre of Alexander Sokurov—and therefore once again reframed as an authorial work.

Further characteristics that are commonly attributed to the essay are its subjectivity, its reflexivity and its self-reflexivity (all of which are evident in *Elegy of a Voyage*). Again, a range of critics may be summoned to support these claims. With reference to subjectivity and the reflection on the self, it is easy to start with Montaigne—whose essayistic work so profoundly shaped the field. Montaigne was, as he famously claimed, the subject of his own book, and wrote not to "pretend to discover things, but to lay open my self." [6] Of comparable importance is Lukács's demand that "the essayist must … become conscious of his own self, must find himself and build something of himself."[7] As for the essay's reflexivity, there is little need to reconfirm that the philosophical engagement with a problem or set of problems is a requirement of the form.

While those critics who have attempted to classify the essay film and its prerequisites disagree on some of them (for instance, voiceover), they all concur on the features listed above.[8] Yet, it seems to me that the cumulative definition that is drawn from these contributions, while incontrovertible, is also all-inclusive, generic and, ultimately, vague. True, the essay makes an argument; it is a field of open experimentation; and it is subjective. And yet, there exists a specific spectatorial experience of the essay film, which is quite distinct from the experience that the audience may have of a documentary (which also always makes an argument), of an avant-garde film (by definition a field of experimentation), or of a film poem (which is eminently subjective). An examination of the essay film's deeper textual structures is in order to identify what is so characteristic of the form, and distinguishes it from other genres.[9]

An essay is the expression of a personal, critical reflection, which is not offered as anonymous or collective, but as originating from a single authorial "voice,"[10] which approaches the subject matter not in order to present a factual report (the field of traditional documentary), but to offer a personal and thought-provoking reflection. At the level of rhetorical structures, then, the filmic essay decidedly points to the enunciating subject. The essay's enunciator, who overtly says "I," and usually admits to being the director of the film, may find expression through simple voiceover, or also embody in the text and, therefore, become a narrator. The relationship between author, enunciator and narrator, however, is never unproblematic or unreflexive; in the essay, the author tends to problematise and question not only her subject matter, but also her subjectivity and authorship. Authorship in the essay film is, thus, interstitial; it is played in the intervening spaces between the empirical author and his or her textual figures.

When defining the essay film, it is however essential to restore importance to the role of the spectator. Because the essay's enunciator is not an anonymous or generalised authority, is a subject who speaks for himself, takes responsibility for his discourse, and overtly embraces his contingent viewpoint, it follows that he does not speak to a broad, generic audience. The argument of the essay film is addressed to a real, embodied spectator, who is asked to enter into a dialogue with the enunciator, to follow his reasoning, and to respond by actively participating in the construction of meaning. The essay film is, then, a fragile field, because it must accept and welcome the ultimate instability of meaning, and thus embrace openness as its unreserved ethos. Rather than "pretend to discover things," as in Montaigne's already quoted passage, thus camouflaging a perfected and closed reflection as an open-ended process of uncovering, the essayist must ask many questions and offer few answers. Answers, then, are allowed to emerge somewhere else: in the position held by the embodied spectator. The essayist's need to problematise authorship itself is justified and required by the need to extend authorship to the audience.

It is around this textual structure, which translates into a constant address of the I/essayist to the you/spectator, that the experience of the essay film materialises and that the spectator's impression of being summoned to fully participate in the construction of essayistic meaning is achieved. The ways in which each essay film does this, however, significantly vary; after all, essays truly are heretical—and thus diverse, disjunctive, paradoxical, contradictory, open and free.

Critics frequently assimilate to the essay other forms such as diary films (the diaristic work of Jonas Mekas, for instance, is often discussed in terms of essay).[11] I propose that these cognate forms do not fully identify with the essay, but are best seen as belonging to the domain of the essayistic, while retaining their own characteristics. Diaries, travelogues and notebooks, like essays, all derive from literary and paraliterary genres. They all imply a strong impression of authorial subjectivity and, even more so than the essay, a clear autobiographical component (essays, which are always personal, may indeed not be autobiographical). Yet, their textual structures and their rhetorical strategies do not rely on the I/you relationship that is typical of the essay. They are, rather, monological texts—highly personal, self-addressed forms in which the enunciator is engaged in a dialogue with the self. This structure is, of course, paradoxical and impossible; as soon as a pen is put to a page, or a camera is turned on, even if allegedly for an entirely private use, a readership and an audience are always already implied.

Elegy of a Voyage is an interstitial text, in-between essay and travelogue. It is, ostensibly, the account of a journey, as suggested by the film's title; it is a sort of travel diary, in which the subject's concerns, as expressed through voiceover, are divided between the account of subjective impressions and perceptions, and the description of landscapes, places and people. The typical daily dimension of the diaristic, however, is eschewed, in favour of a much more uncertain temporality; similarly, space is rendered as indeterminate as possible, as if the travelled locations were mysterious and unknowable. Furthermore, the agency of the I, which is always clearly foregrounded in diaries (diaries, in fact, must say I and must say now), is here deeply problematised.[12] An essayistic drive to muse about large-scale issues—including religion and faith, weakness and fortitude, solitude and the longing for human contact, the meaning of life and the essence of art—emerges continually, and as in waves.

The interstitial positioning of *Elegy of a Voyage* is representative of the tendency of essayistic film forms towards hybridism and the exploration of uncertain generic, narrative, aesthetic, linguistic and ideological territories. It also actualises an implicit characteristic of the essay form: its performativity. The travel narrative, in combination with the essayistic drive, brings out the idea that the essay is performative, because it aims "to preserve something of the *process* of thinking." [13] In other words, the essay weaves the act of thinking into the text; and the verb "to weave" here explicitly suggests the metaphor of the forming of a fabric, thus evoking Adorno's conception of the way in which thought moves in the essay: "In the essay, concepts do not build a continuum of operation, thought does not advance in a single direction, rather the aspects of the argument interweave as in a carpet." [14] Weaving is, indeed, movement— one that does not have a straight direction, but that nevertheless advances, although in a side-to-side manner. This idea is perhaps not far from that of the essay's horizontal montage, as described by André Bazin in his review of Chris Marker's *Lettre de Sibérie* (*Letter from Siberia*, 1957):

> Marker brings to his films an absolutely new notion of montage that I will call 'horizontal,' as opposed to traditional montage that plays with the sense of duration through the relationship of shot to shot. Here, a given image doesn't refer to the one that preceded it or the one that will follow, but rather it refers laterally, in some way, to what is said. [15]

It is the lateral movement that accounts for the digressions that are typical of the essayistic, and generally of thought; digressions that are akin to the diversions and detours in a journey. But if the process of thinking is woven into the essayistic text, thus revealing the well-established metaphor of the text as fabric, [16] this shows that the essay is not a static, dead fabric, but a moving tapestry.

It is the idea of thinking as a route—of the progression of thinking, with its twists and turns and its branching out to the side roads of reflection—that Sokurov attempts to capture and reproduce in *Elegy of a Voyage*. The effect is achieved through the narrator's journey from an unspecified and uncertain point in space and time, a dreamy and snowy "here and now" (a never-mentioned Siberia), to a specific geographical location (the Boijmans Van Beuningen Museum in Rotterdam), which is however unknown to the traveller till the very end (in fact, the name of the museum and of the city are never uttered). But why so much indeterminacy? What does it achieve, and in what ways does it comment on essayistic cinema?

As mentioned, Sokurov's on-screen embodiment is twofold: as voice and as body; no synchronization is achieved between the two. His is the voiceover that speaks incessantly through the film. In terms of auditory space, it was recorded with close miking; it is dry, without reverb, hence creating a sense of I-voice, which occupies its own space. It is, in other words, not a voice projected into a physical environment, but almost the internal voice of consciousness. This effect evokes more decidedly the voice of a diarist engaged in a monologue, or dialogue with the self, than that of an essayist who addresses his audience as an equal partner in the construction of meaning, and is thus well suited to the travelogue, which is—as I have already suggested—a monological form. However, the voice ultimately does address the viewer, who is therefore asked to take up the position of an intimate partner, and is drawn to identify with the speaking self. The spectator is invited to share the effect of first-person experience, and of mild displacement and dizziness, undergone by the narrator/director.

Sokurov's figure also appears, but is always either shot from a distance (as when we see him framed by a snowy expanse), or else in close-up, but fragmented (his feet walking on the snow, or on the museum's parquet; his hands stroking a tree's blossoms, or lightly skimming the paintings), or even shot from behind. When the latter, all we see is his back—he is framed as an observer inside the picture, a *rückenfigur*. Silke Panse has discussed the meaning of the presence of Sokurov as a "back figure" in *Elegy of a Voyage*, with reference to the *rückenfigur* in German romantic painting. For the critic, the presence of Sokurov as a figure viewing a scene spread out before him achieves the effect of representing "the documentary film-maker as powerless, not only in confronting reality but also with regard to his own existence. He does not appear to have authorship on his own life or film, but rather looks at it as a distanced, but nevertheless emotional, observer." [17]

Thus, while being the product of a recognised auteur, who quite overtly places himself in the tradition of high art and in the lineage of modernist filmmakers,[18] through the combination/disjunction of the author's fragmented body or silhouette and of his voiceover, *Elegy of a Voyage* points to an unstable authorship and subjectivity. I invite to view this instability as that of the essay film itself—as a result of its ethos of unreserved openness; and as the essayist's resistance to assert clear authorship and, consequently, a coherent self. This may seem in contradiction with the idea of the essay as the product of a single and clearly situated authorial voice. On the other hand it is not, because the essayist questions established truths and, thus, also stable subjectivity. It is indeed necessary for the essayist to problematise his own authorship and self, in order to problematise truth, and to be able to fully open up to the subjectivity of the embodied spectator.

Elegy of a Voyage's uncertain subjectivity, however, does more than this; the fluidity of the text actualises the idea of thought as motion, and of the thinker/filmmaker as possessed by the motion of thought. At the onset of my chapter, I have briefly anticipated some of the strategies adopted by Sokurov to produce this effect; I will now delve deeper into the film, hoping to disclose the direction of its movement. In particular, I wish to attract the attention to the way in which thought and movement are grafted onto each other. The film opens with the image of an autumn tree, while snow falls before the camera lens; it is a fluctuating, indeterminate image: it is impossible to tell where we are. The voiceover states:

> Strange clouds appeared, as if it were summer, not autumn. The sky was dark and deep. Thunder could be heard. There was movement over the water. There were birds, birds who flew for no other reason than beauty alone. Then the clouds changed. The sky became flat. The light shone upon God's command. A scent of lilacs … Then the flight over water, deep and dangerous. I was afraid of falling. Someone left me … I started to feel better … I breathed deeply. Then movement started. I realised it was winter. I was cold. I could almost touch the road … so smooth and transparent.[19]

While it would be absurd to attempt something like a psychoanalytic interpretation of this stream of consciousness (which is coupled with an equally fragmentary stream of images), it is legitimate to point to the fact that the film opens under the sign of a displaced and dream-like subjectivity—and also in a phase of stasis (although a stasis that already contains movement as potentiality). It is when the initial displacement and the disconnected observation of images and feelings give way to movement that the film itself begins, literally, to move: the camera takes off and drives forward along the road,[20] the voice registers the emergence of a village and speculates about the absence of people in the streets. Suddenly, the film slows down; the narrator finds himself in a clearing, admires the landscape covered in snow, and muses on the invisibility of the world's beauty. The camera then begins to move again and frames a row of houses, while the voiceover goes back to the train of thoughts of before the stopover, and wonders whether it is possible to recall at least one face of those who once lived in the village.

It is in this way, following the alternating rhythm of the journey—which starts, accelerates, slows down, stops, and starts again—that the film unfolds, accompanying but also visually actualising, or indeed producing, Sokurov's stream of consciousness. The rhythm is not imposed by a self-conscious traveller in control of his route; frequently, Sokurov wonders about the ways, whereabouts, and reasons of his travelling ("For some reason, I was walking with a monk"; "What am I doing here? Who sent me?"; "I found myself in a completely different place"). The means of transport are also made indeterminate by verbal commentary and by visual and aural means. For instance, during the first section of the film, while images and montage convey the impression that Sokurov is travelling by car, on the soundtrack we hear his steps in the snow. And again, from being in a church Sokurov suddenly finds himself at a frontier post, but the journey is not visualised, and is indeed erased by the montage, which sutures the two places and deletes the sounds of the road, so that for a while we believe that we are still in the church. When beginning the leg of his journey by sea, then, Sokurov comments in voiceover: "The shore begins to move away," thus describing himself as passively carried by the boat, and almost unaware of his means of transport. While the effect of a dream-like subjectivity never vanishes in the course of the film, there is a progression in the narrator's understanding of his journey. When meeting a man at a roadside café, for instance, Sokurov comments: "Then I begun to realise that my travel had a purpose. I didn't come here by chance." However, agency is never of the subject; later, when arriving at the museum, Sokurov observes: "I was still alone, but someone guided me."

As already noted, this lack of agency is not simply of the traveller, but also of the author. For Panse, by way of this strategy Sokurov "exaggerates the notion of documentary film-making as a passive following of events" [21] and ultimately "opens the possibility of authorship towards infinity." [22] While agreeing with this analysis, *Elegy of a Voyage* is better described as an essay film than as a documentary. Indeed, faithful to the ethos of the form, Sokurov is here specifically engaged in the essayistic operation of constructing an eminently personal discourse, which clearly belongs to a single and well-identified author, while simultaneously problematising authorship and destabilising authority. As I have already argued, the goal of this operation is the creation of an intense involvement of the embodied spectator in the text: an active participation in the weaving of the textual meaning. By describing the reasons and destinations of the journey, and of the film's train of thoughts, as external to his agency, Sokurov opens the possibilities of authorship towards the infinity of the embodied spectators. Ultimately, he achieves this result by presenting thought as a process, a route, a weaving. While inextricably linked to the subject, thought here moves of its own accord, is open-ended, and not fully controlled by the author (who is little more than an observer inside the work of art); therefore, it is receptive of the subjectivity of others.

The fluidity of the text, its mimicking of the flow of thought, is also produced by the film's visual obsession for the element of water in all its forms and textures—gas, liquid, solid. Snowflakes move before the lens for much of the screen time, falling slowly or thickly, dancing and floating; the camera shifts upward to capture fast moving clouds; fog forms and rises before our eyes; snow covers everything, and even falls on the waves of the sea. Shot with special anamorphic lenses that flatten the image, often steeped in a dim light, and at times in semi-darkness, the whole film looks as if it was framed through a veil of trickling water; all the images of *Elegy of a Voyage* are slightly indistinct, and fluctuate, like waves. It is water, then—in its transformative power, its pulse, its mesmerising and mobile amorphousness—that visually conjures the idea of a movement that is mysteriously produced, and that possesses its own direction, rhythm and destination.

Notes

[1] Theodor Adorno *Notes to Literature*, vol. 1, ed. Rolf Tiedemann, trans. Shierry Weber Nicholsen (New York: Columbia University Press, 1991), 23.
[2] Jean Starobinski, quoted in Suzanne Liandrat-Guigues, "Un Art de l'équilibre," in *L'Essai et le cinema*, ed. Suzanne Liandrat-Guigues and Murielle Gagnebin (Seyssel: Champ Vallon, 2004), 8.
[3] Nora Alter, "The Political Im/perceptible in the Essay Film," *New German Critique*, 68 (Spring-Summer 1996): 171.
[4] John Snyder, *Prospects of Power: Tragedy, Satire, the Essay, and the Theory of Genre* (Lexington, Ken.: University Press of Kentucky, 1991), 12.

---

[5] Paul Arthur, "Essay Questions: From Alain Resnais to Michael Moore," *Film Comment*, 39, 1 (Jan/Feb 2003): 62.

[6] Michel de Montaigne, *The Essays of Montaigne*, trans. Charles Cotton, Third Edition (London: Printed for M. Gillyflower, et al, 1700), 254.

[7] György Lukács, "On the Nature and Form of the Essay," in *Soul and Form*, trans. Anna Bostock (London: Merlin Press, 1974), 15.

[8] For Lopate, for instance, "An essay film must have words, in the form of a text, either spoken, subtitled, or intertitled"; see Phillip Lopate, *Totally, Tenderly, Tragically* (Amsterdam: Anchor, 1998), 283. For Corrigan, less prescriptively, one of the main features of the essay film is "the interaction of a personal voice or vision, sometimes in the form of a voice-over"; see Timothy Corrigan, *Film and Literature: An Introduction and Reader* (Upper Saddle River, NJ: Prentice-Hall, 1999), 58.

[9] For a more complete and in-depth exploration of these structures, see Laura Rascaroli, "The essay film: problems, definitions, textual commitments," *Framework*, 49, 2 (Fall 2008): 24-47, and Laura Rascaroli, *The Personal Camera: The Essay Film and Subjective Cinema* (London: Wallflower Press, 2009).

[10] With voice I do not mean voiceover but point of origin, subjectivity, perspective.

[11] See, for instance, Michael Renov, *The Subject of the Documentary* (Minneapolis and London: Minnesota UP, 2004).

[12] The formal precondition of the genre consists, indeed, in "maintaining the enunciatory voice, which remains the same from start to finish, which says I and can only say *I* and *now*." Jean Rousset, *Le Lecteur intime. De Balzac au journal* (Paris: Corti, 1986), 218.

[13] Graham Good, *The Observing Self: Rediscovering the Essay* (London: Routledge, 1988), 20.

[14] Adorno *Notes to Literature*, 160.

[15] André Bazin, "Bazin on Marker" (1958), trans. Dave Kehr, *Film Comment*, 39, 4, (July/August 2003): 44.

[16] A metaphor that dates back at least to Quintilian – "text" of course deriving from the Latin *textus* (tissue) and *texere* (to weave).

[17] Silke Panse, "The Film-maker as *Rückenfigur*: Documentary as Painting in Alexandr Sokurov's *Elegy of a Voyage*," *Third Text*, 20, 1 (January 2006): 9.

[18] Sokurov, an artist with a profound interest in classical culture and in the fine arts, is, indeed, a true auteur in the tradition of modern cinema, who by his own admission recognises as masters only a few film directors, including Bergman, Eisenstein, Griffith, Fellini, Flaherty, Dreyer, and Tarkovsky; see, for instance, Jeremi Szaniawski, "Interview with Aleksandr Sokurov," *Critical Inquiry*, 33, 1 (Fall 2006): 13. For Fredric Jameson, Sokurov is "but one of a whole international generation – a word not taken in the biological or chronological sense – of great auteurs, who seem to renew the claims of high modernism in a period in which that aesthetic and its institutional preconditions seem extinct." Frederic Jameson, "History and Elegy in Sokurov," *Critical Inquiry*, 33, 1, (Fall 2006): 1.

[19] Dialogues are transcribed from the English subtitles of the Facets DVD edition of the film.

---

[20] It is also significant that the way the road is described by the voiceover ("I could almost touch the road, so smooth and transparent") is reminiscent of the film strip.

[21] Panse, "The Film-maker as *Rückenfigur*: Documentary as Painting in Alexandr Sokurov's *Elegy of a Voyage*", 9.

[22] Panse, 23.

CHAPTER TWENTY TWO

THE FILM IS IN FRONT OF US

STEVEN EASTWOOD

> Art, and especially cinematographic art, must take part in this task: not that of addressing a people, which is presupposed already there, but of contributing to the invention of a people.[1]

In *Cinema 2: The Time-Image* Gilles Deleuze suggests that the people depicted in the dominant forms of cinema, regardless of any film's country of origin, are never representative of an actual people. The people are in fact missing, and any attempts by others to create images on this missing people's behalf leads back to the continued absence of that people. The only way to resist this process is to organize one's own representation. But how can we speak of inventing a people (ourselves) and how might we enable the creative becoming of a people not-yet-here, without running into the problem of defining a teleologically rooted collective subject? Deleuze resists any temptation to propose a cine practice by which a people might group themselves, his objective being, rather, to speak to the cinematographic apparatus as a virtual realm capable of engendering new thought. For Deleuze, it is the possibility for new thought that will lead to the formation of a "people." It is an oversight on Deleuze's part however that he concentrates on what has been filmed, rather than on the situation of filmmaking. His concept for the emergence of a missing people finds illustration in the less intense entity of the completed film. Yet the film as outcome is precisely that which Deleuze, when speaking of the art object, says is left when the rush of extensivity we experience around a new thought has reduced in momentum.

In fact, very little film theory or philosophy of any kind gives analysis to the situation of filmmaking, although this would seem to be a fertile spacefor the becoming of a people, precisely because at this stage the representation (if that is the intention of the film) is still half-formed.

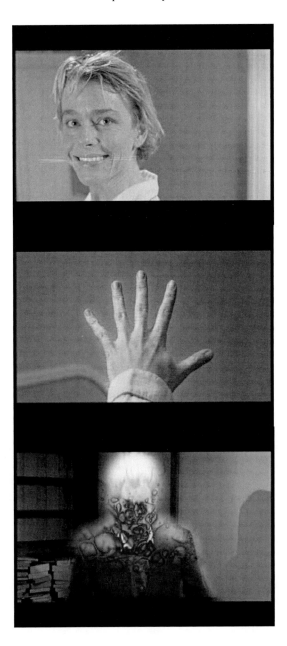

Fig. 1

Fig. 2

Fig. 3

Fig. 4

Fig. 5

Fig. 6

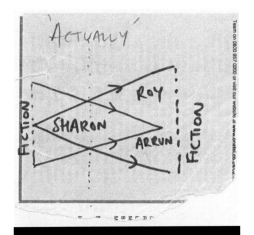

Fig. 7

Fig. 8

Fig. 9

The potency of a concept as event (its expression as action) is strangest during its midpoint, between idea and conclusion. It is not what we desire for our film then, but *how* we desire in our filmmaking. What kind of a tactic for filmmaking might produce such an open cine practice, one that commits our thoughts and our bodies to the not-yet of a film in process? Clearly one which is temporary in application, one which, to use Michel de Certeau's term, rents space in the place of the other (an other who attempts to represent a people), so as to speak in the voice of this other, whilst resisting representation. In the context of the moving image this other is the dominant order of the documentary and the fiction film. This is the minor cinema that Deleuze alludes to, whose practice must be accidental, adrift, contingent, for it has no fixed place, and nothing necessarily to say or show.

I am writing here as a filmmaker, one who regards theories and lenses as interchangeable. I am interested in what form of cinema remains in terms of envisioning and producing a people, whose crystalline and contingent identities are so different to the compressed selves that continue to represent us on the screen, in cliché and through story. Whereas most films work extremely hard to erase the ill-fitting nature of their manufacture, my practice gives emphasis to the event of filmmaking. I am going to tell the story here of a series of films I refer to as *The Actually Trilogy*. Each film in the trilogy acted as a progenitor for the next, the first addressing the event of cinema production through the frame of an experimental fiction, the second by way of a documentary film drift and the third by setting up a deliberately problematic composite of the two. *Of Camera* (2003, Figs. 1, 2 and 3) explores the abortive attempts of two people to be together in the same space. Their disagreement is fuelled by technical difference: the woman exists on videotape and the man on celluloid film. The story corrupts as the woman realises that she and her counterpart are incompatible and that they are being filmed, edited and played back. When watching *Of Camera* the viewer is eavesdropping on a character who senses that an author, crew and audience are in some way present. Topologically, she is boxed in a film system and we are looking in from outside of that system, investing, to varying degrees, in either her plight as a fictional character (can she reconcile her differences with the other character?) or her plight as a mediated subject (can she find stable ground within the mediation system she is close to transgressing?).

Materially, both celluloid and videotape always threaten to transcend the limitations of the virtual image they conduct and become more physically present, and *Of Camera* operates as an essay in the construction and maintenance of a screen order dependent on material conduction. The woman haptically *feels* each edit as a distressing of coherent, action-oriented film space, not so much jumping across impossible continuities of space and time as becoming swallowed-up in them instead, experiencing a tear in diegetic order. However, *Of Camera* is merely a fiction and this screen persona is just a piece in an artifice chain. The complex framework of the lived event of film production is recreated as schema. The performer can only offer the affectation of a crisis in thought and a slippage into self as mediation, for no character can encounter the film they are embedded within. But intermediaries inevitably come into existence in the gap between material process and diegetic narrative systems. The task is to try to inventively occupy this gap.

Where *Of Camera* was a tightly structured production that depicted, through fiction, the situation of becoming the film itself, *The Film* (2004) presents a factual experience of mediation, where the majority of the content is the experience of making the film. Having completed *Of Camera* I sought out a residency in an unfamiliar place, spending May 2004 in the town of Bridport on the south coast of England. It was there and during this period that *The Film* was recorded. Arriving as an outsider, I spent the month wandering the environs of the town without plan or direction, looking for strangers, hoping to find collaborators through unofficial and non-institutional means and to make a film with them. I frequented cafes, pubs and the town square, marking gaffer taped *T* positions for people to potentially hit, leaving a film clapperboard face up on the pavement with the word "real" written on it. This cinema busking was an inversion of street casting, in that I was purposefully casting out, with no opinion about whom I would find.

As a means to head nowhere with this potential film, I adopted the Situationist tactic of the dérive, which is the action of wandering without purpose or goal. The dérive provides a method for reclaiming place as space, and reclaiming time as not delineated in terms of the duality of work or leisure. It is typically a means to differently encounter an urban space, but this drift would be a wandering off into the landscape from an established schematic way of making. This film drift would deploy the very vernacular of cinema against itself and into the lived world, where it is necessarily less proper. Such a tactic makes of film an encounter with the actual, in which the nature of the encounter and the transformation of the subject determines on-screen content. It acts as a rudder that steers in the direction of a strange archipelago, where it is possible to become alien to one's origins, as filmmaker, and to a cultural history of cinema, and therefore new to an other who is filming with you. It is here in this non-place that a missing people has the means to congregate.

For the drifting filmmaker it is never desirable to settle on a landmass, whether in this case such a mass is the fiction film, the documentary, the cinematic essay, or the artist's moving image. It is preferable to move in between these continents, becoming lost, forgetting how to make films in order to give birth to an alien filmmaker inside. This mode of cinema uses artifice to invent spaces; it contravenes established lines, weaving and leaping, leading and misleading. It defiantly occupies the physical space of the film before it has arrived, in other words the pre-filmic as well as the pro-filmic spaces of production, which includes the bodies of the cast and crew as filming is taking place (or is about to take place), and the geographic situation around the event of filming. The film itself, even if it is finished, remains, paradoxically, an open-set, because the most accurate definition of this tactic is that the film is temporally in front of whomever is filming (the not-yet). The task, then, is to temporarily open a space from where these accents and moments of affect can emerge, where difference is generated by the film-as-intention. I describe this as filming our way to a film that is in front of us.

After a long chain of associations and chance encounters, I met Roy White and Arrun Denman, whom for five days allowed their lives to be taken up with very little else but the film production. Both recognized in the attitude of the project sensibilities comparable to their own form of "becoming," which is hill and coastal walking. In their desire to absent themselves from routine social situations and from habitual mental activity (what Roy describes in *The Film* as "The lumpy gravy"), the two men walk daily through repeated landscape sequences, to enable an altered interiority. Much of the filmmaking was conducted on or around their walks, but what walking is like for Roy and Arrun is never expressed. I also resisted developing ideas based upon Roy's rich character, and the temptation to draw Arrun's character out. In the film, neither are described in such a way that they could be understood as fully rounded historical subjects. There are no titles in *The Film*, none of the subjects are named using the standard of a strap line at the bottom of a frame, and the subjects who were unable to participate appear only as fragments of another possible film. The credits, such as they are, are spoken by Roy White over a black screen, as an imageless signature of the bodies, intentions, and places the film traverses. There are no content arcs, no introductions or conclusions, no stories, only events marked by edit and framing decisions, what Andrei Tarkovsky describes as "pointers to life."

We walked our way to the film that was in front of us, through disused cinemas, across hilltops and along beaches, via allotments, into a camera shop and out of the town. The film itself was an imagined veil directed towards the everyday in order to inventively encounter and make alterations to its contingent properties (Fig. 4). But such a virtual film changes, and so do we. As Arrun comments, "The film did become our life basically. It's like, on Wednesday night my life stopped—my normal life—and on Thursday morning, and for the period of those five days, my life completely changed. And on Tuesday or Monday night it will revert again." At times it was unclear when recording had begun and ended. The surplus details that surfaced helped form what might be described as a peculiar kind of structural-materialist documentary. We followed an errant trajectory of mistake and revision. There were no rules governing what we recorded because the film had no subject or content, and therefore there was no way of ascertaining what would be useful to shoot. This dialogic attitude between our utterances as filmmakers, the camera utterance, and the flow of the lived world around our film cannot be compared with speaking. It is the film-act itself, and not the voices of the authors or the history of our actions. Roy observed that it might not be my intention to finish the film, that, "The film might enter a cul-de-sac. It might not go." Without a subject to represent or a story to tell, and without even a pressing aesthetic principle, we were free on our drift to be more tactile with our images, and indiscriminate with where we looked. Without a plan, we were free to pour this film away into the lived world.

The very construction of a pro-filmic space (the camera pointed towards something) automatically creates a complex pre-filmic situation, where a different behaviour resides. *The Film*, during its recurring durational takes, features the camera panning and tracking to *scoop-up* this pre-filmic space, as an inscription of time. Deleuze is attracted to this inattentive gaze into the pro-filmic space, because it conveys the essentially open nature of sets. As D.N. Rodowick writes, the take, when at its greatest intensity (before it has been foreclosed) is an opening onto time; it is a direct image that shows to us the continuous emergence of the new and unforeseen.[2] The take is a virtual delineation of space and time, an interstice paired with the lived world. The words "Action!" and "Cut!" denote an alteration in behavior, as though lived time has temporarily ceased and mediated or performed time has replaced it, except that lived time has not ceased, it remains concurrent but no longer fore-grounded. The take is a form of absence where the person on-camera is returned to their non-filmic body when the take has ended. It is like a piece of time placed over time, because between the announcement and conclusion of the take exists (has existed) both time-time and film-time. A moment of time is not being taken; there is no hole left in the wake of a take because there is *time* time beneath or concurrent with film time. What film takes it still leaves intact. In a take, the subject and the object are therefore not divided in a Cartesian subject/object relation but one and the same. The long take forces the mind and the body to find thought and combat sensation, to wait, to be bored, to be a body craving purpose. This is what George Kouvaros calls, "dead time,"[3] which is the extra cinematic tension that arises as the take outstays its welcome.

Jean-Luc Godard remarked of *Pierrot le Fou* (1965) that, "The sole great problem of film, in each movie, is where and why to begin a shot and why complete it? … Life is the subject, with [Cinema]Scope and color as its attributes ... In short, life filling the screen as a tap fills a bathtub that is simultaneously emptying at the same rate." Godard speaks to the filmmakers' desire to bring the virtuality of time into the concrete of matter. Any film is inevitably the register of the various ways we try to touch time, and of a loss which is the very indiscernability and running away of time. So, the take is what makes film time and lived time concurrent, pressing together the sheets of temporality of the present (the filmed) and the future (the film). Not only is the take the recording of an intentionality—what we decided to film—it is also, in some way, the register of the fact that we had a film in mind during the take, a film which was not yet present. The on (and off) camera conversations with Arrun and Roy in *The Film* were based almost entirely on what they remembered of the film shoot to date, what they thought forthcoming filming should consist of, and what they imagined the finished film would look and sound like. These conjectures were not prompted in order to elicit specific future edit decisions, although this was how they were later applied, so that the vagaries and the fanning out of these commentaries guided the film's direction. When the two men sit together in the Palace Cinema (Fig. 5), addressing their thoughts to the (then blank) screen in front of them, they are envisioning the film when it is finished. In *The Film*, this event plays out as the present-present of that day of the shoot, from where a past is retrieved and brought into the present (the shooting during the days before) and a future is projected (Fig. 6). In the place of exerting a didactic telling of the events, this spoken material prompted rational and nonrational assemblages. Roy and Arrun's on and off-screen voices call up another voice, my voice, the articulation produced by montage, and together these voices, in dialogic relation, form what Rodowick describes as the visual and non-linguistic address of the film itself. The visual field is never bound with any stability to Roy or to Arrun's thinking, nor to their point of view; it is the beginning point of a thought that is mobile and without a thinker, so that gradually the film appears to be thinking by itself.

> There remains the possibility of the author providing himself with 'intercessors', that is, of taking real and not fictional characters, but putting these very characters in the condition of 'making up fiction', of 'making legends', of 'story-telling'. The author takes a step towards his characters, but the characters take a step towards the author: double becoming.[4]

In 2005 I set out to make the film *Actually* with the performers from *Of Camera* and *The Film*. In a Borgesian kind of paradox, the fact that we failed to make the film meant that the original concept, which was to have fictional characters cross over into the realm of the factual, and vice-versa, was fulfilled (Fig. 7). A woman is delivered by car to a remote coastal location, a stranded fictional character equipped with a red suitcase as prop. Not only is she reluctant to be in this place, she is also reluctant to be a character in a film. Is she the same person from *Of Camera*, the performer Sharon Smith who played that character, or someone else? On a beach she encounters Roy White and Arrun Denman. The woman complains when they try to speak to her but remains bound to them through a number of environments and dramatic false starts. These three characters from previous films mix like oil and water, but events finally settle on a hillside at sunset in what appears to be the place of a natural exchange. Inside this film however is another film—the film we didn't make—and this became the film we did make.

The reflexivity in *Of Camera* and the nomadicism of *The Film* conflate in *The Film We Didn't Make* (2006). The lived situation of filmmaking is taken one step further, to the level of predicament. A cast and crew were assembled, film apparatus erected, and then the filmmaker resisted directing anybody to do anything. This lack of intention created a shift in disposition and activity on-set. The fertile awkwardness I had imagined taking place on camera, by allowing pre-existing film personas to occupy screen space together, found a becoming instead behind it, where the camera could not catch it; between intention and contingency, it turned with the turn of the camera. Every planned scene collapsed at the point of execution, and so the group found themselves situated in the act of filmmaking, but without a film to make, left instead with the corporeality and ideation of a film in the "not-making" (Fig. 8). The resultant struggle for narrative belonging, for behavioural similarity, is the register of a gap where cinema and identity are co-existent. As we have already noted, the natural pro-filmic space is rendered unnatural by the film apparatus and the attitudes addressing it (especially when those attitudes are apparently without guide), but this denatured space provides a site for acting out differences and emergent attitudes. At different levels and at different times every member of the cast or crew attempted to rescue the film from its own implosion. One scene devised by the ensemble involved Sharon being discovered by Roy and Arrun at the shoreline, wrapped in a clear tarpaulin and made-up with fake blood. This scene was planned and executed by the group with the exception of myself, who waited with the equipment, further along the beach. As Arrun dryly comments in the coda to the film, "We had this idea that you would be this fictional character and Roy and I would meet you but we would remain natural. But it didn't work, because Roy and I were dragged into your fiction. But what it led to was the shoot on the top of the hill where we were just ourselves. So this idea was actually a failure, but that was the film, the fact that it failed."

Having dragged ourselves along the coastline and hilltops, with variously successful fabrications, I was suddenly keen to turn my back on the mess we had created and on my perceived near breakdown, in the hope of a fortuitous moment. And so I invited the cast and crew to pause on the hill and once more offered them the space of a 400-foot film magazine as a time that could roll away, where those on camera could do as they saw fit. The modern signal of celluloid as fictivity is wrongly cast in this apparently vérité sequence, and the resultant conversation in the wind-blown grass between Arrun and Sharon plots an unexpected curve from artifice to actuality (and back again). What happens? The clapperboard announces change, ushering in a new time, a fresh attitude. All of the characters are together and resting, awash with the rich colours of 16mm, whose indexical and bracketed time somehow draws out a new behaviour. The score, lifted from *Of Camera,* draws the viewer in, but runs out of force as the first words are spoken. Roys says, "I am going to walk off-set a moment and have a gander at Portland [...] and you and Arrun can be *Stars.*" A complex form of flirtation follows, as Sharon offers to feed Arrun chocolate and he declines (Fig. 9). There is a feeling of relief, as though the viewer can also rest now in this duration, comforted by the absence of scenarios, reassured by the strong composition of the frame pointed down from above onto the players, who are laying side by side. Although she is still in costume and with her red suitcase, Sharon's disposition has altered. She is now at once character, intercessor, and performer. Arrun's disposition has also changed. He is no longer silent, and as their banal and at times humorous conversation unfolds he begins to offer private information. Yet we cannot confidently shake off the residue of the previous amateur dramatics. In spite of the seemingly natural content of the conversation, this exchange is for the viewer complicated by subtitles, necessary owing to the poor location sound recording, so that when Arrun makes a deeply personal statement about a bereavement in his former life, there is a tension that comes into existence around his words.

It is accurate to say that this is the most eventful moment in the film and that it constitutes precisely the kind of confessional testimony that the documentary filmmaker obsessively looks for. But Arrun's words have the effect of causing discomfort. Issues of representation, not to mention manipulation, rush to the fore. When a film that is willfully playing with falsity unwittingly makes a space for a truthful declaration, it forces the filmmaker—as arbiter of frames and assemblage—into the role of an agent who is representing, who is suddenly the guardian of this event and the person who speaks for an other. It is this very aura of ambiguity as to the intentions of the filmmaker and the subjects that I find to be the most experimental of environs. To bring to this zone of uncertainty a group of people, on set, and a group of people in an audience, is to take them to a state where they oscillate between doubt and confidence. Affect floods in, and if it can be contained by the film and not subside into the merely useless, then a specific nature of thought and of filming that would commonly be closed down is prolonged as open. *The Film We Didn't Make* comes to an end outside of its storyline, in a peculiar intermediary realm where happenstance intersects with artifice, where characters and the players of those characters are permitted to fraternise with one another, to speak across a chasm—a people in between. The characters have merged with the world and left the film whilst the subjects have given themselves over to the film in front of them and temporarily left the world.

Notes

[1] Gilles Deleuze, *Cinema 1: The Movement-Image* (Minneapolis: University of Minnesota Press, 1986), 217.

[2]D.N. Rodowick, *Gilles* Deleuze's *Time Machine* (Duke University Press, USA, 1997), 111

[3] George Kouvaros (1998): *Where Does it Happen? John Cassavetes and Cinema at the Breaking Point* (Minneapolis: University of Minnesota Press, 251

[4] Gilles Deleuze, *Cinema 1: The Movement-Image*, 222.

BIBLIOGRAPHY

Adorno, Theodor. *Notes to Literature, Vol. 1.* Edited by Rolf Tiedemann, translated by Shierry Weber Nicholsen. New York: Columbia University Press, 1991.

—. "The Essay as Form." In *The Adorno Reader,* edited by Brian O'Connor, 91-111. Oxford: Blackwell, 2000.

Alter, Nora. "The Political Im/perceptible in the Essay Film." *New German Critique,* 68 (Spring-Summer 1996): 165-92.

Agamben, Giorgio. *Language and Death: The Place of Negativity.* Translated by Karen E.Pinkus with Michael Hardt. Minneapolis and Oxford: University of Minnesota Press, 1991.

—. *Idea of Prose.* Translated by Michael Sullivan and Sam Whitsitt. Albany: State University of New York, 1995.

—. *Homo Sacer: Sovereign Power and Bare Life.* Translated by Daniel Heller-Roazen. Stanford, California: Stanford University Press, 1998.

—. *Potentialities: Collected Essays in Philosophy.*Translated by Daniel Heller-Roazen. Stanford, California: Stanford University Press, 1999.

—. "The Dictation of Poetry." In *The End of the Poem: Studies in Poetics.* Translated by Daniel Heller-Roazen. Stanford, California: Stanford University Press, 1999.

—. *Means without End: Notes on Politics.* Translated by Vincenzo Binetti and Cesare Casarino. Minneapolis and London: University of Minnesota Press, 2000.

—. *Infancy and History: On the Destruction of Experience.* Translated by Liz Heron. London and New York: Verso, 2007.

Allert, Beate, ed. *Languages of Visuality: crossings between science, art, politics, and literature.* Detroit: Wayne State University Press, 1996

Alter, Nora. "Translating the Essay into film and installation." *Journal of Visual Culture* 6 (1) (2007): 44-57.

—. *Chris Marker.* Urbana and Chicago: University of Illinois Press, 2006.

Amelunxen, Hubertus, ed. *Photography After Photography.* London: G+B Arts, 1996.

Andrews, Molly and Michael Bamberg, eds. *Considering Counter-Narratives: narrating, resisting, making sense.* Amsterdam; Philadelphia: John Benjamins Publishing Company, 2004

Armes, Roy. *French Cinema since 1946, Volume Two: The Personal Style*. London: Zwemmer Ltd., 1985.

Arthur, Paul. "Essay Questions. The Essay as a Film Genre." *Film Comment* 39 (1) (Jan/Feb 2003): 58-63.

Astruc, Alexandre. "The Birth of a New Avant-Garde: La Caméra-Stylo." In *The New Wave*, edited by Peter Graham. Garden City: Doubleday, 1967.

Auslander, Philip. *Liveness: Performance in a Mediatized Society*. London; New York: Routledge, 2008.

Bakhtin, Mikhail M. *The Dialogic Imagination: Four Essays*. Austin: University of Texas Press, 1981.

Bakhtin, Mikhail. *Rabelais and His World*. Bloomington and Indianapolis: Indiana Press, 1984.

Bal, Mieke. *Looking In: The Art of Viewing*. Amsterdam: Abingdon, 2000.

—. ed. *The Practice of Cultural Analysis: Exposing Interdisciplinary Interpretation*. Stanford: Stanford University Press, 1999.

Barnouw, Erik. *The Magician and the Cinema*. Oxford University Press, 1981.

Barthes, Roland. *Mythologies*. Paris, Seuil, 1957.

—. *Camera Lucida*. New York: Hill and Wang, 1980.

—. *The Pleasure of the Text*. New York: Hill and Wang, 1998.

Bazin, André. *Qu'est-ce que le cinéma?* (Paris: Les Editions du Cerf, 1994)

—. "Bazin on Marker." Translated by Dave Kehr, *Film Comment* 39, 4, (July/August 2003): 44-45.

Bee, Susan, ed. M/E/A/N/I/N/G: *an anthology of artists' writings, theory, and criticism*. Durham, NC: Duke University Press, 2001.

Benjamin, Jessica. *Shadow of the Other: Intersubjectivity and Gender in Psychoanalysis*. London: Routledge, 1998.

Benjamin, Walter. *Illuminations* [1968]. Translated by Harry Zorn. London: Pimlico Press, 1999.

Bensmaïa, Réda. *Barthes à l'essai. Introduction au texte réfléchissant*. Tübingen: Gunter Narr Verlag, 1986.

Bergson, Henri. *Creative Evolution* [1907]. London: Dover Publications, 1998.

Bey, Hakim. *The Temporary Autonomous Zone, Ontological Anarchy, Poetic Terrorism*. Brooklyn, New York: Autonomedia, 1985.

Biemann, Ursula, ed. *Stuff It. The Video Essay in the Digital Age*. Zürich; New York: Voldemeer / Springer, 2003.

Blanchot, Maurice. *Thomas the Obscure*. New York: David Lewis, 1973.

Bleger, José. "Psycho-Analysis of the Pscho-Analytic Frame." *International Journal of Psycho-Analysis* 48 (1967): 511-519.

Bollas, Christopher. "Freudian Intersubjectivity: Commentary on Paper by Julie Gerhardt and Annie Sweetnam." *Psychoanalytic Dialogues* 11 (2001): 93–105.

—. *Free Association.* Duxford, Cambridge: Icon Books Ltd., 2002.

Bourriaud, Nicholas. *Postproduction.* New York: Lukas & Sternberg, 2002.

Boyer, M. Christine. *The City of Collective Memory: Its Historical Imagery and Architectural Entertainments.* Cambridge: MIT Press, 1996.

Braun, Marta. "The Expanded Present: Photographing Movement." In *Beauty of Another Order.* New Haven: Yale University Press, 1997.

Bruzzi, Stella. *New Documentary: A Critical Introduction.* London and New York: Routledge, 2000.

Buchloh, Benjamin. "Allegorical Procedures: Appropriation and Montage in Contemporary Art." *Artforum* 21 (September 1982): 43-56.

Burton, Johanna. "Mystics Rather than Rationalists." In *Open Systems. Rethinking Art c.1970*, edited by Donna de Salvo. London: Tate Publishing, 2005.

Buskirk, Martha. *The Contingent Object of Contemporary Art.* Cambridge, MA: The MIT Press, 2003.

Caillois, Roger. *Man, Play and Games.* Translated by Meyer Barash. University of Illinois Press, 1958/2001.

Calvino, Italo. *Invisible Cities.* London: Secker & Warburg, 1974.

Carroll, Noel, ed. *Beyond Aesthetics: philosophical essays.* Cambridge University Press, 2001

Cixous, Hélène. *The Book of Promethea.* Translated by Betsy Wing. Lincoln and London: University of Nebraska Press, 1991.

Coates, Jennifer and Joanna Thornbarrow, eds. *The Sociolinguistics of Narrative.* Amsterdam: John Benjamins, 2005

Connor, Michael ed. *JODI: COMPUTING 101B.* Liverpool: FACT, the Foundation for Art & Creative Technology, 2004.

Corrigan, Timothy. *Film and Literature: An Introduction and Reader.* Upper Saddle River, NJ: Prentice-Hall, 1999.

Coulter-Smith, Graham, ed. *The Visual-Narrative Matrix: interdisciplinary collisions and collusions.* Fine Art Research Centre, Southampton Institute, 2000.

Crimp, Douglas. "Pictures." New York: Artists Space, 1977.

—. "Pictures." In *Art After Modernism,* edited by Brian Wallis, 175-187. New York: The New Museum of Contemporary Art, 1984.

de Certeau, Michel. *The Practice of Everyday Life,* University of California Press, California. 1984.

Debord, Guy. *Society of the Spectacle and other Films.* London and Seattle: Rebel Press, Left Bank Books, 1992.

Deleuze, Gilles. *Cinema 1: The Movement-Image.* Minneapolis: University of Minnesota Press, 1986.

—. *Cinema 2: The Time-Image.* London: Athlone Press, 1989.

Deleuze, Gilles and Guattari, Félix. *Nomadology: The War Machine.* Cambridge, MA.: Semiotext(e), MIT Press, 1986.

Deleuze, Gilles & Guattari, Félix. *Kafka. Toward a Minor Literature.* Minneapolis; London: University of Minnesota Press, 1986.

Deleuze, Gilles. "Critique." In *Nietzsche and Philosophy*, translated by Hugh Tomlinson. London and New York: Continuum, 2005.

Deller, Jeremy, and Paul Ryan. *The Liverpool of Brian Epstein.* Liverpool: Tate Liverpool, 2007.

Derrida, Jacques. *Politics of Friendship.* London & New York: Verso, 1997.

de Toro, Fernando, ed. *New Intersections: Essays on Culture and Literature in the Post-Modern and Post-Colonial Condition*, Frankfurt am Main: Markus Wiener, 2003.

Doherty, Claire. ed. *From Studio to Situation.* London: Black Dog Publishing, 2004.

Druckrey, Timothy. "From Dada to Digital." In *Metamorphoses: Photography in the Electronic Age.* Edited by Mark Haworth-Booth, 4-7. New York: Aperture, 1994.

Eco, Umberto. "The Poetics of the Open Work" [1962]. In *Participation.* Edited by Claire Bishop, 20-40. Cambridge, Massachusetts: MIT Press, 2006.

—. *On Literature.* London: Vintage, 2006.

Ekeberg, Jonas & Slyngstadli, Ole eds. *How to look at Art Talk, Aesthetics. Capitalism.* Verksted #2/3, 2004.

Elsaesser, Thomas, ed. *Harun Farocki. Working on the Sight-Lines.* Amsterdam: Amsterdam University Press, 2004.

Ezra, Elizabeth and Terry Rowden, eds, *Transnational Cinema: The Film Reader.* London and New York: Routledge, 2006.

Flaxman, Gregory, ed. *The Brain is the Screen: Deleuze and the Philosophy of Cinema.* Minneapolis: University of Minnesota, 2000.

Foster, Hal. *Recodings.* Port Townsend, WA: Bay Press, 1985.

—. *The Return of the Real.* Cambridge, MA: The MIT Press, 1996.

Fraser, Robert. *The Victorian Quest Romance.* Northcote House Publishers Ltd., 1998.

Freud, Sigmund. "On Beginning the Treatment (Further Recommendations on the Technique of Psycho-Analysis I)" [1913] In *The Standard Edition of the Complete Psychological Works of Sigmund Freud, Volume XII (1911-1913): The Case of Schreber, Papers on Technique and Other Works*, edited by James Strachey. London: The Hogarth Press, 1958.

—. "Two Encyclopedia Articles: (A) Psycho-Analysis" [1923] In *The Standard Edition of the Complete Psychological Works of Sigmund Freud, Volume XVIII (1920–1922): Beyond the Pleasure Principle, Group Psychology and Other Works,* edited by James Strachey, London: The Hogarth Press, 1955.

—. "Constructions in Analysis" [1937] In *The Standard Edition of the Complete Psychological Works of Sigmund Freud, Volume XXIII (1937–1939): Moses and Monotheism, An Outline of Psycho-Analysis and Other Works*, edited by James Strachey, London: The Hogarth Press, 1963.

Gade, Rune and Anne Jerslev, eds. *Performative Realism: Interdisciplinary Studies in Art And Media.* Copenhagen: The Museum of Tusculanum Press, 2005

Gauthier, Guy. *Un siècle de documentaires français. Des tourneurs de manivelle aux voltigeurs du multimedia.* Paris: Armand Colin, 2004.

Gevaert, Yves ed. *Qu'est-ce qu'une Madeleine? A Propos du CD-ROM Immemory de Chris Marker.* Paris: Centre Georges Pompidou, 1997.

Gibson, Andrew *Towards a Postmodern Theory of Narrative.* Edinburgh: Edinburgh University Press, 1996.

Gillick, Liam. "Contingent Factors: A Response to Claire Bishop's 'Antagonism and Relational Aesthetics'." *October* 115, (Winter 2006): 95-106.

Good, Graham. *The Observing Self: Rediscovering the Essay.* London: Routledge, 1988.

Green, André. "Potential Space in Psychoanalysis: The Object in the Setting." In *Between Reality and Fantasy:Transitional Objects and Phenomena*, edited by Simon A. Grolnick and Leonard Barkin, 169–189. New York; London: Jason Aronson Inc., 1978.

—. "The Analyst, Symbolization and Absence in the Analytic Setting (On Changes in Analytic Practice and Analytic Experience) – In Memory of D. W. Winnicott." *International Journal of Psycho-Analysis*, 56 (1975): 1-22.

—. "Surface Analysis, Deep Analysis." *International Review of Psycho-Analysis* v. 1 (1974): 415–423.

Guattari, Félix. *Chaosmosis: An Ethico-Aesthetic Paradigm*. Indianapolis: Indiana University Press, 1995.

Guerin, Frances and Roger Hallas eds. *The Image and the Witness*. London: Wallflower Press, 2007.

Guillen, Claudio. *The Anatomies of Roguery: The Origins and the Nature of Picaresque Literature*. New York: Garland Publishing, 1987.

Hacking, Ian. *Representing and Intervening*. Cambridge University Press, 1983.

Hansen, Mark B. N. *New Philosophy for New Media*. Cambridge, MA: The MIT Press, 2004.

Hansen, Miriam. "Mass Culture as Hieroglyphic Writing: Adorno, Derrida, Kracauer." *New German Critique* 56 (Special Issue on Theodor W. Adorno) (1992): 43-73.

Harrison, Andrew. *Philosophy and the Arts: seeing and believing*. Bristol: Thoemmes Press, 1997

Harrison, Thomas. *Essayism: Conrad, Musil and Pirandello*. Baltimore and London: John Hopkins University Press, 1992.

Heaney, Seamus. *Finders Keepers (Selected Prose 1971-2001)*. London: Faber and Faber, 2002.

Heiser, Jörg. "Emotional Rescue." *Frieze,* 71, (2002)

Heiser, Jörg, Susan Hiller, Ellen Kintisch, Christine Seifermann, Jan Verwoert. *Romantic Conceptualism*. Kerber Verlag, 2008.

Holquist, Michael. *Dialogism*. Routledge, London, 1990.

Hubbard, Phil, Rob Kitchin and Gill Valentine eds. *Key Thinkers on Space and Place*. London: Sage Publications, 2004.

Hullot-Kentor, Robert. "Title Essay." *New German Critique* 32. (Spring - Summer, 1984): 141-150.

Hutcheon, Linda. *A Poetics of Postmodernism: History, Theory, Fiction*. London: Routledge, 1988.

—. *A Theory of Parody*. Chicago: University of Illinois Press, 2000.

Huyssen, Andreas. *Present Pasts: Urban Palimpsests and the Politics of Memory*. Stanford: Stanford University Press, 2003.

Jameson, Frederic. "History and Elegy in Sokurov." *Critical Inquiry* 33, 1, (Fall 2006): 1-12.

Jay, Martin. *Songs of Experience: Modern American and European Variations on a Universal Theme*. California: University of California Press, 2005.

Jones, Amelia. *Body Art: Performing the Subject*, University of Minnesota Press, 1998.

Kear, Jon. *Sunless*. Wiltshire: Flicks Books, 1999.

Kelly, Karen and Lynne Cooke, eds. *Francis Alÿs, Fabiola: An Investigation*. New York: Dia Art Foundation, 2008.

Kouvaros, George. *Where Does it Happen? John Cassavetes and Cinema at the Breaking Point,* Minneapolis: University of Minnesota Press, 2004.

Laclau, Ernesto. *New Reflections on the Revolution of our Time*. London, New York: Verso, 1990.

Laclau, Ernesto & and Mouffe, Chantal. *Hegemony and Socialist Strategy: Towards a Radical Democratic Politics*. London, New York: Verso, 2001.

Law, John. *After Method: Mess in Social Science Research*. London: Routledge, 2004

Laxton, Susan, "The Guarantor of Chance: Surrealism's Ludic Practices." *Papers of Surrealism* 1 (2003).
http://www.surrealismcentre.ac.uk/papersofsurrealism/journal1/index.htm

Leach, Neil, ed. *Rethinking Architecture: A Reader in Cultural Theory*. London: Routledge, 1997.

—. *The Anaesthetics of Architecture*. London: MIT Press, 1999.

Liandrat-Guigues, Suzanne. "Un Art de l'équilibre." In *L'Essai et le cinema*. Edited by Suzanne Liandrat-Guigues and Murielle Gagnebin, 7-12. Seyssel: Champ Vallon, 2004.

Lipman, Jean and Richard Marshall. *Art About Art*. New York: E.P. Dutton, 1978.

Lippard, Lucy R. *Six Years: the dematerialization of the art object from 1966-1972*. Berkeley: University of California Press, 1973/2001.

Lister, Martin. *The Photographic Image in Digital Culture*. London: Routledge, 1995.

Lomax, Yve. *Sounding the Event: Escapades in dialogue and matters of art, nature and time*. London and New York: I.B.Tauris, 2005.

Lopate, Phillip. "In Search of the Centaur. The Essay-Film." In *Beyond Document. Essays on Nonfiction Film*. Edited by Charles Warren, 243-270. Middletown: Wesleyan University Press, 1996.

—. *Totally, Tenderly, Tragically*. Amsterdam: Anchor, 1998.

Lorraine, Tamsin. *Irigaray and Deleuze, Experiments in Visceral Philosophy*. Ithaca and London: Cornell University Press, 1999.

Lukács, György. "On the Nature and Form of the Essay." In *Soul and Form*, translated by Anna Bostock, 1-18. London: Merlin Press, 1974.

Maleuvre, Didier. *Museum Memories: History, Technology, Art*. Stanford: Stanford University Press, 1999.

Manovich, Lev.*The Language of New Media*. Cambridge, MA: The MIT Press, 2001.

Marker, Chris. *Commentaires*. Paris: Editions du Seuil, 1961.

Massumi, Brian. *Parables for the Virtual: Movement, Affect, Sensation*. Durham: Duke University Press, 2002.

Mettler, Peter. "Transmitting the Invisible" [interview]. *Dox: Documentary Film Quarterly* 42 (2002), 14-15.

Mignon Nixon. "On the Couch." *October* 113 (Summer 2005): 39–76.

Miller, James. *Quests Surd and Absurd Essays in American Literature*. University of Chicago Press, 1967.

Mitchell, William J. T. *The Reconfigured Eye: Visual Truth in the Post-Photographic Era*. Cambridge, MA: The MIT Press, 2004.

Morison, Heather and Ivan Morison. *Foundation and Empire*. ARTicle Press, 2004.

Momigliano, Luciana Nissin. "The Analytic Setting; a Theme with Variations." In *Continuity and Change in Psychoanalysis: Letters from Milan,* 33–61. London; New York: Karnac Books, 1992.

Montaigne, Michel de. *The Essays: A Selection*. Harmondsworth: Penguin, 1993.

Naficy, Hamid. *An Accented Cinema: Exilic and Diasporic Filmmaking*. Princeton: Princeton University Press, 2001.

Nancy, Jean-Luc. "An Exchange, Jean-Luc Nancy and Chantal Pontbriand." In *Common Wealth*, edited by Jessica Morgan, 111-119. London: Tate Publishing, 2003.

Negri, Antonio. *Time for Revolution*. Translated by Matteo Mandarini. New York and London: Continuum, 2003.

Nora, Pierre, ed. *Realms of Memory*. New York: Columbia University Press, 1996.

O'Brien. F. *The Third Policeman*, London: Flamingo, 1993.

O'Byrne, Darren. *The Dimensions of Global Citizenship*. Portland, OR: Frank Cass & Co. Ltd., 2003.

Ofner, Astrid, ed. *Jacques Demy / Agnès Varda*. Vienna: Viennale, 2006.

—. ed. *Der Weg der Termiten. Beispiele eines essayistischen Kinos 1909-2004*. Wien: Viennale, 2007.

Panse, Silke. "The Film-maker as *Rückenfigur*: Documentary as Painting in Alexandr Sokurov's *Elegy of a Voyage*." *Third Text* 20, 1 (January 2006): 9-25.

Pantenburg, Volker. *Film als Theorie: Bildforschung bei Harun Farocki und Jean-Luc Godard*. Bielefeld: Transscript, 2006.

Parsons, Michael. "Psychic Reality, Negation, and the Analytic Setting" and "Dialogues with André Green." In *The Dead Mother: The Work of André Green,* edited by Gregorio Kohon, 59–75. London: Routledge, published in association with the Institute of Psycho-Analysis, 1999.

Pasolini, Pier Paolo. "The Cinema of Poetry." In *Heretical Empiricism*, edited by Louise K. Barnett. Indiana University Press, Bloomington, 1988.

Paulson, William. "Swimming the Channel." In *Mapping Michel Serres*, edited by Niran Abbas, 25-36. Ann Arbor: University of Michigan Press, 2005.

Pellon, Gustavo and Julio Rodriguez-Luis, (eds.) *Upstarts, Wanderers or Swindlers: Anatomy of the Picaro*. Rodopi Publishing, 1986.

Perec, Georges and Adair, Gilbert. *A Void*. London: Harvill Press, 1995.

—. *Life A User's Manual*. London: Vintage, 2003.

Perniola, Mario (2004) *Art and its Shadow*. London: Continuum.

Phelan, Peggy. *Unmarked: the politics of performance*. London: Routledge, 1993.

Plantinga, Carl (1997) *Rhetoric and Representation in the Nonfiction Film*, Cambridge University Press, UK.

Raban, Jonathan. *Soft City*. London: Harvill Press, 1994.

Rancière, Jacques. "Problems and Transformations in Critical Art." In *Participation*, edited by Claire Bishop, 83-93. Cambridge, Massachusetts: MIT Press, 2004.

Rascaroli, Laura. "The essay film: problems, definitions, textual commitments." *Framework* 49, 2 (Fall 2008): 24-47.

—. *The Personal Camera: The Essay Film and Subjective Cinema*. London: Wallflower Press, 2009.

Reiser, Martin, ed. *New Screen Media: cinema/art/narrative*. London: British Film Institute, 2002

Rendell, Jane. "Architecture-Writing." In *Critical Architecture,* edited by Jane Rendell, special issue of the *Journal of Architecture* v. 10. n. 3 (June 2005): 255–64.

—. "Site-Writing: Enigma and Embellishment." In *Critical Architecture* edited by Jane Rendell, Jonathan Hill, Murray Fraser and Mark Dorrian, xx-xx. London: Routledge, 2007.

—. *Site-Writing: The Architecture of Art Criticism*. London: IB Tauris, forthcoming 2009.

Renov, Michael. *The Subject of the Documentary*. Minneapolis and London: Minnesota UP, 2004.

Reynolds, Anthony. "Romantic Ignorance, The Hope of Nonknowledge." *Angelaki, Journal of Theoretical Humanities*. Vol.10. No.3, (Dec 2005).

Ricoeur, Paul. *Time and Narrative: Volume 1*. Chicago: The University of Chicago Press, 1984.

Rodowick, D.N. *Gilles Deleuze's Time Machine*, Durham, N.C.: Duke University Press, 1997.

Rogoff, Irit. "Wegschauen. Partizipation in der visuellen Kultur," *Texte zur Kunst*, 9. Jahrgang, Heft 36, (Dezember 1999): 8-112

Rousset, Jean. *Le Lecteur intime. De Balzac au journal*. Paris: Corti, 1986.

Russell, Catherine. "Cinephilia and the travel film: *Gambling, Gods and LSD*." *Jump Cut* 48 (Winter 2006) (accessed 27 July 2008) http://www.ejumpcut.org/archive/jc48.2006/GodsLSD/index.html

Rutherford, Anne. "The Poetics of a Potato Documentary that Gets Under the Skin." *Metro* 137 (2003): 126 -131.

Ryle, Gilbert. "The Thinking of Thoughts, What is 'Le Penseur' Doing?" In *Collected Essays, Collected Papers Vol. 2*. Bristol: Thoemmes Antiquarian Books, 1990.

Sadoul, Georges. *Chronique du cinéma français 1939-1967. Ecrits (1)*. Paris: Union générale d'éditions, 1979.

Sandino, Linda, ed. "Telling Stories: Oral Histories and Material Culture." *The Journal of Design History*. Vol. 19, no.4 (Winter 2006)

Scherer, Christina. *Ivens, Marker, Godard, Jarman. Erinnerung im Essayfilm*. München: Fink, 2001.

Scholz, Trebor, *On Open Work by Umberto Eco*. URL (accessed May, 2008): http://distributedcreativity.typepad.com/reading_group/2005/10/post.html.

Sebald, W.G. *Austerlitz*. London: Penguin, 2001.

Serres, Michel. *Hermes: Literature, Science, Philosophy*. Baltimore: John Hopkins University Press, 1982.

—. "Literature and the Exact Sciences." *Substance*, Vol.18, No.2, Issue 59, (1989): 3-34.

—. *Genesis*. Ann Arbor: University of Michigan Press, 1995

—. *The Natural Contract*. Ann Arbor: University of Michigan Press, 1995.

—. *The Troubadour of Knowledge*. Ann Arbor: University of Michigan Press, 1997.

Serres, Michel and Bruno Latour. *Conversations on Science, Culture and Time*. Ann Arbor: University of Michigan Press, 1995.

Shohat, Ella and Robert Stam, eds, *Multiculturalism, Postcoloniality and Transnational Media*. New Brunswick, NJ: Rutgers University Press, 2003.

Silverman, Kaja. *World Spectators*. Stanford: Stanford University Press, 2000.

Smethurst, Paul. *The Postmodern Chronotope: Reading Space and Time in Contemporary Fiction*. Amsterdam: Rodopi, 2000.

Smith, Alison. *Agnes Varda*. Manchester University Press, 1998.

Smithson, Robert. "A Museum of Language in the Vicinity of Art." *Art International* 12, 3 (March 1968): 21.

Snyder, John. *Prospects of Power: Tragedy, Satire, the Essay, and the Theory of Genre.* Lexington, Ken.: University Press of Kentucky, 1991.

Sobchack, Vivian. *The Address of the Eye: Phenomenology of Film Experience.* Princeton University Press, 1992.

Steyn, Juliet. *Act 1: Writing Art (Art Criticism and Theory Series).* London; East Haven, Connecticut: Pluto Press, 1995

Stewart, Susan. *On Longing: Narratives of the Miniature, the Gigantic, the Souvenir, the Collection,* Durham, N.C.: Duke University Press, 1993.

Stoller, Paul. *The Cinematic Griot.* Chicago: University of Chicago Press, 1992.

Sturken, Marita and Lisa Cartwright, eds. *Practices of Looking.* Oxford University Press, 2001

Solnit, Rebecca. *Wanderlust: A History of Walking.* Verso Books, 2006.

—. *A Field Guide to Getting Lost.* Canongate Books, 2006.

Richard Stamelman, *Lost Beyond Telling: Representations of Death and Absence in Modern French Poetry.* Ithaca, New York: Cornell University Press, 1985.

Swift, Rebeccca, ed., *A. S. Byatt and Ignes Sodré: Imagining Characters: Six Conversations about Women Writers.* London: Chatto & Windus, 1995.

Szaniawski, Jeremi. "Interview with Aleksandr Sokurov." *Critical Inquiry* 33, 1 (Fall 2006): 13-27.

Tarkovsky, Andrei (1989) *Sculpting in Time. Reflections on the Cinema,* University of Texas Press, USA.

Thrift, Nigel. "Movement-Space: the Changing Domain of Thinking Resulting from the Development of New Kinds of Spatial Awareness." *Economy and Society,* Vol. 33, No. 4, (2004): 582-604.

—. "Summoning Life." In *Envisioning Human Geographies,* edited by Paul Cloke and Philip Crang, 81-103. London: Arnold, 2004.

—. *Non-Representational Theory: Space, Politics, Affect.* London: Routledge, 2007.

Todd, Peter and Benjamin Cook eds., *Subjects and Sequences: A Margaret Tait Reader.* London: Lux, 2004.

Varda, Agnès. *VARDA par AGNES.* Paris: Cahiers du cinéma, 1994.

Varela, Francisco. "The Reenchantment of the Concrete." In *Incorporations,* edited by Jonathan Crary & Sanford Kwinter, 320-338. New York: Zone, 1992.

Verwoert, Jan. *Bas Jan Ader: In Search of the Miraculous.* London: Afterall, 2006.

Viola, Bill. *Reasons for Knocking at an Empty House: The Visionary Landscape of Perception.* London: Thames and Hudson, 2005.

White, Hayden. *Tropics of Discourse: Essays in Cultural Criticism.* London: John Hopkins University Press, 1978.

Wilson, Rob and Wimal Dissanayake, eds. *Global Local: Cultural Production and the Transnational Imaginary.* Durham NC: Duke University Press, 1996.

Winnicott, D. W. "Metapsychological and Clinical Aspects of Regression Within the Psycho–Analytic Set-Up." *International Journal of Psycho-Analysis*, 36 (1955): 16–26.

Winnicott, D. W. *Playing and Reality.* London: Routledge, 1991.

Wulff, Constantin and Blümlinger, Christa, eds. *Schreiben, Bilder, Sprechen. Texte zum essayistischen Film.* Wien: Sonderzahl, 1992.

CONTRIBUTORS

Åsa Andersson works across images, site-related projects, and prose-poetic text. She holds a PhD in Fine Art and Philosophy (Staffordshire University, 1999) around questions of intimacy and spatiality from a phenomenological perspective. Relating to this is an interest in language, fragile constructions, modernist/contemporary architecture and Japanese aesthetics. Recent activities include the Nagasawa Art Park, Artist-in-Residence Programme in Japanese Water-based Woodblock Printmaking, on Awaji Island, Japan. Åsa is based in Stockholm and acts as a Research Awards Coordinator (0.3) at Leeds Metropolitan University and has taught within the field of Fine Art at several institutions and contributed to a children/philosophy/photography project.

Stuart Brisley is an independent artist working with text, painting, performance and social projects and more recently on the web. His challenging performance work of the 1960s and 1970s endures as an influence, playing a fundamental part in the development of installation and performance art. Founder of the *Artist Project Peterlee*, County Durham in 1976, renamed *The Peterlee Project* in 2004, Brisley continues to produce a living history stretching over 25 years. He is currently working on the *Peterlee Opera* with composer Jay Arden. He has exhibited in recent years at the Arnolfini, John Hansard Gallery, Rooseum Centre, Malmo, South London Gallery and Whitechapel Gallery in 2002. Publications include a novel, *Beyond Reason*: *Ordure* (Bookworks 2003) and a video *The Eye*, recently published by Illuminations.

Martha Buskirk is Professor of Art History and Criticism at Montserrat College of Art in Beverly, Massachusetts. She is author of *The Contingent Object of Contemporary Art* (MIT Press, 2003) and also co-editor of *The Duchamp Effect* (MIT Press, 1996), with Mignon Nixon, and *The Destruction of Tilted Arc: Documents* (MIT Press, 1990), with Clara Weyergraf-Serra. She is currently completing a new book, *Seeing Through the Museum: Art, Life, Commerce,* that examines intersections between museum history and contemporary artistic practices.

Emma Cocker is a Senior Lecturer in Fine Art at Nottingham Trent University, whose current research explores how irresolution, uncertainty, disorientation and the process of 'getting lost' can be discussed as critical conditions of artistic practice. Recent conference papers and essays include "Desiring to be led Astray," *Papers of Surrealism* (2007); "The Art of Misdirection: Anti-Guides and Aimless Wandering," in "Burning Public Art," *Dialogue,* (2007); "Chasing Shadows – Tactics of Getting Lost," *Repeat Repeat,* Chester University (2007) and *PSi #13 Happening/Performance/Event,* New York University (2007). She is a co-editor of the publication, *Transmission: Speaking and Listening* (Volumes 3 - 5).

Stephen Connolly is an artist filmmaker whose practice is concerned with exploring single screen cinematic montage. The resulting work constructs a discourse in fragments, raising questions about the relationships between our belief systems, history and politics. His work has been widely screened in film and media festivals: Ann Arbor Film Festival, Michigan, Rotterdam International Film Festival, Melbourne International Film Festival and in December 2008, a solo screening at the British Film Institute, London. Awards and commissions include New Contemporaries, Liverpool and London, 2006, NOW commission with Patrick Keiller, Nottingham 2007 and LAFVA Award, Film London, 2008.

Steven Eastwood is a filmmaker whose practice spans experimental fiction, documentary, cinematic essay and artists' moving image. International screenings include the ICA, BAFTA, EMAF, the Lux Centre, Anthology Film Archives and Encounters. Recent exhibitions include *Artists Vs Hollywood*, QUT Queensland; *Interior Ritual*, KKprojects, New Orleans; *A Walk Through*, Stephen Lawrence Gallery, London. He has published numerous articles and book chapters and regularly programmes screenings. Eastwood is director of Paradogs productions and the co-founder of the OMSK arts laboratory event. He gained his PhD through UCL, The Slade and has taught widely in the UK and USA. www.cinemaintothereal.org

Maria Fusco is a Belfast-born writer based in London, working across fiction, art criticism and theory. She contributes to a broad range of national and international magazines, journals, catalogues and books, most recently *Hey Hey Glossolalia* published by Creative Time in New York. She is the founder and editor of *The Happy Hypocrite*, a new journal for and about experimental art writing (www.thehappyhypocrite.org), and edited *Put About: A Critical Anthology on Independent Publishing* and is also convening an accompanying conference at Tate Modern. She is currently the Director of Art Writing, at Goldsmiths College in London, where she leads MFA Art Writing.

Polly Gould is an artist and writer based in London. She has shown work widely in the UK and abroad. Recent work has explored landscape, death, our relationships as speaking subjects and our urge to narrate. Gould's short story was included in *The Alpine Fantasy of Victor B. and Other Stories*, a collection of fiction by leading contemporary British artists published by Serpent's Tail in 2006. Her drawing was selected for the Jerwood Drawing Prize 2007. At the ICIA, Bath, 2008 she presented *Peninsular* and a performance of *Libraries and Landscape*. She lectures in Fine Art at Central Saint Martins School of Art and Design.

Geoffrey Gowlland received his PhD in Social Anthropology from the University of Cambridge, and is currently postdoctoral fellow at the London School of Economics. He conducted extensive ethnographic fieldwork among ceramic artisans in the Jiangsu Province of China. His interests include the impact of China's economic reforms on craft learning and apprenticeship, and notions of skill, style and creativity in Chinese crafts

Jakob Hesler is a PhD candidate at Birkbeck, University of London. His research is devoted to the essay film (supervised by Laura Mulvey). His first degree was a Magister Artium in German Language & Literature / Philosophy (Universität Hamburg, Germany). He has also worked as a film critic for many years.

Dr. **Jon Kear** is a lecturer in History and Theory of Art at the University of Kent. He was educated at the Courtauld Institute, London, where he completed his PhD on the painter Paul Cézanne. He is the author of *Sunless* (1999) a study of the French filmmaker Chris Marker and *Impressionism* (2008). He has also published widely on various aspects of 19th and 20th century painting, literature, popular culture and photography, particularly on French art of the period 1860-1900. Currently he is completing two books, one on the painter Paul Cézanne and the other on Fantin Latour.

Robert Knifton is PhD student on the AHRC-funded collaborative programme between Tate Liverpool and MIRIAD, Manchester

Metropolitan University. In 2007 he co-curated the Tate Liverpool exhibition *Centre of the Creative Universe: Liverpool and the Avant-Garde*.

Yve Lomax is a writer and visual artist. She is author of *Writing the Image: An Adventure with Art and Theory* (2000), *Sounding the Event: Escapades in dialogue with matters of art, nature and time* (2005) and *Passionate Being: Language, Singularity and Perseverence* (forthcoming 2009). She is currently Professor in Art Writing at Goldsmiths College and Research Tutor for Fine Art at the Royal College of Art.

Catherine Lupton is Senior Lecturer in Film Studies at Roehampton University. She is the author of *Chris Marker: Memories of the Future* (London: Reaktion, 2005), and has published in *Screen*, *Film Studies* and *Film Comment*.

Craig Martin is Senior Lecturer in Contextual Studies at University for the Creative Arts, United Kingdom. His research interests are in cultural geography, design theory, material culture and social theory. He is currently carrying out research in the Department of Geography at Royal Holloway University of London, where he is investigating the materialities of movement-space, elaborated, in part, through the work of the philosopher Michel Serres. Conference papers have been delivered on a range of topics including spatial heterotopias, logistical space, parasitism, geopolitics and Serresian approaches to writing.

Alex Munt is a Lecturer in the Media Department at Macquarie University, Australia. His PhD is on Low Budget Digital Cinema. His research interests include: digital filmmaking practice/ aesthetics and writing for screen media. He has published features and articles in *Scan Journal, FlowTV, MetroMagazine* and *Senses of Cinema*.

UK based writer and performance artist **Mary Oliver** has been working professionally for almost thirty years. For the last decade she has been creating digital performance works in which the live and the mediatised performer always co-exist. Often comedic in nature these works playfully explore the meeting point of the actual and the digital. She is currently Reader and Associate Head of Research at the School of Media, Music and Performance at the University of Salford, (UK) and lead researcher in the development of a new Digital Performance Laboratory at Salford's Media City.

Mary O'Neill is currently Senior Lecturer in Cultural Context at the University of Lincoln. She studied Fine Art at Dun Laoghaire School of Art and the Crawford College of Art, Cork. She has been awarded several international residencies, most notably at the House of Creativity, Moscow and the Banff Art Center. In 2006 she completed an AHRC funded PhD. Her research interests span a variety of disciplines and include loss, boredom, disappearance and sorrow as well as methodologies of communicating these subjects. A work that combines theoretical text and narrative is included in *Feeling Our Way: Advancing Emotional Geographies,* Ashgate (2008).

Laura Rascaroli is Senior Lecturer in Film Studies at University College Cork, Ireland. She published research focuses on modern and contemporary European Cinema, art film and non-fiction. She is the author, in collaboration with Ewa Mazierska, of *From Moscow to Madrid: European Cities, Postmodern Cinema* (2003), *The Cinema of Nanni Moretti: Dreams and Diaries* (2004), and *Crossing New Europe: Postmodern Travel and the European Road Movie* (2006). Her monograph, *The Personal Camera: The Essay Film and Subjective Nonfiction*, is forthcoming with Wallflower Press. She is currently carrying out research on Irish amateur cinema (1930-1970), and on Michelangelo Antonioni and modernity.

Professor **Jane Rendell** is Director of Architectural Research at the Bartlett, UCL. An architectural designer and historian, art critic and writer, her work has explored various interdisciplinary intersections: feminist theory and architectural history, fine art and architectural design, autobiography and criticism. She is author of *Site-Writing* (forthcoming 2009), *Art and Architecture* (2006), *The Pursuit of Pleasure* (2002) and co-editor of *Pattern* (2007), *Critical Architecture* (2007), *Spatial Imagination* (2005), *The Unknown City* (2001), *Intersections* (2000), *Gender, Space, Architecture* (1999) and *Strangely Familiar* (1995). Her writing has been commissioned by galleries such as the BALTIC, Emmanuel Perrotin, the Hayward and the Serpentine.

Marie Shurkus is the 2007-2009 Mellon Postdoctoral Fellow in Contemporary Art Theory at Pomona College. Her research and teaching interests focus on the intersection of contemporary art and philosophy; she is especially interested in issues of representation, subjectivity, and perception. Her most recent research explores how digital technologies are transforming our understanding of representation, recreating it as an embodied experience that mobilizes affect. Currently, she is at work on a book, based on her dissertation, that constructs a legacy for this perspective through a critical re-interpretation of the Pictures Generation's use of appropriated imagery.

Lisa Stansbie is an artist and Senior Lecturer in Fine Art at the University of Huddersfield. She is currently undertaking a PhD at Leeds Metropolitan University entitled *Multiplicity, encyclopaedic strategies and nonlinear methodologies for a visual practice*. Recent online pieces include work for three editions of www.slashscconds.org an online publishing project and also *The Cloud Collector* (2007) an audio short story for the Canadian based Atlantic Basin Project. Stansbie's films have been shown in The Athens Video Art Festival, Siberia International Film in London, The Olympolis Project in Pieria, Greece and also selected as part of Purescreen 2008 at The Castlefield Gallery, Manchester.

Sissu Tarka is an artist and researcher with an interest in the criticality of emerging practices and economies of media art. Her work addresses themes of non-linearity; modes of resistance; and articulations of democratic, *active* work. Tarka was born in Helsinki and currently lives in London. After completing her PhD in Fine Arts at Central Saint Martins London, she joined CRUMB curatorial resource for upstart media bliss. When not with CRUMB she collaborates with Colm Lally (E:ventGallery London) to explore event structures, dialogical forms, agency and artistic inter-vention in contemporary practices. Recent projects include: "Condensation Revisited: A Lecture on Pigments: 3" (talk & publication with Colm Lally), *ISEA 2008*, Singapore, "Nervous Light Planes" (essay), *Animation*, Vol. 3, No. 2, (2008) SAGE Publications.

Jane Tormey lectures in Critical and Historical Studies at Loughborough University School of Art & Design. Her research explores the exchange of ideas between art practice and other disciplines and the ways in which conceptual and aesthetic traditions can be disturbed by and through photographic/filmic practices. She co-edits the electronic journal *Tracey – Contemporary Drawing* and has work published in *Masquerade: Women's Contemporary Portrait Photography* (Ffotogallery 2003), *The State of the Real* (I.B. Tauris 2005) and *AfterImage*. She is currently completing a book entitled *Contemporary Photographic Realism: practice and theory* (Manchester University Press).

Gillian Whiteley lectures in Critical and Historical Studies at Loughborough University School of Art and Design. Her research focuses on trans-disciplinary practices within socio-political contexts. Recent work includes *Radical Mayhem: Welfare State International and its Followers* (2008 exhibition/catalogue) and an essay published in H. Crawford (ed) *Artistic Bedfellows: Histories, Theories and Conversations in Collaborative Art Practices* (2008). Current projects include *Junk: Art and the Politics of Trash* (forthcoming I.B. Tauris) and www.bricolagekitchen.com, a creative/critical project space for inter-disciplinary explorations of improvisation and the makeshift.

INDEX